THE RICHER, THE POORER

Stories, Sketches, and Reminiscences

Dorothy West

A *Virago* Book

First published in the United States by Doubleday in 1995
First published in Great Britain by Virago Press in 1997

A CIP catalogue record for this book is available
from the British Library.

ISBN 1 86049 066 2

Typeset in Goudy by M Rules
Printed and bound in Great Britain by
Clays Ltd, St Ives plc

Virago
A Division of
Little, Brown and Company (UK)
Brettenham House
Lancaster Place
London WC2E 7EN

To my mother

The author would like to express her thanks to Henry Louis Gates, Jr., who hounded her until this collection became a reality; to Rosemary Csapo, for all of her good offices; and to the *Vineyard Gazette* and its staff, for a relationship that has brought her nothing but joy over the years.

Contents

SKETCHES AND REMINISCENCES

Preface

by
Mary Helen Washington

I first met Dorothy West in February 1980 when I went to the town of Oak Bluffs on Martha's Vineyard, to interview her for an article I was writing on black women's literary history. I was new to the East Coast, living in Cambridge, teaching at the University of Massachusetts in Boston – and not at all sure I wanted to stay in a place where one was constantly being judged by social class, by family background, by academic credentials. I moved to Boston from Detroit, the Motor City, home of Motown – the Supremes and the Temptations; of black revolutionary theaters like Concept East; of one of the early black publishing houses, Broadside Press; of militantly political bookstores like Vaughn's on Dexter; of a working-class university, Wayne State. Boston of the eighties seemed almost apolitical by comparison with Detroit of the seventies, as though the clouds of the radical sixties and seventies had passed over the East, scattering a few raindrops left over from the downpour that deluged Detroit. I discovered later, partly through Dorothy West's groundbreaking first novel, *The Living Is Easy* (1948), that Boston is a city of conflicting, sometimes opposing forces: its history of virulent racism exists side by side with a proud abolitionist past; the same social class that produced its elitism and pretentiousness also produced Monroe Trotter, a Phi Beta

Kappa graduate of Harvard and a prominent member of the black elite who became one of the most active race leaders of the twentieth century.

West is a writer who both reflects and critiques the attitudes and ideals of the black bourgeoisie. By birth and breeding she is 'a proper Bostonian,' which, in the days of her youth, meant that she belonged to a genteel, aspiring middle class. She was born in 1907 in Boston to Isaac West and Rachel Benson West. Her father, an ambitious and industrious ex-slave from Virginia, was a wholesale banana merchant in downtown Boston, known as the Black Banana King. West's light-skinned, beautiful mother, one of twenty-two children, had been sent North by her family, who feared her good looks would get her into trouble with white men in the South. Dorothy West attended the prestigious Girl's Latin School and Boston University and later the Columbia School of Journalism. Isaac West's prosperous business allowed the family to become among the first blacks to own vacation homes and to spend their summers on the island of Martha's Vineyard, specifically in Oak Bluffs, that part of the island that blacks claimed for their own. West's sketches of the island represent the Vineyard of her childhood as an idyllic time and place:

> *The days were full. There were berries to pick, a morning's adventure. There were band concerts for an evening's stroll. There were invitations to lemonade and cookies and whist. There was always an afternoon boat to meet, not so much to see who was getting off, but to see and talk to whatever friends had come for that same purpose.* ('Fond Memories of a Black Childhood')

There were good reasons for the title of her first novel. For these people with education – surrounded by other blacks of achievement and financial security, and access to a summer resort that boasted the largest number of vacationing blacks in the country – the living did seem easy. It even seemed as though, through elegance of style, manners, and bankbook, these proper Bostonians could conquer racism: Dorothy's mother once told her that among people of proper background she would never have to worry about being called a nigger because people of class and breeding never sink to that.

But West's fiction reveals the shadow side of this idyllic picture of island summers and genteel aristocrats. In *The Living Is Easy* she adopted a tone of ironic humor, which she learned from her mother, to satirize the pretensions of the Boston black elite, especially their desire to distinguish themselves from 'ordinary' blacks:

> *Though they scorned the Jew, they were secretly pleased when they could pass for one. Though they were contemptuous of the Latins, they were proud when they looked European. They were not too dismayed by a darkish skin if it were counterbalanced by a straight nose and straight hair that established an Indian origin. There was nothing that disturbed them more than knowing that no one would take them for anything but colored.*

The tradition of writing about black life from the point of view of the privileged narrator or character goes back to the nineteenth century and novels like William Wells Brown's *Clotel* (1853) and Frances Harper's *Iola Leroy* (1892), whose light-skinned, aristocratic characters were examples of racial propriety. Intelligent, superior, and white-looking, these figures embodied the cultural values that supposedly would enable the race to elevate itself from its lowly past in slavery. By the turn of the century, however, these dramas of racial uplift were being severely questioned by novels like James Weldon Johnson's *Autobiography of an Ex-Coloured Man* (1912) and Nella Larsen's

Quicksand (1928), whose main characters, though middle-class themselves, are alienated from the values of the black bourgeoisie. In a contemporary novel, *Sarah Phillips* (1984) by Andrea Lee, the main character, Sarah, reaffirms the ambivalence of the insider who both appreciates and is critical of the black middle class:

> . . . *a group largely unknown to other Americans, which has carried on with cautious pomp for years in eastern cities and suburbs using its considerable funds to attempt poignant imitations of high society, acting with genuine gallantry in the struggle for civil rights, and finally producing a generation of children educated in newly integrated schools and impatient to escape the outworn rituals of their parents.*

Like Johnson, Larsen, and Lee, West writes about the black middle class from the viewpoint of the marginalized insider, both a fierce critic of the bourgeois life and a loyal daughter upholding the values of family and class. In *The Living Is Easy*, the story of privilege is constantly disrupted – by tales of slavery and slave suicide, by stories of blacks fighting de facto segregation in the North and Ku Klux Klan terror in the South, and especially by the figure of the child Judy, who, much like West herself, resents and rejects her mother's desires for status, money, and white acceptance.

It's not surprising, then, that in the twenties West left the insular life of her Boston family and community and ventured to New York to become part of the literary movement known popularly as the Harlem Renaissance. Not yet twenty years old in 1926, West went to New York to receive a second-place award in the *Opportunity* writing contest for the story 'The Typewriter.' As part of a group of younger writers that included Wallace Thurman, Langston Hughes, and Zora Hurston, West led a carefree bohemian life that made her feel she had wasted

time, talent, and money, and when the Harlem Renaissance
party days were over she found herself penitent about her past
life. Eager to redeem herself for what she perceived as lack of
seriousness about her work, she started a magazine called
Challenge to publish the work of younger black writers and 'to
recapture in the mid-thirties the literary vitality of the Harlem
Renaissance, which had not survived the Depression.' Later
called *New Challenge*, the magazine lasted until 1937. This
more serious side of West continued to develop in the thirties as
she worked as a welfare investigator and on the WPA, and as
she produced short stories about issues of race and class
('Mammy,' 'The Richer, the Poorer') that seem as relevant
today as they were during the Depression. In the story
'Mammy,' the black welfare investigator assigned to eliminate
people from public assistance is forced to see how much she has
in common with people of all classes: both the welfare official
and the elevator operator who insults her in front of whites are
doing whatever is necessary to hold on to their jobs. And when
the elderly maid (called 'Mammy' by her white employer)
pleads with the investigator not to cut her assistance, she asks
the woman to recognize their common bond: 'You're my own
people, child. Can you fix up a story for them white folks at the
relief, so's I could get to stay here where it's nice.' In these
stories from the forties we see West's genuine empathy for those
who struggle to feed and clothe children on a meager allowance
and have to depend on welfare, but we also see her larger political statement that, in black communities especially, the
privileged and the poor, like house servant and field slave, are
sometimes desperately united.

After 1945, Dorothy West made her home permanently on
Martha's Vineyard, where she wrote *The Living Is Easy* in 1948
and her second novel, *The Wedding*, in 1994. Spanning almost
seventy years, West's writing career links the Harlem
Renaissance with the social realism of the thirties and forties

and popular fiction of the eighties and nineties. In her most recent fiction she continues to observe the tensions and triumphs in the lives of middle- and upper-class blacks, at times critiquing the false values in their lives, yet always representing these lives in vivid detail. West reminds me that there is a strong sense of place in African-American literature: the Middle Passage, Southern plantations, the urban North, Jim Crow railroads, the church – each place has required specific performances, created specific histories, and shaped specific cultural identities. In her focus on the places she knows well – especially Boston and Martha's Vineyard – which have rarely been written about in African-American literature, Dorothy West has complicated and expanded our knowledge of America.

INTRODUCTION

When I was a child I had a bedroom of my own. My mother and her siblings in their growing years had to sleep on top of each other, and they all swore a sacred oath that a similar fate would never befall their children.

We were a sizable family in a suitably sizable house. There was much coming and going, and a lot of laughter throughout the day. I would not exchange my childhood for any other time or place. But when at five I began to grow into being a self of my own, I wanted to contemplate that private self in solitude.

I asked my mother if I could shut my bedroom door and be by myself sometimes. She asked me why I wanted that privacy. I said because I wanted to think. Since thinking is reasonable, even an admirable exercise she let me. In any case it was easier for her to say yes than to explain the whys of no.

When I was seven I asked her if I could lock my bedroom door. She answered with the expected, why? I said I wanted to write stories and that you had to be by yourself when you wrote them because you had to think hard to make them come out right.

As I grew older my stories began to shape into substance. When I was fourteen I sent my first story, handwritten, to the *Boston Post*, a well-regarded paper which printed a short story by, I assume, a ripening writer each day. There were three weekly prizes, ten dollars, five dollars, and two dollars. I received the ten-dollar prize with commendable regularity. It added to the family income, and I was proud of my contribution. When I got the five-dollar prize I was embarrassed that my contribution was cut in half. I don't remember ever getting the two-dollar prize or no prize at all; if I did I buried that disaster too deep in my memory ever to dig up.

In my sixteenth year an aunt who shared our home was waiting for the trolley that would take her there when a personable young black man approached her, summarily informing her that he was working his way through medical school and thereupon entreating her to buy a subscription to a black magazine called *The Crisis*. Though my aunt had never heard of a magazine so named she believed in ambition and opened her purse.

My mother, who had heard of *The Crisis*, was dismayed when the magazine appeared in our mail slot. The young members in our extended family, all born and raised in Boston, had little if any knowledge of lynching and other obscenities. To see them graphically depicted might discourage us from pursuing our ambition in a world stacked against us.

But there was also in that magazine an announcement of its third or perhaps its fourth literary contest, persuading me to assume that the preceding contests had reaped such a yield of black talent that the contests were ongoing.

I wrote, and then sent to *The Crisis* magazine a story titled 'The Typewriter.' In due time I received an invitation to the awards dinner. I was overwhelmed with joy.

My mother cautioned me that invitations were sent to all contestants, not just to the winners. But I was seventeen, and I refused to believe that God could be so unfeeling as to steer some human hand to write my name on a piece of paper for me to blot with tears. I persuaded my mother to let me go to the magical city of New York, an unforgettable thrill. She was right, of course, in her assessment of award invitations.

But God, with whom I had lengthy conversations in my childhood and presumed had got to know me and my aspirations, allowed me to share a second prize with the now legendary Zora Neale Hurston. At first she had mixed feelings about sharing a prize with an unknown teenager. But in time I became her little sister, and my affection for her has never diminished. In time I was to play my part in the Harlem Renaissance. I was nineteen and its youngest member.

The Harlem Renaissance can never be repeated. It was an age of innocence, when we who were its hopeful members believed that our poems, our plays, our paintings, our sculptures, indeed any facet of our talents would be recognized and rewarded.

My own writing was now more mature. I saw life with a larger eye. But the important magazines were not in the market for stories about blacks. They surmised that neither were their readers. And they did not relish canceled subscriptions from various sections of the country.

In time we became pets of sophisticated whites, the Park Avenue people, as we called them. One of them encouraged me to use his name – that name now long forgotten – and contact George Bye. He was, I was told, the most influential literary agent in New York. Eleanor Roosevelt and other people of importance were his clientele. If anyone could sell a black writer, it was Bye.

But even he couldn't, though the challenge made him continue to try. It took a miracle. The day that I read of a short story contest in a newspaper that somebody had abandoned on a park bench was the day the miracle began to unfold. I made myself believe that a newspaper, since everybody read newspapers, would have relaxed requirements as to color.

I wrote a story called 'Jack in the Pot.' I had come late to knowledge of the contest, and the closing date was only a short time away. But I couldn't find the slip of paper on which I had written the required information, which information, in my panic, completely escaped me. To this day I put important notes on pieces of paper and in less than a day I have no recollection of where I put them for safekeeping. In that area I am incurable.

In my disappointment and self-bashing, I did not know the miracle was waiting to happen. In sackcloth and ashes I sent the story to George Bye, my accompanying letter telling him how I had tried and miserably failed. But if he saw any merit in the story, maybe he would like to give it a try, since I had botched mine.

At that time the *New York Daily News* was devoting a whole page of its Sunday paper to a section called 'Blue Ribbon Fiction.' I did not know that. I knew that the *News* was a tabloid, so of course I read *The New York Times*, or at least I said so, if asked. George Bye sent my story to the editor of the 'Blue Ribbon' section. I did not know about it until he sent me a check for four hundred dollars, an enormous sum in those days, and a congratulatory note.

The owners of the *News* were General Joseph Patterson of the powerful Patterson–McCormick chain, and his lovely wife, Mary King Patterson (who sent me a Christmas card every year until her death. I never sent her a card. I somehow felt she wanted it that way).

I did not see them in person until one day I received a call from a staff member who said that they would be pleased to have me come to their office at some time convenient to me. I readily said I would gladly come at any day and hour·that was suitable to them.

We met within the week. Mrs. Patterson was a true beauty. She had stage presence, and I wondered, and certainly didn't ask, if she had been an actress. Colonel Patterson was also an impressive figure. They told me how much they had liked 'Jack in the Pot,' and they wished me a successful writing career. The 'Blue Ribbon Fiction' page was being replaced by four columns essential to the state of the nation.

The page that gave part of its space to a daily short story of limited length was still intact, however. They would be glad to let me write two such stories a month, an accommodation they invented for me. The sum for a story was fifty dollars, but they knew and I knew it was not the money that mattered. They were helping me keep my writing hand ready and my mind alert. In any case I have never been a person who cared about money; I've always said cheerfully that I would die a happy pauper. I care about people and they care about me. That's all I want.

I was taken to meet the editor of that section. She was Katherine Kelly. We bonded immediately. She gave me advice that I will forever treasure: she said, 'Write your best, always write your best, not for the paper but for pride in your writing.' There were times when I said oh shucks. But there were more times when I followed her advice.

I had spent all my childhood summers on the island of Martha's Vineyard, where we had a small cottage. In my early years, with a child's innocence, I thought it was always summer here, and nobody called you nigger here (to Yankees the word was *verboten*) and no child had to get up on cold mornings to go to school. And maybe there wasn't any school to go to if there wasn't any winter.

The summer of 1947, with my childhood and girlhood over and done with, I was walking on-island with a friend who was sharing my two-week stay. I was casually talking about my mother and her occasional bouts with extravagance when I was a child. My father had a profitable business, and he was indulgent with my mother, who was young enough to be his daughter, and so for my mother the living was easy. I did not know that conversation would linger in my mind nor that I would spend the coming winter writing a book in a summer house where the pipes froze and broke, where the snowplow did not know there was one house still occupied on that shuttered street, and the plumber said that nothing could be done till spring when the ground relaxed its grip on the frozen outdoor pipes. But he found a way to give me water from the main source, which meant an outdoor trip three times a day.

The winter passed without incident, and the incomparable spring on the Vineyard lifted every heart. Every fishing boat waited to set sail .

What was most important to me was that *The Living Is Easy* was finished. George Bye sent it to Houghton Mifflin. They accepted it.

He also sent it to the best-known and most-read women's magazine of that day. Its editors, a husband and wife team, were said to be among the most powerful editors in the country. They loved the book and they wanted to serialize it. George Bye wrote me that wonderful news, but then there was a stretch of silence. And finally he wrote me that a survey showed that many Southern subscribers would cancel their subscriptions if they had to submit to that outrage.

That fall I read an advertisement in the *Vineyard Gazette*, whose reputation for excellence had become an established fact. The ad announced an opening at the paper, though it did not specify in what department. I had been given a favorable review of *The Living Is Easy*, which meant my name should be recognizable. I promptly applied, and the job was mine.

It was a modest job, consisting of filing and billing, no doubt left begging by some young student apprentice returning to college. But I had decided to stay the winter, chiefly because an ailing close relative needed the quiet of the Highlands. The sounds surrounding me at work would enliven my days and make my return home a welcome change of pace.

The water pipes were now underground. The rooms that

were in use had been winterized, and the others were behind closed doors. The cottage was reasonably snug.

Fairly soon the duties I had been hired to do became routine and took less and less time to complete. My working hours, of course, did not diminish. I asked if I could fill that time by writing occasional pieces on whatever came to mind. They were pleased by the question and I was pleased by their ready acquiescence.

In time the paper was bought by James (Scotty) and Sally Fulton Reston, who in turn passed the reins to their son and daughter-in-law, Richard and Mary Jo Reston, an incomparable couple to whom I am devoted. This collection includes many stories that were first printed in the *Gazette*.

STORIES

THE TYPEWRITER

I t occurred to him, as he eased past the bulging knees of an Irish wash lady and forced an apologetic passage down the aisle of the crowded car, that more than anything in all the world he wanted not to go home. He began to wish passionately that he had never been born, that he had never been married, that he had never been the means of life's coming into the world. He knew quite suddenly that he hated his flat and his family and his friends. And most of all the incessant thing that would 'clatter clatter' until every nerve screamed aloud, and the words of the evening paper danced crazily before him, and the insane desire to crush and kill set his fingers twitching.

He shuffled down the street, an abject little man of fifty-odd years, in an ageless overcoat that flapped in the wind. He was cold, and he hated the North, and particularly Boston, and saw suddenly a barefoot pickaninny sitting on a fence in the hot, Southern sun with a piece of steaming corn bread and a piece of fried salt pork in either grimy hand.

He was tired, and he wanted his supper, but he didn't want the beans, and frankfurters, and light bread that Net would undoubtedly have. That Net had had every Monday night since

that regrettable moment fifteen years before when he had told
her – innocently – that such a supper tasted 'right nice. Kinda
change from what we always has.'

He mounted the four brick steps leading to his door and
pulled at the bell; but there was no answering ring. It was broken again, and in a mental flash he saw himself with a
multitude of tools and a box of matches shivering in the
vestibule after supper. He began to pound lustily on the door
and wondered vaguely if his hand would bleed if he smashed
the glass. He hated the sight of blood. It sickened him.

Someone was running down the stairs. Daisy probably. Millie
would be at that infernal thing, pounding, pounding . . . He
entered. The chill of the house swept him. His child was
wrapped in a coat. She whispered solemnly, 'Poppa, Miz Hicks
an' Miz Berry's orful mad. They gointa move if they can't get
more heat. The furnace's bin out all day. Mama couldn't fix it.'
He said hurriedly, 'I'll go right down. I'll go right down.' He
hoped Mrs. Hicks wouldn't pull open her door and glare at
him. She was large and domineering, and her husband was a
bully. If her husband ever struck him it would kill him. He
hated life, but he didn't want to die. He was afraid of God, and
in his wildest flights of fancy couldn't imagine himself an angel.
He went softly down the stairs.

He began to shake the furnace fiercely. And he shook into it
every wrong, mumbling softly under his breath. He began to
think back over his uneventful years, and it came to him as
rather a shock that he had never sworn in all his life. He wondered uneasily if he dared say 'damn.' It was taken for granted
that a man swore when he tended a stubborn furnace. And his
strongest interjection was 'Great balls of fire!'

The cellar began to warm, and he took off his inadequate
overcoat that was streaked with dirt. Well, Net would have to
clean that. He'd be damned – ! It frightened him and thrilled
him. He wanted suddenly to rush upstairs and tell Mrs. Hicks if

she didn't like the way he was running things, she could get out. But he heaped another shovelful of coal on the fire and sighed. He would never be able to get away from himself and the routine of years.

He thought of that eager Negro lad of seventeen who had come North to seek his fortune. He had walked jauntily down Boylston Street, and even his own kind had laughed at the incongruity of him. But he had thrown up his head and promised himself: 'You'll have an office here some day. With plate-glass windows and a real mahogany desk.' But, though he didn't know it then, he was not the progressive type. And he became successively, in the years, bell boy, porter, waiter, cook, and finally janitor in a downtown office building.

He had married Net when he was thirty-three and a waiter. He had married her partly because – though he might not have admitted it – there was no one to eat the expensive delicacies the generous cook gave him every night to bring home. And partly because he dared hope there might be a son to fulfill his dreams. But Millie had come, and after her, twin girls who had died within two weeks, then Daisy, and it was tacitly understood that Net was done with childbearing.

Life, though flowing monotonously, had flowed peacefully enough until that sucker of sanity became a sitting room fixture. Intuitively at the very first he had felt its undesirability. He had suggested hesitatingly that they couldn't afford it. Three dollars the eighth of every month. Three dollars: food and fuel. Times were hard, and the twenty dollars apiece the respective husbands of Miz Hicks and Miz Berry irregularly paid was only five dollars more than the thirty-five a month he paid his own Hebraic landlord. And the Lord knew his salary was little enough. At which point Net spoke her piece, her voice rising shrill. 'God knows I never complain 'bout nothin'. Ain't no other woman got less than me. I bin wearin' this same dress here five years, an' I'll wear it another five. But I don't want nothin'. I ain't never wanted nothin'. An' when I does as', it's only for my children. You're a poor sort of father if you can't give that child jes' three dollars a month to rent that type-writer. Ain't 'nother girl in school ain't got one. An' mos' of 'ems bought an' paid for. You know yourself how Millie is. She wouldn't as' me for it till she had to. An' I ain't going to disappoint her. She's goin' to get that typewriter Saturday, mark my words.'

On a Monday then it had been installed. And in the months that followed, night after night he listened to the murderous 'tack, tack, tack' that was like a vampire slowly drinking his blood. If only he could escape. Bar a door against the sound of it. But tied hand and foot by the economic fact that 'Lord knows we can't afford to have fires burnin' an' lights lit all over the flat. You'all gotta set in one room. An' when y'get tired setting y'c'n go to bed. Gas bill was somep'n scandalous last month.'

He heaped a final shovelful of coal on the fire and watched the first blue flames. Then, his overcoat under his arm, he mounted the cellar stairs. Mrs. Hicks was standing in her kitchen door, arms akimbo. 'It's warmin',' she volunteered.

'Yeh,' he was conscious of his grime-streaked face and hands, 'it's warmin'. I'm sorry 'bout all day.'

She folded her arms across her ample bosom. 'Tending a fur-nace ain't a woman's work. I don't blame you wife none 'tall.'

Unsuspecting, he was grateful. 'Yeh, it's pretty hard for a woman. I always look after it 'fore I goes to work, but some days it jes' ac's up.'

'Y'oughta have a janitor, that's what y'ought,' she flung at him. 'The same cullud man that tends them apartments would be willin'. Mr. Taylor has him. It takes a man to run a furnace, and when the man's away all day –'

'I know,' he interrupted, embarrassed and hurt. 'I know. Tha's right, Miz Hicks, tha's right. But I ain't in a position to make no improvements. Times is hard.'

She surveyed him critically. 'Your wife called down 'bout three times while you was in the cellar. I reckon she wants you for supper.'

'Thanks,' he mumbled and escaped up the back stairs.

He hung up his overcoat in the closet, telling himself, a little lamely, that it wouldn't take him more than a minute to clean it up himself after supper. After all, Net was tired and probably worried what with Mrs. Hicks and all. And he hated men who made slaves of their womenfolk. Good old Net.

He tidied up in the bathroom, washing his face and hands carefully and cleanly so as to leave no – or very little – stain on the roller towel. It was hard enough for Net, God knew.

He entered the kitchen. The last spirals of steam were rising from his supper. One thing about Net, she served a full plate. He smiled appreciatively at her unresponsive back, bent over the kitchen sink. There was no one who could bake beans just like Net's. And no one who could find a market with frankfurters quite so fat.

He sat down at his place. 'Evenin', hon.'

He saw her back stiffen. 'If your supper's cold, 'tain't my fault. I called and called.'

He said hastily, 'It's fine, Net, fine. Piping.'

She was the usual tired housewife. 'Y'oughta et your supper 'fore you fooled with that furnace. I ain't bothered 'bout them niggers. I got all my dishes washed 'cept yours. An' I hate to mess up my kitchen after I once get it straightened up.'

He was humble. 'I'll give that old furnace an extra lookin' after in the mornin'. It'll last all day tomorrow, hon.'

'An' on top of that,' she continued, unheeding him and giving a final wrench to her dish towel, 'that confounded bell don't ring. An' –'

'I'll fix it after supper,' he interposed quickly.

She hung up her dish towel and came to stand before him looming large and yellow. 'An' that old Miz Berry, she claim she

was expectin' comp'ny. An' she know they must 'a' come an'
gone while she was in her kitchen an' couldn't be at her winder
to watch for 'em. Old liar.' She brushed back a lock of naturally
straight hair. 'She wasn't expectin' nobody.'

'Well, you know how some folks are –'

'Fools! Half the world,' was her vehement answer. 'I'm goin'
in the front room an' set down a spell. I bin on my feet all day.
Leave them dishes on the table. God knows I'm tired, but I'll
come back an' wash 'em.' But they both knew, of course, that
he, very clumsily, would.

At precisely quarter past nine when he, strained at last to the
breaking point, uttering an inhuman, strangled cry, flung down
his paper, clutched at his throat, and sprang to his feet, Millie's
surprised young voice, shocking him to normalcy, heralded the
first of that series of great moments that every humble little
middle-class man eventually experiences.

'What's the matter, Poppa? You sick? I wanted you to help
me.'

He drew out his handkerchief and wiped his hot hands. 'I
declare I must 'a' fallen asleep an' had a nightmare. No, I ain't
sick. What you want, hon?'

'Dictate me a letter, Poppa. I c'n do sixty words a minute.
You know, like a business letter. You know, like those men in
your building dictate to their stenographers. Don't you hear
'em sometimes?'

'Oh sure, I know, hon. Poppa'll help you. Sure. I hear that
Mr. Browning. Sure.'

Net rose. 'Guess I'll put this child to bed. Come on now,
Daisy, without no fuss. Then I'll run up to Pa's. He ain't bin well
all week.'

When the door closed behind them, he crossed to his daughter, conjured the image of Mr. Browning in the process of
dictating, so arranged himself, and coughed importantly.

'Well, Millie –'

'Oh, Poppa, is that what you'd call your stenographer?' she teased. 'And anyway pretend I'm really one – and you're really my boss, and this letter's real important.'

A light crept into his dull eyes. Vigor through his thin blood. In a brief moment the weight of years fell from him like a cloak. Tired, bent, little old man that he was, he smiled, straightened, tapped impressively against his teeth with a toil-stained finger, and became that enviable emblem of American life: a businessman.

'You be Miz Hicks, huh, honey? Course we can't both use the same name. I'll be J. Lucius Jones. J. Lucius. All them real big men use their middle names. Jus' kinda looks big doin', doncha think, hon? Looks like money, huh? J. Lucius.' He uttered a sound that was like the proud cluck of a strutting hen. 'J. Lucius.' It rolled like oil from his tongue.

His daughter twisted impatiently. 'Now, Poppa – I mean Mr. Jones, sir – please begin. I am ready for dictation, sir.'

He was in that office on Boylston Street, looking with visioning eyes through its plate-glass windows, tapping with impatient fingers on its real mahogany desk.

'Ah – Beaker Brothers, Park Square Building, Boston, Mass. Ah – Gentlemen: In reply to yours of the seventh instant would state –'

Every night thereafter in the weeks that followed, with Daisy packed off to bed, and Net 'gone up to Pa's' or nodding unobtrusively in her corner, there was the chameleon change of a Court Street janitor to J. Lucius Jones, dealer in stocks and bonds. He would stand, posturing, importantly flicking imaginary dust from his coat lapel, or, his hands locked behind his back, he would stride up and down, earnestly and seriously debating the advisability of buying copper with the market in such a fluctuating state. Once a week, too, he stopped in at Jerry's, and after a preliminary purchase of cheap cigars, bought the latest trade papers, mumbling an embarrassed explanation:

'I got a little money. Think I'll invest it in reliable stock.'

The letters Millie typed and subsequently discarded, he rummaged for later, and under cover of writing to his brother in the South, laboriously, with a great many fancy flourishes, signed each neatly typed sheet with the exalted J. Lucius Jones.

Later, when he mustered the courage, he suggested tentatively to Millie that it might be fun – just fun, of course – to answer his letters. One night – he laughed a good deal louder and longer than necessary – he'd be J. Lucius Jones, and the next night – here he swallowed hard and looked a little frightened – Rockefeller or Vanderbilt or Morgan – just for fun, y'understand! To which Millie gave consent. It mattered little to her one way or the other. It was practice, and that was what she needed. Very soon now she'd be in the hundred class. Then maybe she could get a job!

He was growing very careful of his English. Occasionally – and it must be admitted, ashamedly – he made surreptitious ventures into the dictionary. He had to, of course. J. Lucius Jones would never say 'Y'got to' when he meant 'It is expedient.' And, old brain though he was, he learned quickly and easily, juggling words with amazing facility.

Eventually, he bought stamps and envelopes – long, important-looking envelopes – and stammered apologetically to Millie, 'Honey, Poppa thought it'd help you if you learned to type envelopes, too. Reckon you'll have to do that, too, when y'get a job. Poor old man,' he swallowed painfully, 'came round selling these envelopes. You know how 'tis. So I had to buy 'em.' Which was satisfactory to Millie. If she saw through her father, she gave no sign. After all, it was practice, and Mr. Hennessey had promised the smartest girl in the class a position in the very near future. And she, of course, was smart as a steel trap. Even Mr. Hennessey had said that – though not in just those words.

He had gotten in the habit of carrying those self-addressed envelopes in his inner pocket where they bulged impressively.

And occasionally he would take them out – on the car usually – and smile upon them. This one might be from J. P. Morgan. This one from Henry Ford. And a million-dollar deal involved in each. That narrow, little spinster who, upon his sitting down, had drawn herself away from his contact, was shunning J. Lucius Jones!

Once, led by some sudden, strange impulse, as an outgoing car rumbled up out of the subway, he got out a letter, darted a quick shamed glance about him, dropped it in an adjacent box, and swung aboard the car, feeling, dazedly, as if he had committed a crime. And the next night he sat in the sitting room quite on edge until Net said suddenly, 'Look here, a real important letter come today for you, Pa. Here 'tis. What you s'pose it says?' And he reached out a hand that trembled. He made brief explanation. 'Advertisement, hon. Thassal.'

They came quite frequently after that, and despite the fact that he knew them by heart, he read them quite slowly and carefully, rustling the sheet, and making inaudible, intelligent comments. He was, in these moments, pathetically earnest.

Monday, as he went about his janitor's duties, he composed in his mind the final letter from J. P. Morgan that would consummate a big business deal. For days now, letters had passed between them. J.P. had been at first quite frankly uninterested. He had written tersely and briefly. Which was meat to J. Lucius. The compositions of his brain were really the work of an artist. He wrote glowingly of the advantages of a pact between them. Daringly he argued in terms of billions. And at last J.P. had written his next letter would be decisive. Which next letter, this Monday, as he trailed about the office building, was writing itself in his brain.

That night Millie opened the door for him. Her plain face was transformed. 'Poppa – Poppa, I got a job! Twelve dollars a week to start with! Isn't that swell!'

He was genuinely pleased. 'Honey, I'm glad. Right glad,' and went upstairs, unsuspecting.

He ate his supper hastily, went down into the cellar to see about his fire, returned and carefully tidied up, informing his reflection in the bathroom mirror, 'Well, J. Lucius, you c'n expect that final letter any day now.'

He entered the sitting room. The phonograph was playing. Daisy was singing lustily. Strange. Net was talking animatedly to Millie, busy with needle and thread over a neat, little frock. His wild glance darted to the table. The pretty little center-piece of the bowl and wax flowers all neatly arranged: the typewriter gone from its accustomed place. It seemed an hour before he could speak. He felt himself trembling. Went hot and cold.

'Millie – your typewriter's – gone!'

She made a deft little in-and-out movement with her needle. 'It's the eighth, you know. When the man came today for the money, I sent it back. I won't need it no more – now! The money's on the mantelpiece, Poppa.'

'Yeh,' he muttered. 'All right.'

He sank down in his chair, fumbled for the paper, found it.

Net said, 'Your poppa wants to read. Stop your noise, Daisy.'

She obediently stopped both her noise and the phonograph, took up her book, and became absorbed. Millie went on with her sewing in placid anticipation of the morrow. Net immediately began to nod, gave a curious snort, slept.

Silence. That crowded in on him, engulfed him. That blurred his vision, dulled his brain. Vast, white, impenetrable . . . His ears strained for the old, familiar sound. And silence beat upon them . . . The words of the evening paper jumbled together. He read 'J. P. Morgan goes –'

It burst upon him. Blinded him. His hands groped for the bulge beneath his coat. Why this – this was the end! The end of those great moments – the end of everything! Bewildering pain tore through him. He clutched at his heart and felt, almost, the jagged edges drive into his hand. A lethargy swept down upon him. He could not move, nor utter a sound. He could not pray, nor curse.

Against the wall of that silence J. Lucius Jones crashed and died.

THE FIVE-DOLLAR BILL

Judy could read before she was seven. Mother said that when she was four she could read the weather reports to her father. The only one she fell down on was the variable wind one. Only she didn't really fall down, for when she came to that difficult word and got it out somehow, the father caught her up in his arms and hugged and kissed her hard.

Judy loved the father. She did not know very much about him. She guessed he was her relative because they had the same name. She would have liked to know if this kinship were closer than an uncle; or was it like a grandfather, for the father was much older than Mother, with the top of his head broken and wrinkles around his kind eyes.

But Judy was a shy child who did not like to ask questions, for either the grown-up people said, run and play, or gave you ridiculous answers with superior smiles.

Judy could answer the little questions herself. It was the big questions about babies and God, and telling a lie for your mother, that grown-up people were never truthful about.

The stork did not bring babies. It was not true about a stork flying over clouds and dropping babies down chimneys. Santa Claus could come down a chimney because he was a man and wouldn't get hurt. But would God let a stork drop a dear little baby down a dirty chimney?

No, a woman prayed to God very hard for a baby. Then it began to grow in her stomach. When it was quite grown a doctor cut a hole in her side and the baby came out. After that the woman stayed in bed until the hole healed up. In that moment of the baby's birth the woman became a mother. But how a man became a father Judy did not know.

And about God: Did He really punish people in a fire with a pitchfork? Did He stick them with the pitchfork himself? Why, Judy could not have hurt a fly. She could kill a mosquito all right because it was teenier. Sometimes, though, when you killed a mosquito a lot of blood squished out. That made your stomach feel queer for a minute. But then Mother said beamingly, got him good, didn't you, darling, and everything was all right.

Mother could kill anything without feeling queer. She killed flies and ants and even big roaches, and put down traps for mice. She said anything that belonged outdoors should stay outdoors if it didn't want her to kill it. And she would grab a wad of paper and go banging at a fly, which was fun to watch if you did not think too hard about the fly's family

God was supposed to be gooder than Mother. God was not supposed to have Mother's temper. Mother said damn and sometimes Goddamn. If Judy overheard she would frown and have a temper. She would say Goddamn to the father. Then she would have a temper when the father reproached her for saying such words before Judy.

They would begin the queer thing called quarreling. The words would fly between them and it would seem to Judy that her mother's words hit hardest. Yet at such times, as fond as she was of the father, she would want to run to her mother, saying protectively, there, there, my darling.

Judy often wondered if the father lived with them. She

always went to bed while he was still sitting up, and he was never there in the morning like her mother. There were only two bedrooms, hers and her mother's. And once she heard her mother say to the college man, Jim and I have not lived together as man and wife for months.

Mother was careless with money. She was always losing it. Judy never saw her lose it really, but she would tell Judy about it and after a while Judy would remember exactly how it happened. When the father sat down to dinner, Mother would tell him about it, too, adding, Judy remembers. Judy would say proudly, yes, Mother.

Mother always lost the money on the day the college man came. Mother said he was poor and came to sell things to help him through college. She said Judy had better not tell the father because he was not a college man and got mad if anybody mentioned college men to him.

Judy did not know what the college man sold and she would not ask her mother. It always cost just what the father had left for the gas bill or the milk bill, and once even what the father had left for a birthday frock for Judy.

When the college man came, mother would let Judy take her dolly out in its carriage. But it would not be the same as on other days. She would dress her doll hurriedly, and it would not seem to be a real baby, but just an old doll. She would feel silly, and would just want to get away from the college man and his teasing voice.

Then one night the father and Mother had a terrible quarrel about Mother losing money. You could hear their voices all over the house, only this time it was the father's words hitting hardest. Neither Judy nor her mother had ever mentioned the college man to him, but he knew all about him just the same, and called himself a fool and the college man a rat, and said he was going to divorce Mother and take Judy away from her.

Judy did not know what divorce meant, but when the father

said he would take her away from her mother, she knew that as mad as he was he would take her for keeps, and never let them see each other.

She got out of bed and ran into the kitchen, and threw herself into her mother's arms. She was sobbing wildly and saying hysterical things. Her mother held her close and began to cry, too, saying, there, there, my precious, just like Judy had always wanted to say to her.

After a long time she felt the father's hand on her head. She heard him say something about the child's sake, and knew he meant he would let her stay. All in a moment she fell asleep, with her hand sliding down her mother's soft cheek.

After that the father did not leave any more money for bills. The college man came once and said, where was the money for his books? He looked very scornful while he said it, and he kept his hat in his hand.

Mother forgot about Judy and cried and clung to the college man. He pushed her away and said she knew where to reach him when she had the money for his books. The outer door slammed after him.

Then Judy knew that the college man sold books and was mad because Mother would not pay him. Still it was strange. She had never seen her mother so heartbroken. Even with the father it had not been like that. For she had never heard her proud mother plead. She had never seen her stalwart mother cling to anyone.

Judy had to say it. Give him back his old books.

Her mother stopped in the midst of a sob. You go and play, she said coldly.

After a while Judy almost forgot about the college man and the money her mother owed him. It was only when her mother walked up and down and around the room looking burningly beautiful that Judy felt sick and afraid and saw the college man's image.

Then it was that Judy, who could read almost anything at seven, read in the Sunday supplement about the moving picture machine. You sent away for some reproductions of famous paintings. When they came you sold them. When you had sold them all you sent the money to Mr. Fisher in Chicago, and he sent you a moving picture machine. If you put up a sheet and charged a penny to all the children in the neighborhood once a week, pretty soon you'd have enough money to give your mother to pay that old college man for his old books.

Judy talked it over with the father, except the part about the college man. He said he was proud of his little businesswoman and helped her write the letter to Mr. Fisher. He took her out and lifted her up to the mailbox so she could post it herself.

In less than a week the pictures came. The father said they were beautiful and made the first purchase himself. There were twenty to dispose of at a quarter apiece.

Judy sold one to her teacher, one to the barber who cut her hair, one to the corner grocer at whose store they had an account, one to kind Mr. McCarthy who ran the poolroom, one to an uncle, one to an aunt, and two to company ladies. The father said she had done simply wonders and took the rest of the pictures to the office building, where he was superintendent, and sold them.

He brought her the money in silver. Judy was very excited. She counted out her money and wanted to have it all changed to a five-dollar bill.

Mother got up and said she would take Judy to the corner grocer's right now. And tomorrow they would go to the post office, where Judy was to send the money order herself.

Mother held out her hand and was radiant. Judy slipped her small palm into hers. They smiled at each other and shut out the male, their husband and father. In this moment Judy was saying, it is for your sake, my darling. Her mother's mounting excitement answered, I know it, my sweet, my precious.

They went to the corner grocer's, still holding hands. Judy skipped along. It was seven o'clock of a winter's evening. The stars were shining. The snow crunched under her feet. Everything was dear and familiar, the car line, the icicles on the cables, the signboards with their bright illustrations luminous under the electric lights, the vacant lot with the snowmen silent and stout, the fire alarm, the post box. All things good, and best of all her mother's bright and beautiful face, her mother's parted, red-lipped mouth, with her breath on the winter night.

The corner grocer rang up No Sale and gave Judy a five-dollar bill. Judy said, you take it for me, Mommy, with the same indulgence that mothers use in saying to small children, you may carry the package, dear.

Mother opened her purse and fished around in it. After a while she looked her amused surprise at Mr. Brady and gave him a lovely, humble smile, full of sweet pleading. She took Mr. Brady into her confidence and said she must make an urgent call. Would Mr. Brady give her a nickel and put it on the bill.

All of a sudden Judy felt sick. She knew her mother's burning beauty had not been for her, nor was it now for Mr. Brady. She did not want to hear her mother make the telephone call. She went and stood at the door and stared up at a little star snug among its elders. The star began blinking so hard that it made her eyes water.

When she heard the nickel ring in the telephone box, she began to sing shrilly and kept on singing until her mother came out of the booth and bade Mr. Brady a wonderful good night.

All the way home Judy would not look at her mother. She played a skipping game that kept her a pace ahead. Her mother kept saying loving things, but Judy pretended not to hear and would give no loving answers.

At the door her mother reminded her, my precious, don't bother to mention to your father about the telephone call. I dialed the wrong number and lost my nickel, so I didn't really make it after all.

When Judy went in she said, good night, Father, with her head hanging down. She hated him, too, and ran off to bed without once begging to stay up.

In the morning Judy made herself believe that last night had been a bad dream. She ran all the way home from school. Her mother greeted her with a hug and kiss. She looked very alive and kept smiling at Judy, with the blood flooding her cheeks and her eyes star bright in her head.

Judy ate her lunch. The table was pretty, but there was unwashed company china in the sink. The plate her mother placed before her was not a company plate.

The lunch was soft things, but they stuck in Judy's throat. She felt excited and sad. Suddenly her mother was saying, darling, I sent your money off myself. I was passing the post office this morning, and it seemed rather silly to make a second trip this noon. You won't tell your father, will you? He thought it would please you to send it yourself. But you're Mother's big girl, aren't you, my precious? And you aren't disappointed, are you?

No'm, said Judy, and she never said no'm. Her heart was standing in her throat. She thought it would burst.

That night she went to bed before the father came for dinner. She said she felt sick in her stomach, and in fact she did. She did not want the light, nor a book, nor her doll. She shut her eyes tight. The father tiptoed into the room. She lay very still. His lips brushed her forehead. He tiptoed out. She put her mouth in the pillow and sobbed herself to sleep.

It was not so bad the first week. After every mail she would make herself believe the moving picture machine would surely come on the next. But the week passed. Another week began. The father said, it ought to come this week anyway. Her mother added cheerfully, oh yes. The second week ended. The third week began. Then the father said, shall I help you write them a letter, Judy?

Her eyes met her mother's bright unwavering ones. I forgot the address, she said.

Thereafter the father did not speak of the matter again. He said Judy must just consider it an unfortunate experience and profit by it.

Saturday morning of the fourth week it was Judy who got the mail that the elevator boy had pushed under the doorsill. There was a letter addressed to herself. It bore Mr. Fisher's return address. The other letters fell from her hand. She stumbled blindly into her room and opened the envelope.

It was not really a letter. It was a newspaper page. There was a picture of a little girl and a story with easy words about how she had kept some pictures that belonged to Mr. Fisher, though he had written her twice to return them. The police had come and taken her to jail, where she had stayed forever and ever. Her mother got sick and died from worrying. Her father lost his job because his daughter was a thief and had to beg on the streets.

Judy was so terrified she could not stir. Her eyes dilated. She could not swallow. She began to itch all over.

After a long time she folded the newspaper page and hid it under her mattress. She flung herself across the bed, quivering and unable to cry. She would suffer like this at the peal of a bell, at an unfamiliar voice, at an unexpected sound, and she would share this pain with no one. For she knew even if she screwed up the courage to go to a grown-up, she would get the untruthful answer, children don't go to jail, when there was that picture of that little girl which proved that they did.

The doorbell jangled. Judy jumped off the bed, scuttled under it, and drew herself up into a ball, banging her head against the floor, and holding her breath hard.

God, she prayed, let me die.

But children do not die. They grow up to be the strange things called mothers and fathers. Very few parents profit by childhood experiences. When they look back they do not really remember. They see through a sentimental haze. For childhood is full of unrequited love, and suffering, and tears.

JACK IN THE POT

When she walked down the aisle of the theater, clutching the money in her hand, hearing the applause and laughter, seeing, dimly, the grinning black faces, she was trembling so violently that she did not know how she could ever regain her seat.

It was unbelievable. Week after week she had come on Wednesday afternoon to this smelly, third-run neighborhood movie house, paid her dime, received her beano card, and gone inside to wait through an indifferent feature until the house lights came on, and a too jovial white man wheeled a board onto the stage and busily fished in a bowl for numbers.

Today it had happened. As the too jovial white man called each number, she found a corresponding one on her card. When he called the seventh number and explained dramatically that whoever had punched five numbers in a row had won the jackpot of fifty-five dollars, she listened in smiling disbelief that there was that much money in his pocket. It was then that the woman beside her leaned toward her and said excitedly, 'Look, lady, you got it!'

She did not remember going down the aisle. Undoubtedly her neighbor had prodded her to her feet. When it was over, she tottered dazedly to her seat, and sat in a dreamy stupor, scarcely able to believe her good fortune.

The drawing continued, the last dollar was given away, the theater darkened, and the afternoon crowd filed out. The little gray woman, collecting her wits, followed them.

She revived in the sharp air. Her head cleared and happiness swelled in her throat. She had fifty-five dollars in her purse. It was wonderful to think about.

She reached her own intersection and paused before Mr. Spiro's general market. Here she regularly shopped, settling part of her bill fortnightly out of her relief check. When Mr. Spiro put in inferior stock because most of his customers were poor-paying reliefers, she had wanted to shop elsewhere. But she could never get paid up.

Excitement smote her. She would go in, settle her account, and say good-bye to Mr. Spiro forever. Resolutely she turned into the market.

Mr. Spiro, broad and unkempt, began to boom heartily, from behind the counter. 'Hello, Mrs. Edmunds.'

She lowered her eyes and asked diffidently, 'How much is my bill, Mr. Spiro?'

He recoiled in horror. 'Do I worry about your bill, Mrs. Edmunds? Don't you pay something when you get your relief check? Ain't you one of my best customers?'

'I'd like to settle,' said Mrs. Edmunds breathlessly.

Mr. Spiro eyed her shrewdly. His voice was soft and insinuating. 'You got cash, Mrs. Edmunds? You hit the number? Every other week you give me something on account. This week you want to settle. Am I losing your trade? Ain't I always treated you right?'

'Sure, Mr. Spiro,' she answered nervously. 'I was telling my husband just last night, ain't another man treats me like Mr. Spiro. And I said I wished I could settle my bill.'

'Gee,' he said triumphantly, 'it's like I said. You're one of my best customers. Worrying about your bill when I ain't even worrying. I was telling your investigator . . .' he paused significantly, 'when Mr. Edmunds gets a job, I know I'll get the balance. Mr. Edmunds got himself a job maybe?'

She was stiff with fright. 'No, I'd have told you right off, and her, too. I ain't one to cheat on relief. I was only saying how I wished I could settle. I wasn't saying that I was.'

'Well, then, what you want for supper?' Mr. Spiro asked soothingly.

'Loaf of bread,' she answered gratefully, 'two pork chops, one kinda thick, can of spaghetti, little can of milk.'

The purchases were itemized. Mrs. Edmunds said good night and left the store. She felt sick and ashamed, for she had turned tail in the moment that was to have been her triumph over tyranny.

A little boy came toward her in the familiar rags of the neighborhood children. Suddenly Mrs. Edmunds could bear no longer the intolerable weight of her mean provisions.

'Little boy,' she said.

'Ma'am?' He stopped and stared at her.

'Here.' She held out the bag to him. 'Take it home to your mama. It's food. It's clean.'

He blinked, then snatched the bag from her hands, and turned and ran very fast in the direction from which he had come.

Mrs. Edmunds felt better at once. Now she could buy a really good supper. She walked ten blocks to a better neighborhood and the cold did not bother her. Her misshapen shoes were winged.

She pushed inside a resplendent store and marched to the meat counter. A porterhouse steak caught her eye. She could not look past it. It was big and thick and beautiful.

The clerk leaned toward her. 'Steak, moddom?'

'That one.'

It was glorious not to care about the cost of things. She bought mushrooms, fresh peas, cauliflower, tomatoes, a pound of good coffee, a pint of real cream, a dozen dinner rolls, and a maple walnut layer cake.

The winter stars were pricking the sky when she entered the dimly lit hallway of the old-law tenement in which she lived. The dank smell smote her instantly after the long walk in the brisk, clear air. The Smith boy's dog had dirtied the hall again. Mr. Johnson, the janitor, was mournfully mopping up.

'Evenin', Mis' Edmunds, ma'am,' he said plaintively.

'Evening,' Mrs. Edmunds said coldly. Suddenly she hated Mr. Johnson. He was so humble.

Five young children shared the uninhabitable basement with him. They were always half sick, and he was always neglecting his duties to tend to them. The tenants were continually deciding to report him to the agent, and then at the last moment deciding not to.

'I'll be up tomorrow to see 'bout them windows, Mis' Edmunds, ma'am. My baby kep' frettin' today, and I been so busy doctorin'.'

'Those children need a mother,' said Mrs. Edmunds severely. 'You ought to get married again.'

'My wife ain' daid,' cried Mr. Johnson, shocked out of his servility. 'She's in that T.B. home. Been there two years and 'bout on the road to health.'

'Well,' said Mrs. Edmunds inconclusively, and then added briskly, 'I been waiting weeks and weeks for them window strips. Winter's half over. If the place was kept warm –'

'Yes'm, Mis' Edmunds,' he said hastily, his bloodshot eyes imploring. 'It's that ol' furnace. I done tol' the agent time and again, but they ain' fixin' to fix up this house 'long as you all is relief folks.'

*

The steak was sizzling on the stove when Mr. Edmunds' key turned in the lock of the tiny three-room flat. His step dragged down the hall. Mrs. Edmunds knew what that meant: 'No man wanted.' Two years ago Mr. Edmunds had begun, doggedly, to canvass the city for work, leaving home soon after breakfast and rarely returning before supper.

Once he had had a little stationery store. After losing it, he had spent his small savings and sold or pawned every decent article of furniture and clothing before applying for relief. Even so, there had been a long investigation while he and his wife slowly starved. Fear had been implanted in Mrs. Edmunds. Thereafter she was never wholly unafraid. Mr. Edmunds had had to stand by and watch his wife starve. He never got over being ashamed.

Mr. Edmunds stood in the kitchen doorway, holding his rain-streaked hat in his knotted hand. He was forty-nine, and he looked like an old man.

'I'm back,' he said. 'Cooking supper.'

It was not a question. He seemed unaware of the intoxicating odors.

She smiled at him brightly. 'Smell good?'

He shook suddenly with the cold that was still in him. 'Smells like always to me.'

Her face fell in disappointment, but she said gently, 'You oughtn't to be walking 'round this kind of weather.'

'I was looking for work,' he said fiercely. 'Work's not going to come knocking.'

She did not want to quarrel with him. He was too cold, and their supper was too fine.

'Things'll pick up in the spring,' she said soothingly.

'Not for me,' he answered gloomily. 'Look how I look. Like a bum. I wouldn't hire me, myself.'

'What you want me to do about it?' she asked furiously.

'Nothing,' he said with wry humor, 'unless you can make money, and make me just about fifty dollars.'

She caught her breath and stared at his shabbiness. She had seen him look like this so long that she had forgotten that clothes would make a difference.

She nodded toward the stove. 'That steak and all. Guess you think I got a fortune. Well, I won a little old measly dollar at the movies.'

His face lightened, and his eyes grew soft with affection. 'You shouldn't have bought a steak,' he said. 'Wish you'd bought yourself something you been wanting. Like gloves. Some good warm gloves. Hurts my heart when I see you with cold hands.'

She was ashamed, and wished she knew how to cross the room to kiss him. 'Go wash,' she said gruffly. 'Steak's 'most too done already.'

It was a wonderful dinner. Both of them had been starved for fresh meat. Mrs. Edmunds' face was flushed, and there was color in her lips, as if the good blood of the meat had filtered through her skin. Mr. Edmunds ate a pound and a half of the two-pound steak, and his hands seemed steadier with each sharp thrust of the knife.

Over coffee and cake they talked contentedly. Mrs. Edmunds wanted to tell the truth about the money, and waited for an opening.

'We'll move out of this hole some day soon,' said Mr. Edmunds. 'Things won't be like this always.' He was full and warm and confident.

'If I had fifty dollars,' Mrs. Edmunds began cautiously, 'I believe I'd move tomorrow. Pay up these people what I owe, and get me a fit place to live in.'

'Fifty dollars would be a drop in the bucket. You got to have something coming in steady.'

He had hurt her again. 'Fifty dollars is more than you got,' she said meanly.

'It's more than you got, too,' he said mildly. 'Look at it like this. If you had fifty dollars and made a change, them relief folks would worry you like a pack of wolves. But say, f' instance, you had fifty dollars, and I had a job, we could walk out of here without a howdy-do to anybody.'

It would have been anticlimactic to tell him about the money. She got up. 'I'll do the dishes. You sit still.'

He noticed no change in her and went on earnestly, 'Lord's bound to put something in my way soon. Things is got to break for us. We don't live human. I never see a paper 'cept when I pick one up a the subway. I ain't had a cigarette in three years. We ain't got a radio. We don't have no company. All the plea-sure you get is a ten-cent movie one day a week. I don't even get that.'

Presently Mrs. Edmunds ventured, 'You think the investiga-tor would notice if we got a little radio for the bedroom?'

'Somebody got one to give away?' His voice was eager.

'Maybe.'

'Well, seeing how she could check with the party what give it to you, I think it would be all right.'

'Well, ne' mind –' Her voice petered out.

It was his turn to try. 'Want to play me a game of cards?'

He had not asked her for months. She cleared her throat. 'I'll play a hand or two.'

He stretched luxuriously. 'I feel so good. Feeling like this, bet I'll land something tomorrow.'

She said very gently, 'The investigator comes tomorrow.'

He smiled quickly to hide his disappointment. 'Clean forgot. It don't matter. That meal was so good it'll carry me straight through Friday.'

She opened her mouth to tell him about the jackpot, to promise him as many meals as there was money. Suddenly someone upstairs pounded on the radiator for heat. In a moment someone downstairs pounded. Presently their side of the house resounded. It was maddening. Mrs. Edmunds was bitterly aware that her hands and feet were like ice.

' 'Tisn't no use,' she cried wildly to the walls. She burst into tears. ' 'Tisn't nothing no use.'

Her husband crossed quickly to her. He kissed her cheek. 'I'm going to make all this up to you. You'll see.'

By half past eight they were in bed. By quarter to nine Mrs. Edmunds was quietly sleeping. Mr. Edmunds lay staring at the ceiling. It kept coming closer.

Mrs. Edmunds waked first and decided to go again to the grand market. She dressed and went out into the street. An ambulance stood in front of the door. In a minute an intern emerged from the basement, carrying a bundled child. Mr. Johnson followed, his eyes more bleary and bloodshot than ever.

Mrs. Edmunds rushed up to him. 'The baby?' she asked anxiously.

His face worked pitifully. 'Yes, ma'am, Mis' Edmunds. Pneumonia. I heard you folks knockin' for heat last night but my hands was too full. I ain't forgot about them windows, though. I'll be up tomorrow bright and early.'

Mr. Edmunds stood in the kitchen door. 'I smell meat in the morning?' he asked incredulously. He sat down, and she spread the feast, kidneys, and omelet, hot buttered rolls, and strawberry jam. 'You mind,' he said happily, 'explaining this mystery? Was that dollar of yours made out of elastic?'

'It wasn't a dollar like I said. It was five. I wanted to surprise you.'

She did not look at him and her voice was breathless. She had decided to wait until after the investigator's visit to tell him the whole truth about the money. Otherwise they might both be nervous and betray themselves by their guilty knowledge.

'We got chicken for dinner,' she added shyly.

'Lord, I don't know when I had a piece of chicken.'

They ate, and the morning passed glowingly. With Mr. Edmunds' help, Mrs. Edmunds moved the furniture and gave the flat a thorough cleaning. She liked for the investigator to find her busy. She felt less embarrassed about being on relief when it could be seen that she occupied her time.

The afternoon waned. The Edmundses sat in the living room, and there was nothing to do. They were hungry but dared not start dinner. With activity suspended, they became aware of the penetrating cold and the rattling windows. Mr. Edmunds began to have that wild look of waiting for the investigator.

Mrs. Edmunds suddenly had an idea. She would go and get a newspaper and a package of cigarettes for him.

At the corner, she ran into Mr. Johnson. Rather he ran into her, for he turned the corner with his head down, and his gait as unsteady as if he had been drinking.

'That you, Mr. Johnson?' she said sharply.

He raised his head, and she saw that he was not drunk.

'Yes, ma'am, Mis' Edmunds.'

'The baby – is she worse?'

Tears welled out of his eyes. 'The Lord done took her.'

Tears stood in her own eyes. 'God knows I'm sorry to hear that. Let me know if there's anything I can do.'

'Thank you, Mis' Edmunds, ma'am. But ain't nothin' nobody can do. I been pricin' funerals. I can get one for fifty dollars. But I been to my brother, and he ain't got it. I been everywhere. Couldn't raise no more than ten dollars.' He was suddenly embarrassed. 'I know all you tenants is on relief. I wasn't fixin' to ask you all.'

'Fifty dollars,' she said strainedly, 'is a lot of money.'

'God'd have to pass a miracle for me to raise it. Guess the city'll have to bury her. You reckon they'll let me take flowers?'

'You being the father, I guess they would,' she said weakly.

When she returned home the flat was a little warmer. She entered the living room. Her husband's face brightened.

'You bought a paper!'

She held out the cigarettes. 'You smoke this kind?' she asked lifelessly.

He jumped up and crossed to her. 'I declare I don't know how to thank you! Wish that investigator'd come. I sure want to taste them.'

'Go ahead and smoke,' she cried fiercely. 'It's none of her business. We got our rights same as working people.'

She turned into the bedroom. She was utterly spent. Too much had happened in the last twenty-four hours.

'Guess I'll stretch out for a bit. I'm not going to sleep. If I do drop off, listen out for the investigator. The bell needs fixing. She might have to knock.'

At half past five Mr. Edmunds put down the newspaper and tip-toed to the bedroom door. His wife was still asleep. He stood for a moment in indecision, then decided it was long past the hour when the investigator usually called, and went down the hall to the kitchen. He wanted to prepare supper as a surprise. He opened the window, took the foodstuffs out of the crate that in winter served as icebox, and set them on the table.

The doorbell tinkled faintly.

He went to the door and opened it. The investigator stepped inside. She was small and young and white.

'Good evening, miss,' he said.

'I'm sorry to call so late,' she apologized. 'I've been busy all day with an evicted family. But I knew you were expecting me, and I didn't want you to stay in tomorrow.'

'You come on up front, miss,' he said. 'I'll wake up my wife. She wasn't feeling so well and went to lie down.'

She saw the light from the kitchen, and the dark rooms beyond.

'Don't wake Mrs. Edmunds,' she said kindly, 'if she isn't well. I'll just sit in the kitchen for a minute with you.'

He looked down at her, but her open, honest face did not disarm him. He braced himself for whatever was to follow.

'Go right on in, miss,' he said.

He took the dish towel and dusted the clean chair. 'Sit down, miss.'

He stood facing her with a furrow between his brows, and his arms folded. There was an awkward pause. She cast about for something to say, and saw the table.

'I interrupted your dinner preparations.'

His voice and his face hardened for the blow.

'I was getting dinner for my wife. It's chicken.'

'It looks like a nice one,' she said pleasantly.

He was baffled. 'We ain't had chicken once in three years.'

'I understand,' she said sincerely. 'Sometimes I spend my whole salary on something I want very much.'

'You ain't much like an investigator,' he said in surprise. 'One we had before you woulda raised Ned.' He sat down suddenly, his defenses down. 'Miss, I been wanting to ask you this for a long time. You ever have any men's clothes?'

Her voice was distressed. 'Every once in a while. But with so many people needing assistance, we can only give them to our employables. But I'll keep your request in mind.'

He did not answer. He just sat staring at the floor, presenting an adjustment problem. There was nothing else to say to him.

She rose. 'I'll be going now, Mr. Edmunds.'

'I'll tell my wife you was here, miss.'

A voice called from the bedroom. 'Is that you talking?'

'It's the investigator lady,' he said. 'She's just going.'

Mrs. Edmunds came hurrying down the hall, the sleep in her face and tousled hair.

'I was just lying down, ma'am. I didn't mean to go to sleep. My husband should've called me.'

'I didn't want him to wake you.'

'And he kept you sitting in the kitchen.'

She glanced inside to assure herself that it was sufficiently spotless for the fine clothes of the investigator. She saw the laden table, and felt so ill that water welled into her mouth.

'The investigator lady knows about the chicken,' Mr. Edmunds said quickly. 'She –'

'It was only five dollars,' his wife interrupted, wringing her hands.

'Five dollars for a chicken?' The investigator was shocked and incredulous.

'She didn't buy that chicken out of none of your relief money,' Mr. Edmunds said defiantly. 'It was money she won at a movie.'

'It was only five dollars,' Mrs. Edmunds repeated tearfully.

'We ain't trying to conceal nothing,' Mr. Edmunds snarled. He was cornered and fighting. 'If you'd asked me how we come by the chicken, I'd have told you.'

'For God's sake, ma'am, don't cut us off,' Mrs. Edmunds moaned. 'I'll never go to another movie. It was only ten cents. I didn't know I was doing wrong.' She burst into tears.

The investigator stood tense. They had both been screaming at her. She was tired and so irritated that she wanted to scream back.

'Mrs. Edmunds,' she said sharply, 'get hold of yourself. I'm not going to cut you off. That's ridiculous. You won five dollars at a movie and you bought some food. That's fine. I wish my family could win five dollars for food.'

She turned and tore out of the flat. They heard her stumbling and sobbing down the stairs.

'You feel like eating?' Mrs. Edmunds asked dully.

'I guess we're both hungry. That's why we got so upset.'

'Maybe we'd better eat, then.'

'Let me fix it.'

'No.' She entered the kitchen. 'I kinda want to see you just sitting and smoking a cigarette.'

He sat down and reached in his pocket with some eagerness. 'I ain't had one yet.' He lit a cigarette, inhaled, and felt better immediately.

'You think,' she said bleakly, 'she'll write that up in our case?'

'I don't know, dear.'

'You think they'll close our case if she does?'

'I don't know that neither, dear.'

She clutched the sink for support. 'My God, what would we do?'

The smoke curled around him luxuriously. 'Don't think about it till it happens.'

'I got to think about it. The rent, the gas, the light, the food.'

'They wouldn't hardly close our case for five dollars.'

'Maybe they'd think it was more.'

'You could prove it by the movie manager.'

She went numb all over. Then suddenly she got mad about it.

It was nine o'clock when they sat down in the living room. The heat came up grudgingly. Mrs. Edmunds wrapped herself in her sweater and read the funnies. Mr. Edmunds was happily inhaling his second cigarette. They were both replete and in good humor.

The window rattled and Mr. Edmunds looked around at it lazily. 'Been about two months since you asked Mr. Johnson for weather strips.'

The paper shook in her hand. She did not look up. 'He promised to fix it this morning, but his baby died.'

'His baby! You don't say!'

She kept her eyes glued to the paper. 'Pneumonia.'

His voice filled with sympathy. He crushed out his cigarette. 'Believe I'll go down and sit with him a while.'

'He's not there,' she said hastily. 'I met him when I was going to the store. He said he'd be out all evening.'

'I bet the poor man's trying to raise some money.'

She let the paper fall in her lap, and clasped her hands to keep them from trembling. She lied again, as she had been lying steadily in the past twenty-four hours, as she had not lied before in all her life.

'He didn't say nothing to me about raising money.'

'Wasn't no need to. Where would you get the first five cents to give him?'

'I guess,' she cried jealously, 'you want me to give him the rest of my money.'

'No,' he said. 'I want you to spend what little's left on yourself. Me, I wish I had fifty dollars to give him.'

'As poor as you are,' she asked angrily, 'you'd give him that much money? That's easy to say when you haven't got it.'

'I look at it this way,' he said simply. 'I think how I'd feel in his shoes.'

'You got your own troubles,' she argued heatedly. 'The Johnson baby is better off dead. You'd be a fool to put fifty dollars in the ground. I'd spend my fifty dollars on the living.'

' 'Tain't no use to work yourself up,' he said. 'You ain't got fifty dollars, and neither have I. We'll be quarreling in a minute over make-believe money. Let's go to bed.'

Mrs. Edmunds waked at seven and tried to lie quietly by her husband's side, but lying still was torture. She dressed and went into the kitchen, and felt too listless to make her coffee. She sat down at the table and dropped her head on her folded arms. No tears came. There was only the burning in her throat and behind her eyes.

She sat in this manner for half an hour. Suddenly she heard a man's slow tread outside her front door. Terror gripped her. The steps moved on down the hall, but for a moment her knees were water. When she could control her trembling, she stood up and knew that she had to get out of the house. It could not contain her and Mr. Johnson.

She walked quickly away from her neighborhood. It was a raw day, and her feet and hands were beginning to grow numb. She felt sorry for herself. Other people were hurrying past in overshoes and heavy gloves. There were fifty-one dollars in her purse. It was her right to do what she pleased with them. Determinedly she turned into the subway.

In a downtown department store she rode the escalator to the dress department. She walked up and down the rows of lovely garments, stopping to finger critically, standing back to admire.

A salesgirl came toward her, looking straight at her with soft, expectant eyes.

'Do you wish to be waited on, madam?'

Mrs. Edmunds opened her mouth to say 'Yes,' but the word would not come. She stared at the girl stupidly. 'I was just looking,' she said.

In the shoe department, she saw a pair of comfort shoes and sat down timidly in a fine leather chair.

A salesman lounged toward her. 'Something in shoes?'

'Yes, sir. That comfort shoe.'

'Size?' His voice was bored.

'I don't know,' she said.

'I'll have to measure you,' he said reproachfully. 'Give me your foot.' He sat down on a stool and held out his hand.

She dragged her eyes up to his face. 'How much you say those shoes cost?'

'I didn't say. Eight dollars.'

She rose with acute relief. 'I ain't got that much with me.'

She retreated unsteadily. Something was making her knees weak and her head light.

Her legs steadied. She went quickly to the down escalator.

She reached the third floor and was briskly crossing to the next down escalator when she saw the little dresses. A banner screamed that they were selling at the sacrifice price of one dollar. She decided to examine them.

She pushed through the crowd of women, and emerged triumphantly within reach of the dresses. She searched carefully. There were pinks and blues and yellows. She was looking for white. She pushed back through the crowd. In her careful hands lay a little white dress. It was spun gold and gossamer.

Boldly she beckoned a salesgirl. 'I'll take this, miss,' she said.

All the way home she was excited and close to tears. She was in a fever to see Mr. Johnson. She would let the regret come later. A child lay dead and waiting burial.

She turned her corner at a run. Going down the rickety basement stairs, she prayed that Mr. Johnson was on the premises.

She pounded on his door and he opened it. The agony in his face told her instantly that he had been unable to borrow the money. She tried to speak, and her tongue tripped over her eagerness.

Fear took hold of her and rattled her teeth. 'Mr. Johnson, what about the funeral?'

'I give the baby to the student doctors.'

'Oh my God, Mr. Johnson! Oh my God!'

'I bought her some flowers.'

She turned and went blindly up the stairs. Drooping in the front doorway was a frost-nipped bunch of white flowers. She dragged herself up to her flat. Once she stopped to hide the package under her coat. She would never look at that little white dress again. The ten five-dollar bills were ten five-pound stones in her purse. They almost hurled her backward.

She turned the key in her lock. Mr. Edmunds stood at the door. He looked rested and confident.

'I been waiting for you. I just started to go.'

'You had any breakfast?' she asked tonelessly.

'I made some coffee. It was all I wanted.'

'I shoulda made some oatmeal before I went out.'

'You have on the big pot time I come home. Bet I'll land something good,' he boasted. 'You brought good luck in this house. We ain't seen the last of it.' He pecked her cheek and went out, hurrying as if he were late for work.

She plodded into the bedroom. The steam was coming up fine. She sank down on the side of the bed and unbuttoned her coat. The package fell on her lap. She took the ten five-dollar bills and pushed them between a fold of the package. It was burial money. She could never use it for anything else. She hid the package under the mattress.

Wearily she buttoned up her coat and opened her purse again. It was empty, for the few cents remaining from her last relief check had been spent indiscriminately with her prize money.

She went into the kitchen to take stock of her needs. There was nothing left from their feasts. She felt the coffeepot. It was still hot, but her throat was too constricted for her to attempt to swallow.

She took her paper shopping bag and started out to Mr. Spiro's.

MAMMY

The young Negro welfare investigator, carrying her brief-case, entered the ornate foyer of the Central Park West apartment house. She was making a collateral call. Earlier in the day she had visited an aging colored woman in a rented room in Harlem. Investigation had proved that the woman was not quite old enough for Old Age Assistance, and yet no longer young enough to be classified as employable. Nothing, therefore, stood in the way of her eligibility for relief. Hers was a clear case of need. This collateral call on her former employer was merely routine.

The investigator walked toward the elevator, close on the heels of a well-dressed woman with a dog. She felt shy. Most of her collaterals were to housewives in the Bronx or supervisors of maintenance workers in office buildings. Such calls were never embarrassing. A moment ago as she neared the doorway, the doorman had regarded her intently. The service entrance was plainly to her left, and she was walking past it. He had been on the point of approaching when a tenant emerged and dispatched him for a taxi. He had stood for a moment torn between his immediate duty and his sense of outrage. Then he had gone away dolefully, blowing his whistle.

The woman with the dog reached the elevator just as the

doors slid open. The dog bounded in, and the elevator boy bent and rough-housed with him. The boy's agreeable face was black, and the investigator felt a flood of relief.

The woman entered the elevator and smilingly faced front. Instantly the smile left her face, and her eyes hardened. The boy straightened, faced front, too, and gaped in surprise. Quickly he glanced at the set face of his passenger.

'Service entrance's outside,' he said sullenly.

The investigator said steadily, 'I am not employed here. I am here to see Mrs. Coleman on business.'

'If you're here on an errand or somethin' like that,' he argued doggedly, 'you still got to use the service entrance.'

She stared at him with open hate, despising him for humiliating her before and because of a woman of an alien race.

'I am here as a representative of the Department of Welfare. If you refuse me the use of this elevator, my office will take it up with the management.'

She did not know if this was true, but the elevator boy would not know either.

'Get in, then,' he said rudely, and rolled his eyes at his white passenger as if to convey his regret at the discomfort he was causing her.

The doors shut and the three shot upward, without speaking to or looking at each other. The woman with the dog, in a far corner, very pointedly held her small harmless animal on a tight leash.

The car stopped at the fourth floor, and the doors slid open. No one moved. There was a ten-second wait.

'You getting out or not?' the boy asked savagely.

There was no need to ask whom he was addressing.

'Is this my floor?' asked the investigator.

His sarcasm rippled. 'You want Mrs. Coleman, don't you?'

'Which is her apartment?' she asked thickly.

'Ten-A. You're holding up my passenger.'

When the door closed, she leaned against it, feeling sick, and trying to control her trembling. She was young and vulnerable. Her contact with Negroes was confined to frightened relief folks who did everything possible to stay in her good graces, and the members of her own set, among whom she was a favorite because of her two degrees and her civil service appointment. She had almost never run into Negroes who did not treat her with respect.

In a moment or two she walked down the hall to Ten-A. She rang, and after a little wait a handsome middle-aged woman opened the door.

'How do you do?' the woman said in a soft drawl. She smiled. 'You're from the relief office, aren't you? Do come in.'

'Thank you,' said the investigator, smiling, too, relievedly.

'Right this way,' said Mrs. Coleman, leading the way into a charming living room. She indicated an upholstered chair. 'Please sit down.'

The investigator, who never sat in overstuffed chairs in the homes of her relief clients, plumped down and smiled again at Mrs. Coleman. Such a pleasant woman, such a pleasant room. It was going to be a quick and easy interview. She let her brief-case slide to the floor beside her.

Mrs. Coleman sat down in a straight chair and looked searchingly at the investigator. Then she said somewhat breathlessly, 'You gave me to understand that Mammy has applied for relief.'

The odious title sent a little flicker of dislike across the investigator's face. She answered stiffly, 'I had just left Mrs. Mason when I telephoned you for this appointment.'

Mrs. Coleman smiled disarmingly, though she colored a little.

'She has been with us ever since I can remember. I call her Mammy, and so does my daughter.'

'That's a sort of nurse, isn't it?' the investigator asked coldly. 'I had thought Mrs. Mason was a general maid.'

'Is that what she said?'

'Why, I understood she was discharged because she was no longer physically able to perform her duties.'

'She wasn't discharged.'

The investigator looked dismayed. She had not anticipated complications. She felt for her briefcase.

'I'm very confused, Mrs. Coleman. Will you tell me just exactly what happened, then? I had no idea Mrs. Mason was – was misstating the situation.' She opened her briefcase.

Mrs. Coleman eyed her severely. 'There's nothing to write down. Do you have to write down things? It makes me feel as if I were being investigated.'

'I'm sorry,' said the investigator quickly, snapping shut her briefcase. 'If it would be distasteful . . . I apologize again. Please go on.'

'Well, there's little to tell. It all happened so quickly. My daughter was ill. My nerves were on edge. I may have said something that upset Mammy. One night she was here. The next morning she wasn't. I've been worried sick about her.'

'Did you report her disappearance?'

'Her clothes were gone, too. It didn't seem a matter for the police. It was obvious that she had left of her own accord. Believe me, young woman, I was very relieved when you telephoned me.' Her voice shook a little.

'I'm glad I can assure you that Mrs. Mason appears quite well. She only said she worked for you. She didn't mention your daughter. I hope she has recovered.'

'My daughter is married,' Mrs. Coleman said slowly. 'She had a child. It was stillborn. We have not seen Mammy since. For months she had looked forward to nursing it.'

'I'm sure it was a sad loss to all of you,' the investigator said gently. 'And old Mrs. Mason, perhaps she felt you had no further use for her. It may have unsettled her mind. Temporarily,' she added hastily. 'She seems quite sane.'

'Of course, she is,' said Mrs. Coleman with a touch of bitterness. 'She's just old and contrary. She knew we would worry about her. She did it deliberately.'

This was not in the investigator's province. She cleared her throat delicately.

'Would you take her back, Mrs. Coleman?'

'I want her back,' cried Mrs. Coleman. 'She has no one but us. She is just like one of the family.'

'You're very kind,' the investigator murmured. 'Most people feel no responsibility for their aging servants.'

'You do not know how dear a mammy is to a Southerner. I nursed at Mammy's breast. I cannot remember a day in my life without her.'

The investigator reached for her briefcase and rose.

'Then it is settled that she may return?'

A few hours ago there had been no doubt in her mind of old Mrs. Mason's eligibility for relief. With this surprising turn there was nothing to do but reject the case for inadequate proof of need. It was always a feather in a field worker's cap to reject a case that had been accepted for home investigation by a higher-paid office worker.

Mrs. Coleman looked at the investigator almost beseechingly.

'My child, I cannot tell you how much I will be in your debt if you can persuade Mammy to return. Can't you refuse to give her relief? She really is in need of nothing as long as I am living. Poor thing, what has she been doing for money? How has she been eating? In what sort of place is she staying?'

'She's very comfortable, really. She had three dollars when she came uptown to Harlem. She rented a room, explained her circumstances to her landlady, and is getting her meals there. I know that landlady. She has other roomers who are on relief. She trusts them until they get their relief checks. They never cheat her.'

'Oh, thank God! I must give you something to give to that woman. How good Negroes are. I am so glad it was you who came. You are so sympathetic. I could not have talked so freely to a white investigator. She would not have understood.'

The investigator's smile was wintry. She resented this well-meant restatement of the trusted position of the good darky.

She said civilly, however, 'I'm going back to Mrs. Mason's as soon as I leave here. I hope I can persuade her to return to you tonight.'

'Thank you! Mammy was happy here, believe me. She had nothing to do but a little dusting. We are a small family, myself, my daughter, and her husband. I have a girl who comes every day to do the hard work. She preferred to sleep in, but I wanted Mammy to have the maid's room. It's a lovely room with a private bath. It's next to the kitchen, which is nice for Mammy. Old people potter about so. I've lost girl after girl who felt she was meddlesome. But I've always thought of Mammy's comfort first.'

'I'm sure you have,' said the investigator politely, wanting to end the interview. She made a move toward departure. 'Thank you again for being so cooperative.'

Mrs. Coleman rose and crossed to the doorway.

'I must get my purse. Will you wait a moment?'

Shortly she reappeared. She opened her purse. 'It's been ten days. Please give that woman this twenty dollars. No, it isn't too much. And here is a dollar for Mammy's cab fare. Please put her in the cab yourself.'

'I'll do what I can.' The investigator smiled candidly. 'It must be nearly four, and my working day ends at five.'

'Yes, of course,' Mrs. Coleman said distractedly. 'And now I just want you to peep in at my daughter. Mammy will want to know how she is. She's far from well, poor lambie.'

The investigator followed Mrs. Coleman down the hall. At an open door they paused. A pale young girl lay on the edge of a big tossed bed. One hand was in her tangled hair, the other clutched an empty bassinet. The wheels rolled down and back, down and back. The girl glanced briefly and without interest at her mother and the investigator, then turned her face away.

'It tears my heart,' Mrs. Coleman whispered in a choked voice. 'Her baby, and then Mammy. She has lost all desire to live. But she is young and she will have other children. If she would only let me take away that bassinet! I am not the nurse that Mammy is. You can see how much Mammy is needed here.'

They turned away and walked in silence to the outer door. The investigator was genuinely touched, and eager to be off on her errand of mercy.

Mrs. Coleman opened the door, and for a moment seemed at a loss as to how to say good-bye. Then she said quickly, 'Thank you for coming,' and shut the door.

The investigator stood in indecision at the elevator, half persuaded to walk down three flights of stairs. But this she felt was turning tail, and pressed the elevator button.

The doors opened. The boy looked at her sheepishly. He swallowed and said ingratiatingly, 'Step in, miss. Find your party all right?'

She faced front, staring stonily ahead of her, and felt herself trembling with indignation at this new insolence.

He went on whiningly, 'That woman was in my car is mean as hell. I was just puttin' on to please her. She hates niggers 'cept when they're bowin' and scrapin'. She was the one had the old doorman fired. You see for yourself they got a white one now. With white folks needin' jobs, us niggers got to eat dirt to hang on.'

The investigator's face was expressionless except for a barely perceptible wincing at his careless use of a hated word.

He pleaded, 'You're colored like me. You ought to understand. I was only doing my job. I got to eat same as white folks, same as you.'

They rode the rest of the way in a silence interrupted only by his heavy sighs. When they reached the ground floor, and the doors slid open, he said sorrowfully, 'Good-bye, miss.'

She walked down the hall and out into the street, past the glowering doorman, with her face stern, and her stomach slightly sick.

The investigator rode uptown on a northbound bus. At One Hundred and Eighteenth Street she alighted and walked east. Presently she entered a well-kept apartment house. The elevator operator deferentially greeted her and whisked her upward.

She rang the bell of number fifty-four, and visited briefly with the landlady, who was quite overcome by the unexpected payment of twenty dollars. When she could escape her profuse thanks, the investigator went to knock at Mrs. Mason's door.

'Come in,' called Mrs. Mason. The investigator entered the small, square room. 'Oh, it's you, dear,' said Mrs. Mason, her lined brown face lighting up.

She was sitting by the window in a wide rocker. In her black, with a clean white apron tied about her waist, and a white bandana bound around her head, she looked ageless and full of remembering.

Mrs. Mason grasped her rocker by the arms and twisted around until she faced the investigator.

She explained shyly, 'I just sit here for hours lookin' out at the people. I ain' seen so many colored folks at one time since I left down home. Sit down, child, on the side of the bed. Hit's softer than that straight chair yonder.'

The investigator sat down on the straight chair, not because the bedspread was not scrupulously clean, but because what she had come to say needed stiff decorum.

'I'm all right here, Mrs. Mason. I won't be long.'

'I was hopin' you could set awhile. My landlady's good, but she's got this big flat. Don't give her time for much settin'.'

The investigator, seeing an opening, nodded understandingly.

'Yes, it must be pretty lonely for you here after being so long an intimate part of the Coleman family.'

The old woman's face darkened. 'Shut back in that bedroom behin' the kitchen? This here's what I like. My own kind and color. I'm too old a dog to be learnin' new tricks.'

'Your duties with Mrs. Coleman were very slight. I know you are getting on in years, but you are not too feeble for light employment. You were not entirely truthful with me. I was led to believe you did all the housework.'

The old woman looked furtively at the investigator. 'How come you know diff'rent now?'

'I've just left Mrs. Coleman's.'

Bafflement veiled the old woman's eyes. 'You didn't believe what all I tol' you?'

'We always visit former employers. It's part of our job, Mrs. Mason. Sometimes an employer will rehire our applicants. Mrs. Coleman is good enough to want you back. Isn't that preferable to being a public charge?'

'I ain't-a goin' back,' said the old woman vehemently.

The investigator was very exasperated. 'Why, Mrs. Mason?' she asked gently.

'That's an ungodly woman,' the old lady snapped. 'And I'm Godfearin'. Tain't no room in one house for God and the devil. I'm too near the grave to be servin' two masters.'

To the young investigator this was evasion by superstitious mutterings.

'You don't make yourself very clear, Mrs. Mason. Surely Mrs. Coleman didn't interfere with your religious convictions. You left her home the night after her daughter's child was born dead. Until then, apparently you had no religious scruples.'

The old woman looked at the investigator wearily. Then her head sank forward on her breast.

'That child warn't born dead.'

The investigator said impatiently, 'But surely the hospital –?'

' 'T warn't born in no hospital.'

'But the doctor –?'

'Little sly man. Looked like he'd cut his own throat for a dollar.'

'Was the child deformed?' the investigator asked helplessly.

'Hit was a beautiful baby,' said the old woman bitterly.

'Why, no one would destroy a healthy child,' the investigator cried indignantly. 'Mrs. Coleman hopes her daughter will have more children.' She paused, then asked anxiously, 'Her daughter is really married, isn't she? I mean, the baby wasn't . . . illegitimate?'

'Its ma and pa were married down home. A church weddin'. They went to school together. They was all right till they come up North. Then *she* started workin' on 'em. Old ways wasn't good enough for her.'

The investigator looked at her watch. It was nearly five. This last speech had been rambling gossip. Here was an old woman clearly disoriented in her Northern transplanting. Her position as mammy made her part of the family. Evidently she felt that gave her a matriarchal right to arbitrate its destinies. Her small grievances against Mrs. Coleman had magnified themselves in her mind until she could make this illogical accusation of infanticide as compensation for her homesickness for the folkways of the South. Her move to Harlem bore this out. To explain her reason for establishing a separate residence, she had told a fantastic story that could not be checked, and would not be recorded, unless the welfare office was prepared to face a libel suit.

'Mrs. Mason,' said the investigator, 'please listen carefully. Mrs. Coleman has told me that you are not only wanted, but very much needed in her home. There you will be given food and shelter in return for small services. Please understand that I sympathize with your imaginings, but you cannot remain here without public assistance, and I cannot recommend to my superiors that public assistance be given you.'

The old woman, who had listened worriedly, now said blankly, 'You mean I aint-a gonna get it?'

'No, Mrs. Mason, I'm sorry. And now it's ten to five. I'll be glad to help you pack your things, and put you in a taxi.'

The old woman looked helplessly around the room as if seeking a hiding place. Then she looked back at the investigator, her mouth trembling.

'You're my own people, child. Can' you fix up a story for them white folks at the relief, so's I could get to stay here where it's nice?'

'That would be collusion, Mrs. Mason. And that would cost me my job.'

The investigator rose. She was going to pack the old woman's things herself. She was heartily sick of her contrariness, and determined to see her settled once and for all.

'Now where is your bag?' she asked with forced cheerfulness. 'First I'll empty these bureau drawers.' She began to do so, laying things neatly on the bed. 'Mrs. Coleman's daughter will be so glad to see you. She's very ill, and needs your nursing.'

The old woman showed no interest. Her head had sunk forward on her breast again. She said listlessly, 'Let her ma finish what she started. I won't have no time for nursin'. I'll be down on my knees rasslin' with the devil. I done tol' you the devil's done eased out God in that house.'

The investigator nodded indulgently, and picked up a framed photograph that was lying face down in the drawer. She turned it over and involuntarily smiled at the smiling child in old-fashioned dress.

'This little girl,' she said, 'it's Mrs. Coleman, isn't it?'

The old woman did not look up. Her voice was still listless. 'That was my daughter.'

The investigator dropped the photograph on the bed as if it were a hot coal. Blindly she went back to the bureau, gathered up the rest of the things, and dumped them over the photograph.

She was a young investigator, and it was two minutes to five. Her job was to give or withhold relief. That was all.

'Mrs. Mason,' she said, 'please, please understand. This is my job.'

The old woman gave no sign of having heard.

THE RICHER, THE POORER

Over the years Lottie had urged Bess to prepare for her old age. Over the years Bess had lived each day as if there were no other. Now they were both past sixty, the time for summing up. Lottie had a bank account that had never grown lean. Bess had the clothes on her back, and the rest of her worldly possessions in a battered suitcase.

Lottie had hated being a child, hearing her parents' skimping and scraping. Bess had never seemed to notice. All she ever wanted was to go outside and play. She learned to skate on borrowed skates. She rode a borrowed bicycle. Lottie couldn't wait to grow up and buy herself the best of everything.

As soon as anyone would hire her, Lottie put herself to work. She minded babies, she ran errands for the old.

She never touched a penny of her money, though her child's mouth watered for ice cream and candy. But she could not bear to share with Bess, who never had anything to share with her. When the dimes began to add up to dollars, she lost her taste for sweets.

By the time she was twelve, she was clerking after school in a small variety store. Saturdays she worked as long as she was wanted. She decided to keep her money for clothes. When she entered high school, she would wear a wardrobe that neither she nor anyone else would be able to match.

But her freshman year found her unable to indulge so frivolous a whim, particularly when her admiring instructors advised her to think seriously of college. No one in her family had ever gone to college, and certainly Bess would never get there. She would show them all what she could do, if she put her mind to it.

She began to bank her money, and her bankbook became her most private and precious possession.

In her third year of high school she found a job in a small but expanding restaurant, where she cashiered from the busy hour until closing. In her last year of high school the business increased so rapidly that Lottie was faced with the choice of staying in school or working full time.

She made her choice easily. A job in hand was worth two in the future.

Bess had a beau in the school band, who had no other ambition except to play a horn. Lottie expected to be settled with a home and family while Bess was still waiting for Harry to earn enough to buy a marriage license.

That Bess married Harry straight out of high school was not surprising. That Lottie never married at all was not really surprising either. Two or three times she was halfway persuaded, but to give up a job that paid well for a homemaking job that paid nothing was a risk she was incapable of taking.

Bess's married life was nothing for Lottie to envy. She and Harry lived like gypsies, Harry playing in second-rate bands all over the country, even getting himself and Bess stranded in Europe. They were often in rags and never in riches.

Bess grieved because she had no child, not having sense enough to know she was better off without one. Lottie was certainly better off without nieces and nephews to feel sorry for. Very likely Bess would have dumped them on her doorstep.

That Lottie had a doorstep they might have been left on was only because her boss, having bought a second house, offered Lottie his first house at a price so low and terms so reasonable that it would have been like losing money to refuse.

She shut off the rooms she didn't use, letting them go to rack and ruin. Since she ate her meals out, she had no food at home, and did not encourage callers, who always expected a cup of tea.

Her way of life was mean and miserly, but she did not know it. She thought she lived frugally in her middle years so that she could live in comfort and ease when she most needed peace of mind.

The years, after forty, began to race. Suddenly Lottie was sixty, and retired from her job by her boss's son, who had no sentimental feeling about keeping her on until she was ready to quit.

She made several attempts to find other employment, but her dowdy appearance made her look old and inefficient. For the first time in her life Lottie would gladly have worked for nothing, to have some place to go, something to do with her day.

Harry died abroad, in a third-rate hotel, with Bess weeping as hard as if he had left her a fortune. He had left her nothing but his horn. There wasn't even money for her passage home.

Lottie, trapped by the blood tie, knew she would not only have to send for her sister, but take her in when she returned. It didn't seem fair that Bess should reap the harvest of Lottie's lifetime of self-denial.

It took Lottie a week to get a bedroom ready, a week of hard work and hard cash. There was everything to do, everything to replace or paint. When she was through the room looked so fresh and new that Lottie felt she deserved it more than Bess.

She would let Bess have her room, but the mattress was so lumpy, the carpet so worn, the curtains so threadbare that

Lottie's conscience pricked her. She supposed she would have to redo that room, too, and went about doing it with an eagerness that she mistook for haste.

When she was through upstairs, she was shocked to see how dismal downstairs looked by comparison. She tried to ignore it, but with nowhere to go to escape it, the contrast grew more intolerable.

She worked her way from kitchen to parlor, persuading herself she was only putting the rooms to rights to give herself something to do. At night she slept like a child after a long and happy day of playing house. She was having more fun than she had ever had in her life. She was living each hour for itself.

There was only a day now before Bess would arrive. Passing her gleaming mirrors, at first with vague awareness, then with painful clarity, Lottie saw herself as others saw her, and could not stand the sight.

She went on a spending spree from the specialty shops to beauty salon, emerging transformed into a woman who believed in miracles.

She was in the kitchen basting a turkey when Bess rang the bell. Her heart raced, and she wondered if the heat from the oven was responsible

She went to the door, and Bess stood before her. Stiffly she suffered Bess's embrace, her heart racing harder, her eyes suddenly smarting from the onrush of cold air.

'Oh, Lottie, it's good to see you,' Bess said, but saying nothing about Lottie's splendid appearance. Upstairs Bess, putting down her shabby suitcase, said, 'I'll sleep like a rock tonight,' without a word of praise for her lovely room. At the lavish table, top-heavy with turkey, Bess said, 'I'll take light and dark, both,' with no marveling at the size of the bird, or that there was turkey for two elderly women, one of them too poor to buy her own bread.

With the glow of good food in her stomach, Bess began to

spin stories. They were rich with places and people, most of them lowly, all of them magnificent. Her face reflected her telling, the joys and sorrows of her remembering, and above all, the love she lived by that enhanced the poorest place, the humblest person.

Then it was that Lottie knew why Bess had made no mention of her finery, or the shining room, or the twelve-pound turkey. She had not even seen them. Tomorrow she would see the room as it really looked, and Lottie as she really looked, and the warmed-over turkey in its second-day glory. Tonight she saw only what she had come seeking, a place in her sister's home and heart.

She said, 'That's enough about me. How have the years used you?'

'It was me who didn't use them,' said Lottie wistfully. 'I saved for them. I saved for them. I forgot the best of them would go without my ever spending a day or a dollar enjoying them. That's my life story in those few words, a life never lived.

'Now it's too near the end to try.'

Bess said, 'To know how much there is to know is the beginning of learning to live. Don't count the years that are left us. At our time of life it's the days that count. You've too much catching up to do to waste a minute of a waking hour feeling sorry for yourself.'

Lottie grinned, a real wide-open grin, 'Well to tell the truth, I felt sorry for you. Maybe if I had any sense I'd feel sorry for myself, after all. I know I'm too old to kick up my heels, but I'm going to let you show me how. If I land on my head, I guess it won't matter; I feel giddy already, and I like it.'

FUNERAL

Judy could not feel her mother. Nowhere in the wide expanse of bed was her large, warm body. And Judy dared not peer under the bed to see if some desperado had killed and concealed her. Tremors ran up and down her small body. Her hands grew hot and damp, and her feet quite cold and clammy. She wanted to scream for one of the aunts, but could not.

Someone was creaking up the stairs. It was probably the desperado come back to finish her off. She shut her eyes tightly and tried to think of Jesus.

The blackness was suddenly thinned with silver. A drawer opened and shut. She heard her mother's unmistakable sniff and opened her eyes.

'You go back to sleep,' said the mother.

But Judy sat up and stared solemnly. 'You're crying.'

'You go back to sleep,' said the mother.

There was movement in the aunts' room. Judy could hear her father blowing his nose. A terrible fear wrenched her heart.

'Mums, Mums, is my kitty dead?'

The mother laughed sharply and bitterly. 'The hospital phoned. Poor Uncle Eben has passed away.'

Judy lay back on her pillow. 'Has he gone somewhere?' she asked doubtfully.

'He's gone home to God,' said the mother with conviction.

Judy closed her eyes to shut out the comic image of an angelic Uncle Eben. When she opened them again it was day and time to get up for school.

She dressed leisurely. She had the realization that it did not matter whether she was late for school. She thought, 'There is death in my family,' and was proud.

She would go and say good morning to the aunts. The frail spinster sisters of her father adored her, and she liked to be petted. She always let a lock of hair hang over one eye, so that the favorite aunt might brush it away with a caressing hand and kiss her forehead.

The aunts sat silently by their coal fire. They were dressed in black. Their plain, dark faces were gaunt. Their hands were not steady in their laps.

Judy felt chilled and distressed. She went awkwardly to the favorite aunt and leaned against her knee. But the somber face was alien, and the unquiet hands did not flutter to her hair.

The elder aunt turned quietly to her sister. 'Do you think the child has heard?'

'God spare her,' said the favorite aunt, piously.

'Do you mean,' Judy asked shrilly, 'about Uncle Eben?'

The sharpness of it knifed their pathetic silence. Their mute mouths quivered. Their stricken eyes overflowed.

The image of Uncle Eben returned. But he was no longer amusing in robe and wings. Judy's breast burned. Her throat ached. She knew with intense agony that she was going to cry.

She turned and fled the room, gained her own, and flung herself prone on the bed. She burrowed her mouth in the pillow. She did not weep because Uncle Eben was dead. She wept out of a vast pity at the anguish of the living.

When she had quieted, she rose and bathed her heated face. She got together her little pile of books, set her cap on her tousled hair, slung her thick sweater over her arm, and went down the stairs.

The aunts had preceded her. They sat at the kitchen table drinking black coffee. The large and lovely yellow mother was eating heartily ham and eggs.

That strengthened Judy. She sat down and smiled.

'Don't you be late,' said the mother.

The familiar greeting shut the door fast on Uncle Eben. The aunts were simply in dark clothes. This was the usual Tuesday morning.

'Can I have two pieces of cake in my lunch?' asked Judy.

Presently she was going down the long hill to the school-house. She walked in the sun and lifted her face to the intermittent calls of wooing birds. Spring was just around the nearest corner, and Judy was glad.

She shot into her seat as the last bell rang.

Eulalie whispered to the back of her head: 'I spent two hours on this beastly history.'

Judy's mind raced back to the schoolroom. 'I've not studied it!'

'Oh, Judy! First period, too.'

'I went and forgot! What on earth made me go and forget? I always do it first thing every morning.' She thought sharply. 'It was my uncle's dying! My Uncle Eben died, Eulalie.'

'Oh!' said Eulalie, looking sorry.

Nora leaned out into the aisle. Her eyes were wide with sympathy. 'Is there death in your family, Judy?'

A thrill of pride ran down Judy's spine. Her breath quick-ened. Her eyes were like stars.

'It's my Uncle Eben who lived in a Home on account of being blind.'

'Did he die on account of being blind?' Eulalie ventured.

'I expect,' quoted Judy glibly, 'he had another stroke.'

'But why did you come to school?' Nora wanted to know.

'Death's very sad. My mummy puts away all our toys and pulls down the shades.'

'I think,' advised Eulalie, 'you ought to tell the teacher.'

Judy was suddenly shy. She had not thought Uncle Eben's death quite warranted her telling Miss Doran. It was strange and thrilling to her, because she had never before known death in its immediacy. It would embarrass her acutely if Miss Doran stared coldly and questioningly. Still, Eulalie had spoken with some authority. And Judy liked to watch the transformation of people's faces.

She got up from her seat, flung up her small head, and went down the aisle. The class with one accord straightened and craned. Judy, under this undeviating concentration, felt that her head was waggling, and was conscious of her isolated darkness.

Miss Doran looked up, frowned, and laid down her pen. At a glance Judy saw that she had been preparing a history quiz. She grew panicky, and this nervousness sent quick tears to her eyes. Miss Doran's face smoothed and softened. The unexpected gentleness further confused her. She said miserably, with a catch in her voice, 'My Uncle Eben's dead.'

Her words rang out clearly in the quiet room. There was an audible gasp. Then Judy could hear the triumphant whispering of Eulalie and Nora.

Miss Doran's arms went around her. 'Judy, dear child. I'm sorry. Do you want to return home, darling, or did your mother think it best to get you away from it all this morning?'

Judy was ashamed. She did not know how to tell Miss Doran that the momentous Thing was not lying importantly in her mother's parlor, but was somewhere in a vast hospital whose name she could not remember. She dreaded Miss Doran's jerking away from her in scorn. After all, families were huge affairs. Perhaps, to an experienced woman like Miss Doran, only death in the house really mattered.

Judy could not lie. 'No'm,' she said unhappily.

Miss Doran did not understand. 'Then, of course. I excuse you, Judy. I cannot expect you to have your mind on your studies. Stay out in the open as much as you can. You need not return until after the funeral.'

With a gentle pat she sent the child out. The class stared after her as one might stare after a favorite heroine.

Judy went racing down the corridor, her mind caught away to adventure. She knew that tomorrow her mother would pack her off to school again. But today was hers. And she had a quarter in her pocket. For the first time in her ten years, she was out on her own. She would poke her nose down various streets and browse in the library. She would eat her lunch on a park bench and buy a bag of candy. She would ride to the end of the car line and back. If she cared, she would even venture into an inexpensive movie. Death in the family was a holiday.

The exciting morning passed.

Father continually flipped out an enormous black-bordered handkerchief. He had on a black tie and an uncomfortable collar. He also had on Uncle Eben's shoes and hat and overcoat. Mother had said that with Uncle Eben's closetful of good, black clothes simply hanging in the Home, it was foolish of Father to buy a funeral outfit. Father had called a cab. Judy had begged the ride. They had come back fairly sitting on top of Uncle Eben's belongings.

The aunts were shrouded in long, black veils. Only the whites of their eyes glimmered, and their sparse teeth when they talked.

The lovely, flushed mother had flung back her becoming short veil. Judy thought her mother was beautiful. They smiled at each other.

Judy had on the dark dress that she wore on rainy days. The favorite aunt had bought her a pair of black silk stockings.

When she passed the hall mirror, she slyly admired them.

Somebody rang the bell. The father said meaningly: 'It's the automobile, I guess.' The mother, with an apologetic look, pulled down her veil.

Judy did not want to get out of the car. She wished that she were a baby and could kick and scream, or that she were nearer the mother and could wheedle. But then she remembered that she meant to be a great writer and must welcome every experience. She got out bravely.

A light-skinned lady in a crumpled frock led them into a parlor. She made little noises in her throat and told them she was sorry. Judy caught the terrifying word *body*, and went and cowered against the window. The father and the mother and the aunts disappeared.

But in a moment the favorite aunt was back and beckoning her.

'You must come and look at him, Judy. He's beautiful.'

Judy prayed, 'God, don't let his teeth click,' and crossed the threshold.

A dozen familiar and unfamiliar people sat in a small room on insecure chairs. A pretty woman peered into an open box and made the sign of the cross. About the box were unattractive bunches of fresh and wilted flowers. Judy knew suddenly that this was a coffin and that Uncle Eben was in it. She trailed after the favorite aunt like a young lamb to the slaughter.

'Smile down at him, Judy.'

A curious Thing made in the image of an unhappy man lay in a satin-lined casket. If Judy dared touch the smooth, dark cheek, she would find it brown clay in her hand. She wished she could ask her mother, who alone might understand, whether Uncle Eben was somewhere else and this was a plaster cast.

'Go sit by your mother,' whispered the favorite aunt.

Judy tiptoed to the uncertain seat in the front row and sat quietly, her hands folded in her lap and her ankles crossed.

Slowly she became aware that the dim blob protruding above the rim of the casket was the tip of a nose. She was bewitched and held and gradually horrified.

But her horror was caught away by the violent sound of the father's sobs. She jerked up her head and stared at him.

In all of her life she had never seen a man cry. To her tears were the weakness of children and women, who had not the courage of men. She was fascinated and appalled. The father's head wobbled weakly. He made strangled snorts in his throat. Tears streamed down his cheeks and ran into the corners of his mouth. His nose dripped.

She was ashamed. Her own eyes filled with tears. Her body burned. She thought in extremest torture, 'My father is weak, and I am the child of my father . . .'

The mother bent to her. 'Judy, comfort your father.'

She swayed as if she had been struck.

'He mustn't cry like that, Judy.'

She raised her sick eyes to her mother's face. 'Mummy, what do I do?'

'Just slip your hand into his. He loves you, Judy.'

That did not move her. A stranger wept beside her. She felt her stomach collapse. With a great effort she kept herself steady. Had the father's life depended upon it, she could not have stretched out a soothing hand.

'Mummy,' she cried, 'I can't!' and burrowed against her.

An oily yellow man in a night frock coat leaned down to the mother. 'Are you pleased with the body?'

'He's beautiful,' said the mother.

'For much or little I turn 'em out the same. I'd appreciate your coming to me whenever – God forbid! – you have to.'

He swung out a heavy watch and said humorously, 'Our kind of people.'

'Yes. Service was set for three,' said the mother primly.

'Our kind of people,' he repeated. 'That cullud preacher is

probably somewheres chewing the rag with Sister Fullbosom.'

The mother and the undertaker laughed softly.

There was a small stir in the back of the room. Somebody importantly rushed down the length of it. The undertaker bustled to the newcomer's side and led him to the small pulpit. With a careless glance at the body, the young preacher shifted out of his coat, glanced at his watch, cleared his throat, and plunged into a wailing spiritual that grew in volume and poignancy as the rest of the mourners joined in.

The aunts, too, swayed and moaned in unison. Presently the father lifted his head and keened. But Judy did not want the mother to sing. She did not want to feel the swell of song from stomach to bosom to throat. She held her head tight against the mother to stem the rise of it.

The song hushed at the last stanza. The chorus whimpered out in a muted medley of unmusical voices. The preacher fumbled in his pocket, took out several soiled bits of paper, extracted and unfolded a rumpled sheet, and clamped on his glasses.

He stared at the illegible name of the deceased and slurred over it. He read automatically: 'Born March 2, 1868, in Charleston, South Carolina. Died April 3, 1919, in this city. He rounded fifty-one years. Professed religion at age of eighteen. Married wife, Mary, who died in childbirth in 1894. Came North, entered Pullman service, and was a faithful servitor for twenty years. Was retired and pensioned, after total blindness, in 1914. He was never known to touch liquor or cards. He lived humble, and served his God, and died in the arms of Jesus at 2 A.M. Tuesday morning. He leaves a sorrowing brother and his wife, and two sorrowing sisters, and a sorrowing niece to mourn their loss.'

Judy pulled at her mother. 'Mums, why did he read that? What did he say it for? What did he mean about our sorrowing?'

The mother shrugged impatiently, thought a bit, and yielded kindly: 'It's an obituary, Judy, and God knows we are sorry.'

Suddenly to Judy this word that she had never heard before became a monstrous symbol, not of life but of one's living. She drew away from her mother. Her mind strained toward the understanding of this new discovery. She must think it through like a woman.

She thought with shame: I have not really cried for Uncle Eben. I am not really a sorrowing niece . . . She shut her eyes against the unreality of the casket. And then she was a little girl again, just five, and had on Uncle Eben's glasses, and was bouncing on his knee. But she found herself sliding to the floor. The ludicrous glasses fell from her nose and shattered. She pricked her finger, blood spurted, and she screamed. Above her scream rose Uncle Eben's tortured wail: 'God in heaven, I'm blind!' Then the blood did not matter. She tried to piece together Uncle Eben's glasses, in panic that she would be blamed for his blindness.

Later there was the strange Uncle Eben with bandages over his eyes, and pain on his mouth, and hot, trembling hands that went ceaselessly over her face. And there was the sightless Uncle Eben, very old and shriveled and shaky, going uncertainly on a cane that tapped and tapped and tapped. Then there was the mother with a pursed mouth, and the father gesturing angrily, and the mother's unforgettable words: 'I married you, not your whole helpless family.' Then Uncle Eben went off to a Home on a cane that tapped and tapped.

Judy cried now, unchildishly and terribly, in regret that Uncle Eben had ever lived. She had the sharp thought: Uncle Eben's life and Uncle Eben's death do not really matter . . . She was no longer a small child reasoning. Even her word images were mature. She was seeing deeply the tragedy of commonplace existence.

Her attention was acute now. She was keenly aware of her own absorption. The egotism that at all times swayed her was compelling her to store up impressions. She knew with bitterness that when she was older and abler, the events of this day would crowd into her mind with the utmost clearness and find release through her own particular medium of words. Only as it might serve her as a plot for a story – and the horror of this over-whelmed her – had the poor life and death of Uncle Eben any meaning.

He had left no child, nor book, nor even ennobling longings to thread into eternity the wisp of his spirit.

A big black man was shyly speaking. He called Uncle Eben a brother worker. He said that he was glad to be here to represent the Pullman company, and pointed out their unlovely flowers. He made a large gesture of introducing his wife, and sat down relievedly.

She advanced toward the casket. She was brown and buxom and soiled. Her voice was not beautiful.

'I never knew our dear brother personally, but I feel very close to all Pullman porters on account of my husband's being one of the head ones. I tries to come to their funerals as often as I can. I am proud to say that last year I didn't miss one.

'I'm not much on poem writing, but most people seems to like these little verses which I composed for Pullman Brother Jessey's death in 1916. I generally reads it at funerals. With your kind indulgence, I'll read it at this one.'

She ducked her head as a child might, and recited in an unmusical tremolo:

My tears overflow as I look down upon our dear brother.
The eyes that could open are shut.
The tongue that could speak is mute.
The feet that traversed o'er the earth are still by our Maker's
     will.
We weep beside this casket, we the wife, we the children, we
     the sorrowing friends.

We cannot realize that this is but the shell.
Already in spirit our dear brother stands before his Maker.
And God sits on His golden throne passing judgment.
We who knew this dear man know with confidence that the
*   gates have been opened to him.*
He lived clean and died humble, and that counts.
Do not take it too much to heart, dear relatives and friends.
We all got a time to go, and some go soon, and some go late.
Just lay your burden on the Lord, and he will gladly lighten
*   your load.*
The Devil is a toad!

She went and sat down.

Judy could hear little sputters of praise. The aunts were pressing the soiled lady's hands. Over her head the father bent to the
mother and said earnestly: 'Real sad and appropriate.'

The young preacher went to stand above the body. He was
suddenly so wild-eyed that Judy thought he must be drunk.

He said heatedly: 'This man ain't happy. This poor brother
died in despair. No undertaker's art could smooth out all his suffering. He was worried to death, that's what. Why ain't he
having a big funeral in some dicty church 'stead of you asking
somebody you never seen before to come round here? 'Cause
none of you thought he was worth a highfalutin funeral. I feels
for this man.'

Judy simply held her breath. She dared not stare up at her
parents, but she was aware of her mother's nervous twitching.

The preacher went on: 'I didn't come here to preach this
funeral in hopes of getting five or ten dollars. I don't want no
money. Get this straight. I wouldn't take it. I ain't doing a bit
more for this dead brother than I want somebody, out of the
kindness of his heart, to do some day for me.'

Judy thought that rather admirable.

'You all been bragging 'bout him being a Pullman porter.

That's first cousin to being a slave. Why ain't you put it right? For twenty years our dead brother's been an 'umble cog in a wheel.

'The trouble with our kind of people is we don't stick together. The white man does, and the white man rules the world. We got to organize! Us that is on top has got to help us at the bottom. But what uppity Negro will? But don't you all get me started. I never know when to stop. Jesus, guide this soul over Jordan. Amen.'

He practically leaped into his coat and came to shake hands with the mother.

'Thank you, sister,' Judy heard, as he patted her hat and passed on to the father.

Judy tugged at her mother. 'Mums, why did he thank you? Oughtn't you to have thanked him?'

'Ssh! For the money, child. Stop asking questions.'

'What money, Mums? Did you give him money?'

'Judy, I'm warning you! For the funeral, child. You got to give them a little something.'

Judy was simply struck. 'But, Mummy, he said he wouldn't take it!'

The mother whispered wearily: 'They got to say something, child.'

Two efficient men came to close the casket. The father was led by the light-skinned lady to take a last look. He came back considerably stricken and leaned against Judy. She slipped her arm around him. Through her small body wave upon wave of maternal passion surged. She was no longer contemptuous. Her heart swelled with compassion.

The efficient men trundled the box out on castors. The father and the mother followed. Judy went between the aunts into the sunny street.

The casket went neatly into a wooden box in the hearse. The flowers were piled around it. The door would not shut, and the undertaker fiddled and frowned.

Judy thought in alarm: I couldn't bear it if Uncle Eben spilled in the street . . .

But presently the door banged shut. Judy followed the family into the first car.

The mother immediately flung back her veil. Her lovely face was flushed and excited. The father squirmed in his shoes. The aunts tried hard to go on with their weeping, but could not.

The undertaker poked in his head. 'We're ready to start. Mister and Missus Tilly, and Missus Mamie Wicks, and Miss Eva Jenkins are following in the second car. It'll be quite a ride, so you all settle comfortable.' He made a gesture. 'That little thing there is an ashtray. Ashes to ashes.' He laughed kindly and shut them in.

The hearse started off. In a moment their motor was rolling smoothly. Judy settled back, liking it very much, and wishing she could look out the window.

'No mind that preacher was right,' said the father, loosing his laces.

'He wasn't nobody's fool,' said the elder aunt.

The contrary mother said smartly: 'I didn't like his talking like that at a funeral.'

'We got to organize,' the father remembered. 'There ain't no set time to preach that.'

'Funerals should be sad,' said the mother.

'God knows!' sighed the favorite aunt.

'Still,' agreed the father, 'I didn't like him flinging up to us about Eben.'

The mother voiced coldly: 'Sounded to me like he was posted.'

The favorite aunt drew up her delicate body. 'Then it must be your conscience. God is my witness that until that man stood in the pulpit, I couldn't have told you he was white or black.'

'Eben died careworn and weary,' said the elder aunt. 'That young man didn't need his glasses to tell him that.'

The mother's voice shook. 'I got as much pity as anybody, but, more than that, I got a child. And that child comes close to me as God Himself! Now that Eben's gone to glory, I can praise his virtues loud as anyone. But Eben had his faults, and I won't shut my eyes to them. He let himself go in his blindness. He wasn't careful. He wasn't always . . . clean. I mean to bring up my child like a white child. There ain't nothing going to sicken her little stomach. There ain't nothing going to soil her little mind.'

Judy rhymed under her breath: 'Funerals should be sad and Mums has got a mad.' But she was ashamed and thought tenderly: How much my mummy loves me, as much as God, and that's a sin, and she knows it. She isn't afraid. Does she love me because I'm me, or does she love me because I mean to be a great writer? I have talent. But there are geniuses. Am I a genius? What is a genius? If I have a child, I shan't want her to be a genius. I should be jealous. It's wicked to be jealous. I don't care. Nobody knows it because I'm so sweet, but I like to be first in everything. If I can't be first, I don't want to be anything. I don't want a baby, anyway. They hurt, and the way they come isn't nice. But, of course, I don't really believe it. I'd die if I thought my mummy and daddy could do a thing like that. I wish everything could be beautiful. People, and the things they say, and the things they do. Daddy has a flat nose. When I was small, I didn't love my daddy. My mummy is beautiful. I like light people. Why is it wicked to like light people? I'm glad Uncle Eben's dead. Once I saw Uncle Eben being nasty. If I had a little boy baby, I'd be ashamed to touch him. I'm very wicked. I'm afraid of dead people. I'm afraid, afraid! At night they fly about in white shrouds. I don't want to be sent up to bed without Mummy.

She made a little cradle of her hands.

'You all didn't hear Eva Jenkins moaning and groaning,' said the elder aunt.

The mother seemed to increase. 'Carrying on like a fool!'

The father added: 'I reckon she realized Eben's bit of money won't never come to her now.'

The favorite aunt said gently: 'I think she really loved him.'

The elder aunt made a coarse joke. 'Yeh, him and his money.'

'Eva Jenkins ain't young,' said the favorite aunt. 'It wasn't love she wanted . . .'

'You struck it right,' the father cut in unkindly. 'It was easy in her old age, and a blind old shoe what couldn't keep track of her comings and goings.'

The mother said with definiteness: 'Ever since that trouble in lodge meeting eight years ago, Eva Jenkins had it in for me. It's my opinion she wanted poor Eben just on account of spite, so's to take his little lump of money away from me and mine.'

'I fixed her good,' the father triumphed, 'when I got my brother Eben to sign every penny over to me.'

'And you broke her heart,' said the favorite aunt. 'She knew that, alone, she could never give Eben the little comforts his nature demanded.' She went on broodingly: 'I guess she wonders now did we. People has got to lie flat on their backs before they find out what's false and what's true.'

Judy thought with pride: My aunty is good. I want to be good like my aunty. But I love my mummy best, even though my mummy tells lies. My mummy and daddy care about money. I never, never want to . . .

The elder aunt snapped up the back curtain. 'Still at it,' she reported grimly.

'Jerk it down in her face,' the father commanded, 'to show her how much she's wanted at my brother Eben's funeral. You got to be common with some folks before they understand.'

The aunt did so with such vengeance that one of the side shades flew up, and Judy caught a little pool of sun in her cradle, and folded her hands to shut the glare out of her baby's eyes.

'I could eat a horse and wagon,' said the mother.

'I don't know why 'tis,' said the father, 'but funerals make me hungry.'

'I set a nice dinner back on the stove. I'll suttinly be glad to pitch into it. There's nothing I like more than I like chicken and rice and thick brown gravy.'

The father reminisced sentimentally: 'There's nothing I like more than I like black-eyed peas and ham and cabbage my mammy used to give us.'

The favorite aunt contributed frigidly: 'I don't see how you two can put your minds on food. All I want is a strong cup of tea and maybe a sliver of toast.'

'The dead are dead,' said the father. 'The living has needs of the body.'

'The mother weeps for her child. Outside of that, I guess there ain't much honest sorrow wasted.'

'Them as trusts God and believes in the resurrection has no need to weep. I shall meet my brother Eben in the promised land.'

Judy thought sharply how awful it must be to be old! To know that your sun may set tomorrow! She would guard her growing. She would end each day with some little delight. She would do good deeds! When she had reached Uncle Eben's age, she must not die unhonored. But then she had the image of the baker's wife shrieking in the back of the shop: 'My baby's dead! My little baby's dead!' The young could die, too. Death was not the weak surrender of the old. Death was God in his heaven counting out souls.

But how could God let a little baby die? Why did he let it be born? If God is good, how can he bear to see its mother cry? People should be glad. To be glad is to be beautiful. When I am sad, my lip droops. When I am glad, I'm like my mummy. Everything should be beautiful. Why does a God let things be ugly? There is not really a Santa Claus. Can I be me if there is not a God? I wish I could ask my mummy. But my mummy tells lies. It's wicked to lie to your little girl. When I tell lies, my throat burns, and I tremble. I'll never, never lie to my little girl. But I'll never, never have one. She might die. And then I should hate God. And if I could not say, 'God! God!' I should want to die too . . .

The car had stopped. Judy peered ahead and saw the undertaker dash up a pebbled path. After a bit a bell tolled once, then again, and again. The hearse wound up a narrow road. The white slabs stood out sharply in the gathering dusk. A few fresh flowers reared their lovely heads. Green grass sprouted.

The hearse halted. Irish workmen came ambling. The undertaker again poked in his head, and said that he had got a nice plot, and that their brother was to be laid under six feet only. Judy didn't know just why that mattered. But the father thanked him and bent to tie his laces.

They got out of the car. The undertaker shepherded them in order. The casket went perilously. Presently they stood above the open earth. The undertaker began giving crisp commands.

The mother said sharply: 'Judy, go stand on that board. It's an old saying, "The cold you catch at a funeral lasts until your own."'

Judy went to stand on the board, teetering a little.

She heard Mrs. Tilly whispering: 'I hope there ain't no long rigamarole. We got that other funeral.'

Eva Jenkins came to stand beside her. 'You're growing, Judy. I'm sorry your Uncle Eben couldn't live to be proud of you.'

Judy stared up at the gentle-voiced woman. 'I'm going to be a great writer.'

'You are going to be something that's beautiful. And God knows there is need of beauty in this world.'

'To be beautiful is to be glad. I hate funerals!'

'To be really beautiful, Judy, is to come through pain and sorrow and parting without bitterness.'

Judy looked hard at Eva Jenkins and thought that she was beautiful.

The casket was lowered. The undertaker got a shovelful of earth and came first to the father. 'Assist us in the burial of our dead,' he suggested. The father took a handful and weakly scattered it. Shortly the workmen were at it in earnest.

The undertaker fussily arranged the flowers. He detached a wilted carnation and offered it to the mother. Judy thought innocently: I guess they have favors at funerals just like at parties. But when she was passed a flower she clasped her hands behind her back and looked very stubborn. She had heard the father say, 'I'll keep mine forever,' and had not believed him, and had been distressed.

The undertaker began to shake hands all around. They turned toward the cars.

Mr. Tilly said softly to the father: 'The company pays for the funeral, brother.'

The father exclaimed in gratitude: 'God bless them! I'll write them a letter of thanks in the morning. All this talk 'bout organization! Sometimes I think the Pullman porter is biting the hands what feeds him.'

The hearse had started. Judy watched it careen down the road in a wild dash to Mrs. Tilly's other funeral. Mrs. Tilly, in the second car, madly followed. Their car, too, went swiftly and the driver whistled snatches of popular songs.

Two blocks away from their street, a motor swung around the corner into their fender. Their driver, who had to make Mrs. Tilly's other funeral, too, cursed softly, halted his car, and went to make investigations.

The father, who loved excitement, followed him into the thick of it.

'Folks don't have no respect for funerals nor nothing nowadays,' said the elder aunt.

The favorite aunt argued: 'With the blinds up and the chauffeur singing, how was they to tell this was a funeral?'

The mother neatly concluded: 'If we was standing on our heads, he hadn't no right to run into us.'

They impatiently fidgeted. But they did not think it proper to get out and walk home from a funeral.

The father and the chauffeur returned in triumph. The father gave the chauffeur his card and urged him to summon him for a witness. When he was settled again, he said easily, 'Looks like I lost my posy.'

Judy was glad to be home. She did not want any supper. But the aunts and the mother in fresh aprons ignored her.

The steaming supper was set on the table. They gathered round. The father said, 'Do you remember how Eben loved chicken?' and tore into it. Judy, remembering, could not swallow.

The mother said impatiently: 'Quit that fiddlin' and eat your supper.'

'I'm not hungry,' Judy said faintly.

'Of course you are,' the elder aunt protested contentedly.

The father added facetiously: 'All cullud children like chicken.'

For the overwrought child the day culminated in this. She snatched up her plate and flung it on the floor. Her speech was almost indistinguishably thick. She was never to know where she got the words.

'I won't eat funeral-baked meats! I won't! Nobody can make me!'

It was almost as if she saw the hot food turn to straw in their open mouths.

'You march yourself out of here and go to bed,' shrilled the mother, 'and God give me strength to spank you in the morning.'

Judy went, with her head high and her spirit quaking.

She went up the unlighted stairs with her eyes shut tight against the apparition of Uncle Eben. But the darkness so terrified her that she made a lattice of her fingers, and slowly opened her eyes on the lesser horror.

She gained her room, and snapped on the light, and leaned against the door. She was so weak that for a long moment there was no sound nor movement save her strangled breathing and the beating of her heart. She dared not go into the closet for her nightgown, nor did she dare stand long on the treacherous floor. She got to the bed and huddled in its center.

With one terrified motion she ripped off her dress. Her shoes followed, then her stockings. In her bloomers and waist she got under the covering and frantically hid her face under the sheet.

She could not uncover it. Surely, if she did, a grinning ghost would swoop down upon her. She lay and shivered and tortured herself with the floating image of Uncle Eben. In sheer terror she began to sob, and went on sobbing, and could not stop.

By and by she slept.

THE PENNY

The little boy ran happily down the village street. His bunchy sweater and gaping shoes were inadequate to keep out the cold, but he felt nothing but joy. For the first time in weeks he had a penny to spend. His father had given it to him just five minutes before.

His father had brought home his piddling pay for his part-time job and dropped it into his mother's lap. His mother had counted it carefully with her customary sigh. As usual, there was never enough to last the week. Midway through the week there would not be food enough or fuel enough to carry them until next payday.

The little boy's stomach would growl in school. His face and faded shirt would show the scarcity of hot water and soap. His mother would leave her unheated flat and her empty kerosene heater and sit by the glowing heaters of her neighbors, gratefully gulping the coffee they gave her, and slyly pocketing the big, buttered slices of homemade bread. His father would beg a beer from some familiar at the bar to steel himself against the heartbreak of his wife and the hunger of his son. There was no joy in any hour of their day.

He was their husband and father. They had shared his good times. They loved him no less when his luck was bad. But his boy was so little, only six, and six was so young for sacrifices. Other boys had baseball bats and boxing gloves, and milk and butter in their bellies, and stout shoes and clean shirts, and pennies mixed with the marbles in their pockets.

The man could not remember the last time he had given the boy a penny to spend. It was surely in another and better world. To this pale creature with the pinched face and hollow eyes he had never given anything.

The man had snatched a penny from the aproned lap of his wife and folded the boy's fingers over it. Instantly there had been a miraculous transformation. The gnome who clutched the penny had turned into a child.

And so the child raced toward the candy store, and his heart almost burst with happiness. There were beautiful things in the candy store. All the wonderful things the other kids pulled out of their pockets at recess. The things that could make a boy's mouth water with wanting.

He could have his choice of any of these. He could show his penny to the shopkeeper and take as long as he liked to choose. He could stand outside and press his nose against the glass and not feel bad, for after a while he could go inside and put his penny on the counter. He could turn the knob of an ordinary door and walk straight into heaven.

The little boy's head was in the clouds. He did not know he had reached the curb. His feet slid into space. When he picked himself up, his hands were empty. His frantic eye saw the penny rolling toward the gutter. It vanished as he lunged.

He limped back to the curb and sat down. A bruise was swelling on his cheek. His body was wrenched and sore. But just as he had not felt the cold, now he did not feel the pain. The penny, the round, shining penny, was gone. The end of the world has come at its bright beginning. The boy dropped his head on his knees and whimpered like a whipped puppy.

Miss Hester Halsey came down the street, walking in her

prim way, with her nose, as always, a little disdainful. She had worked in the same office for twenty years and saved her money. She had no patience with people who were poor. They were simply shiftless. Miss Halsey saw the huddled figure of the boy. His back was to her, but she recognized his rags. He was the son of that worthless drunk and that lazy slattern. Miss Halsey's mouth grew grim. Her small, neat feet quickened their pace. Presently she stood over the boy. Delicately she touched him with her foot.

'Little boy?'

His head jerked up. He scowled and snuffled. His grief was too immense for speech with this strange woman. He turned his face away and went on whimpering quietly.

Miss Halsey saw the ugly bruise. She touched the boy with her foot again.

'Who hit you?' she asked in a soft, strained voice.

The boy did not answer.

'Your mother?' she urged. 'Your father?'

The little boy was frightened. He could not have answered if he had wanted to. He moved crabwise along the curb.

Miss Halsey moved along the curb with him. She did not move crabwise. She made a fluid movement after him. Her gloved hand touched his cheek. He winced and drew a sobbing breath.

'Does it hurt bad?' asked Miss Halsey eagerly. 'Anyone who could beat a child . . .' her voice grew hoarse with righteousness, 'ought to be reported to the proper authorities.' She stooped, and her mouth was level with his ear. 'Tell me, who did it, little boy?'

The boy took a quick, terrified look at her. Her burning eyes pulled him to his feet. He tried to escape, but his stiffening leg buckled under him. He sat down hard on the curb again.

'Your leg, your leg, too,' the relentless voice insisted. 'Did they take a stick to you? Did they take a . . . a poker?'

The little boy felt as if he were drowning. This strange woman was pushing him down, down, and he was too tired to struggle. Once when he was three he had leaned too far over the rain barrel. He had fought his way to the surface, and his father had heard his cries. How he wanted the water to close over him to shut this woman out of sight and sound.

Feverishly Miss Halsey dug in her purse. She selected a coin, a shining penny, and held it out to him.

'Look, little boy, a nice, new penny. Wouldn't you like a nice, new penny?

Once more he looked at her. His eyes were black with pleading. He did not want the penny. He only wanted to drown.

'You can have the penny,' said Miss Halsey warmly, seeing the pleading look. 'You can have it as soon as you tell me what happened. Poor little neglected boy, you'd be better off in a Home.'

Home, thought the little boy. If he drowned, he could never go back home. Tonight there would be fire and food. There would be hot water and a bath. He didn't want to drown. Oh, why didn't this lady let him go?

Miss Halsey was purring softly. 'You can go and buy candy if I give you the penny. If you tell me what happened, you can go and buy candy.'

He could feel the water receding. She was going to let him go. She was going to give him a penny for candy. Everything would be as it was before. He stood up and smiled shyly at Miss Halsey. He was not afraid of her now. He felt happy and excited. Heaven was half a block away. In another minute he would enter it.

Miss Halsey let the penny lie in her open palm. The boy looked at it with an open mouth that began to moisten with wanting. Miss Halsey was as happy and excited as the boy. In a moment the long day would have some meaning. The dreary day of dull endeavor would end on a high note of moral victory.

'It was your father, wasn't it?' said Miss Halsey in a rich, full voice. 'He came home drunk as usual and struck you with a poker. Your mother wasn't there to stop him. She was off galli-vanting at some neighbor's. You crawled as far as this corner, and I found you.'

The thought of candy was driving him crazy. He was a timid little boy, but he could not restrain his hand any longer. The penny snuggled inside it, but Miss Halsey's fingers did not quite release it. He looked at her brightly, expectantly, ready to die for the penny.

'That's how it was, little boy, wasn't it?'

'Yes'm,' he said joyously.

Miss Halsey released the penny. The little boy turned and scooted away. His leg was not sore anymore. He was not walk-ing on earth anyway. He was walking on air.

Miss Halsey continued down the street. She, too, was afloat in the clouds. She was thinking about the letter she would write to the minister.

In the whole town there were no two people happier than Miss Halsey and the little boy.

THE BIRD LIKE NO OTHER

Colby ran through the woods. He ran hard, as if he were putting his house and family behind him forever. The woods were not a dark forest of towering trees. They were just scrub oak and stunted pine with plenty of room for the sun to dapple the road. The road, really a footpath worn by time, was so much a part of Colby's summers that at any point he knew how many trees to count before he reached the one with the hollow that caught the rain and gave the birds a drinking cup.

As the clearing came in sight with its cluster of cottages, Colby began to call Aunt Emily, the stridency in his voice commanding her to shut out the sweeter sounds of summer.

Whatever Aunt Emily was doing, Colby knew, she would stop what she was doing. Wherever she was, she would start for the porch, so that by the time Colby pounded up the stairs, she would be sitting on her old porch glider, waiting for him to fling himself down beside her and cool his hot anger in her calm.

Aunt Emily was a courtesy aunt, a family friend of many years. When Colby's mother was a little girl, she played with Aunt Emily's little boy when they came on holiday from their separate cities. Then Aunt Emily lost her little boy in a winter accident on an icy street. When vacation time came again, it took all her courage to reopen her cottage. But she knew she must do it this saddest summer of all if she was ever to learn to live in a world that could not bend its tempo to the slow cadence of grief.

Colby's sister made frequent visits with her dolls. She brought the dolls that didn't cry or didn't wet because they were always rewarded with a tea party for their good behavior. She eased the summer's sorrow for Aunt Emily, who felt an obligation to show this trusting child a cheerful face and to take an interest in her eager talk.

All the same, though Aunt Emily felt a bit ungrateful thinking it, a little girl dressing her dolls for a tea party is no substitute for a little boy playing cowboys and Indians at the top of his lungs.

Colby's family would have agreed with her. His mother adored him because he was her long-awaited son, five years younger than the youngest of his three sisters. His father was pleased and proud to have another male aboard.

But Colby couldn't see where he came first with anybody. As far as he was concerned he was always at the bottom of a heap of scrapping sisters. No matter how good he tried to be, his day most generally depended on how good his sisters decided to be. His rights were never mightier than their wrongs.

Aunt Emily had been Colby's sounding board ever since the summer he was four. One day that summer, his mother postponed a promised boat ride because his sisters had fought with each other all morning over whose turn it was to use the paint box that somebody had given them together. When they began to make each other cry, they were sent upstairs as punishment, and the outing was postponed.

Colby felt he was being punished for blows he hadn't struck and tears he hadn't caused. He had to tell somebody before he burst. Since he knew the way to Aunt Emily's, he went to tell her.

She took a look at his clouded-over face, plumped him down on her old porch glider, then went inside to telephone his mother that Colby wasn't lost, just decamped. His mother told her what had happened, and Aunt Emily listened with uncommitted little clucks. She wasn't any Solomon to decide if it was more important to punish the bad than to keep a promise to the good.

She could hear him banging back and forth on the glider, waiting in hot impatience to tell his tale of woe. The old glider screeched and groaned at his assault on its unoiled joints.

Standing inside her screen door, wincing in sympathy, Aunt Emily knew that neither she nor any nearby neighbor could take that tortured sound much longer. She tried to think of something to distract Colby's mind until he calmed down. A blue jay flew across her line of vision, a bird familiar to the landscape, but the unexciting sight bloomed into an idea.

Shutting the screen door soundlessly, approaching Colby on whispering feet, she put her finger to her lips and sat down beside him.

As he stared at her round-eyed, his swinging suspended, she said softly, 'Colby, before you came the most beautiful bird I ever saw was sitting on my hydrangea bush. He almost took my breath. I never saw a bird of so many colors. When you came running, he flew away. But if we don't talk or make any noise, he may come back.'

After a moment of reflection, Colby's curiosity pulled out the plug in his sea of troubles, and he settled back.

That was the way this gentle fiction began. When Aunt Emily decided that the beautiful bird was gone for the day, Colby was wearing an agreeable face of a normal color. Taking the initiative, a shameless triumph over a small boy, Aunt Emily plunged into a story before Colby could get his mouth open to begin his own.

For the rest of that summer, and in the summers that followed, when Colby came glad or when Colby came only a little bit mad, the right to speak first was his automatically. But when Colby came breathing fire, by uncanny coincidence, the bird like no other had just left the yard.

It was soon routine for Colby to seal his lips and settle down to wait.

Now he was eight, and on this angry morning when he flung himself up Aunt Emily's stairs, and flung himself down beside her on the poor old glider that responded as expected to a sudden shock, it was plainly a morning to search the sky for the bird like no other.

Before Aunt Emily could comb a fresh story out of her memory, Colby got a speech in ahead of her. He said in an excited whisper, 'I see it, I see it. I see the bird you said was so beautiful. I guess he's every color in the world.'

Jerking upright in stunned surprise, making the glider wearily protest, Aunt Emily asked in a shaken voice, 'Where?'

'On that tree over there, see, over there.'

By a confluence of golden sunlight and blue sky and green leaves and shimmering summer air, a bird on a swinging bough took on an astonishing beauty.

For a moment Aunt Emily couldn't believe her eyes. But in another moment her eyes stopped playing tricks. And suddenly she wanted to stop playing tricks, too.

'Colby, look again. That's a jay. There never was a bird like the one I told you about. I made him up.'

As if to give credence to her confession, the bird on the bough released itself from its brief enchantment and flew away in the dress of a blue jay.

Colby spoke slowly. 'Why did you make up a bird to tell me about?'

Aunt Emily started to answer, but asked instead, 'Don't you know why, Colby?'

'I think so,' he said soberly.

'Will you tell me?'

'To make me sit still so I wouldn't say bad things about my family when I was mad. But you didn't want to make me sit still like a punishment. So you made me sit still like we were waiting to see something wonderful.'

'I see the wonderful thing I've been waiting for. I see a little boy who's learned about family loyalty. It's as beautiful to look at as that bird.'

Colby got up. He scuffed his sneakers. 'Well, I guess I'll go home now. See you, Aunt Emily.'

He bounded down the stairs and began to run home, running faster and faster. Aunt Emily's eyes filled with sentimental tears. He was trying to catch up with the kind of man he was going to be. He was rushing toward understanding.

THE HAPPIEST YEAR, THE
SADDEST YEAR

She did not remember ever playing with dolls. But she did not remember much of anything before she was four. That being so, she would not have denied – if the facts were paraded before her – that in the year she was three, her mother had come toward her, cradling a doll to show her the art of cradling a doll, and then attached it to her unready arms, wrapping her weak embrace around the china creature, and thereupon stepped back to admire the picture of miniature mother and make-believe child.

What, she asked, was Deedee going to name her new baby, helpfully reciting a list of lovely real-life names for her to choose from. Deedee brushed them aside. 'Her name is "Doll,"' she said in a voice that would have sounded dry had she been older.

Maybe in time she gave her doll a more agreeable name and learned to treat it tenderly. Or maybe in time, a surer guess, she abandoned it, leaving her mother with no choice but to threaten to give the poor thing away to some more worthy child, and to have to follow through in the face of Deedee's instant acquiescence.

If her mother worried about Deedee's rejection of mothering, she tried to find an explanation in the fact that Deedee, the youngest of three daughters, was probably holding fast to her

special place as the resident baby, and was simply not ready to
share it with a blond and blue-eyed doll. Deedee's family was
colored – the description 'black' not yet in compulsory use –
and 'colored' fitting them perfectly since they ran the whole
spectrum of colors, every shade and variation, with Deedee at
the farthest end from the blond and blue-eyed doll.

Her mother's diagnosis of Deedee's condition was as wrong as
most empirical judgments. At Christmas time in her fourth
year, the year her remembering began, when asked what she
wanted for Christmas, she said with immediate readiness, 'A
real baby.'

Her mother could not have been more undone. 'You don't
even like dolls. What would you do with a baby?'

'I'd take care of it.'

'I'm still taking care of you. How can you take care of a
baby?'

'You can teach me.'

'You're not much more than a baby yourself.'

'I'm going to be five ' She held up five fingers to prove it,
which in itself was a very childish demonstration for anyone
trying to prove her importance.

Mother and daughter seesawed back and forth in a fruitless
search for a resolution of the impasse. Until finally her mother
told her she was sick of her foolishness, and to go and play.

She was five, then six, then seven, and through those years,
particularly when Christmas was approaching, their aging bat-
tle about babies would reactivate, the two facing each other in
the most aggrieved way, presenting the same unacceptable pros
and cons, and, as usual, ending in a draw.

At eight, Deedee was old enough to know that she had been
asking for a Christmas miracle, when there really weren't that
many to go around. She said to her mother, 'I want some books
and some games for Christmas, and that's all.' She gave her
mother a lovely smile that said, 'I really mean it.'

Then the Christmas she was nine, the miracle happened. Her mother said, 'I have a surprise for you. You have two little cousins coming from Chicago to live with us. Chicago is too cold for them. We'll try to keep them warm and well. They're a brother and sister, and that's what they call each other, so we will too. He's not quite three, she's not quite two. They're really only babies, and you can help me take care of them. They'll be here in time for Christmas.'

There was such a swelling in Deedee's throat that she could not speak. Her mother gave her a lovely smile that said, 'I know how you feel.'

The parents of the children, too young themselves, had found it impossible to keep two children warm and fed. There was no welfare for the poor then. They could only feed on poverty. Deedee's parents were well enough off to help when help was needed. An extended family was part of daily living. Sharing was a lifeline.

A Boston friend living in Chicago and coming home for Christmas brought the children to their new home on Christmas Eve. When Deedee and her sisters came in from play, coming in the back way as they always did to see what was happening in the kitchen, their mother said, 'Sister and Brother are here. I've put them to bed upstairs. They had a long trip. Go see them before they fall asleep.'

Her sisters raced upstairs, and Deedee couldn't follow. She had waited so long for this moment to happen, and now it was more than she could bear. Her mother said gently, 'Go see your babies. They're waiting.'

She went upstairs, walking slowly because she could walk no faster. It seemed a journey that lasted forever. She reached the open door and stepped inside. She saw the little boy tucked in at the foot of the bed, half sitting up, while her sisters stood over him, telling each other how darling he was. Deedee loved him at once. He looked like a Christmas card angel, very blond and very fair, little trace of his black blood showing, and wriggling all over with friendliness.

She started toward him, and felt something pull her, though nothing and no one was touching her. The little boy was smiling straight at her, wanting her to come and hug him, and she took another step forward. Something pulled her again. Now she turned, feeling her smile erase itself from her face, and some nameless ache rising inside her. A little brown girl, with an almost unearthly beauty, was tucked in at the head of the bed. She was not sitting up like her brother, who was full of euphoria at being in a warm house, in a warm bed, with good food warming his belly. She lay flat, she lay still. They stared at each other, silent, not smiling, their hearts interlocking. And Deedee heard her own heart say as clearly as if the words were said aloud, 'I'm going to love you best of all.'

It was over. But the spell was not broken. It had become part of her. She felt at ease. She joined her sisters and gave the little boy a big welcome hug and a big welcome kiss. They played with him until their mother called them to supper. They tiptoed past the little girl because she had fallen asleep.

Deedee filled a large part of the little boy's life. But the little girl was Deedee's life, and she was the little girl's existence. The affinity between the two could not be explained. It was as if they had both been born for this encounter, as if they had once been one flesh.

Then one day Deedee came home from school, and Sister was not at the door to greet her. She was upstairs in bed, as she was the next day, and the next day, and the day after that. And then one day she was not there at all. They had taken her to the hospital. A week passed, and another week passed. The grown-ups closed their faces, and nothing could be read in them.

There came a night when the telephone rang, and Deedee jerked awake, and then fell asleep again, surface sleep that was easily shattered. There were sounds in her room. She woke up. There was a bureau across the room with a mirror above it. Her mother and her Aunt Minnie were facing the mirror. Their faces were reflected, but they were not seeing what the mirror saw. They were standing there because it was the farthest away from Deedee's bed.

Her mother spoke: 'I don't know what to do about Deedee. If I wake her up and tell her, she'll never forget it. If I don't wake her up, she may never forgive me.'

Perhaps Deedee stirred. For suddenly her mother and aunt were really looking in the mirror, and they saw her lying in bed with her eyes wide open.

Her mother came quickly and stood over her. 'Deedee,' she said, 'the hospital just called. Sister died. She doesn't have to suffer any more. She's in heaven now. Now you close your eyes and go back to sleep.'

She closed her eyes and went back to sleep. When she awoke, it was morning. She felt excited. Something had happened in the night. What was it? Then she remembered. Sister had died. She jumped up and ran into her sisters' room. 'Genia, Helen, wake up, wake up. Sister died last night.' She saw tears splash their faces. Then she was right. Something exciting had really happened.

Her mother said she didn't have to go to school that day. She looked surprised. She wanted to go. She went to school and told everybody that her little cousin was dead. Somebody told her teacher. Her teacher said she could go home. She was surprised again.

The day of the funeral was a lovely day to go see Sister. Now they were all in the funeral parlor, where there were flowers and sad-faced friends. Deedee's mother pointed to a coffin and said, 'Go look at Sister.' Deedee went to the coffin and peered into it. She came back to her mother. 'There's a little dead girl in there. Where's Sister? I came to see Sister.'

Her mother said, 'That was Sister you saw.' That was the moment she came out of the shock that she had been in for three days. She had come to the funeral to take Sister home. It was not that she did not know about death. It was just that she did not know it could touch her. How could she know until it touched her. The smell of carnations was all around her. For years she could not bear their smell, for even more years she could not touch one.

They were home now, she dry-eyed, icy. Brother had stayed with an aunt. He ran to greet her. She turned away without touching him. She called her mother and took her aside. What she had to say she had to say outside of anyone else's hearing. She stared hard at her mother, and said the terrible thing, asked the haunting question.

'We're a colored family, aren't we? Why did God take our brown baby and let our white baby live?' Then she ran out of the room, knowing there was no answer to so cruel a question, knowing that only a mother would never reveal her wickedness. She had to strike out at someone, someone who would forgive her.

For days, for weeks she was mean to the little boy, dropping his bread on the floor to make him eat dirt, squeezing his hand so tightly when she held it that tears started in his eyes, doing every little hurtful thing she could get away with. And the little boy clung to her through it all, because he needed her now more than ever with Sister not there to play with, to sleep with, to talk to. Deedee had loved him once, and he did not know she had stopped.

It was summer, and the family came down from Boston to their summer cottage on the Island. Deedee's little meannesses continued, and Brother continued to trust her because love is forgiving.

One early evening, Deedee's sisters went to visit some friends their age, saying firmly that she was too young to go with them, but she was used to that, and watched them go. Then her mother said she was going to walk to a cottage down the road to sit awhile with an ailing friend. She put Brother to bed and told Deedee to go to him if he called.

Deedee went outside and sat on the porch, sitting as still as a mouse, so that Brother would think she had gone out, too, and feel scared being by himself. After a while she could hear him talking, and she wouldn't answer. She wouldn't comfort him by saying, 'Go back to sleep, I'm right here.'

He went on talking, and she wasn't answering, and he didn't sound scared. It made her feel funny. Now it was she who began to feel scared. Who was he talking to? What was happening? She had to get up and see.

She went to the little bedroom at the back of the house. He scarcely noticed her coming. He was talking away, and he didn't stop. 'What are you talking about?' she said crossly. 'You go straight to sleep or you'll catch it.'

'I'm talking to Sister,' he said.

'Where is she?' Deedee asked softly.

'Right here,' he said in surprise at the question.

'Do you see her?'

'Don't you?'

'No,' said Deedee. 'She doesn't want to see me. Will you tell her I'm sorry?

'Deedee's sorry.'

The tears that she had never shed began to fall. 'Oh, Brother,' she said, 'I love you, let me love you.'

She lay down beside him, and his hand crept into hers, the dark hand, the fair hand, entwined together.

That was the way her mother found them, asleep together. And the mother smelled a faint scent of carnations.

Then it was home again. Then summer ended. They were home again, and it was Christmas again. And there they were around the tree, all of the faces filled with Christmas joy.

Deedee went over to Brother. She bent down to him. 'Is she here?'

He understood: 'Yes.'

'Can you see her?'

'No.'

And the ghost was laid.

THE ENVELOPE

George Henty reached his doorstep and sighed with relief. His working day was over. The long day that began with leaving the living heart of a house that had heard his first cries, that had opened its doors to his frantic retreats from his first inglorious fights, that had given him security in the folds of his mother's wide skirts, that had blessed his marriage to Lottie, who understood him.

George Henty shut the door behind him, escaping the sound and fury of the world outside. Let those who enjoyed it push and shove each other now. He was out of that maddening stream. Here was sanctuary, here was home.

He hung his hat and coat in the closet, and casually glanced at the hall table where Sarah, the general maid, always put the mail. There were never any letters for him. He was not any good at making men friends. And, of course, he didn't correspond with women. How could anyone stray from the cheery comfort of a pair of house slippers and a fireside?

George's casual glance turned to one of surprise. There was a black-bordered envelope on the table. It was undoubtedly for him, for Lottie would long since have opened and read her mail. He picked it up gingerly. He disliked hearing news of the dead.

The envelope was soft and oblong in his hand. It did not have the stiff square feel of a formal announcement. It must be a personal letter from someone bereaved. He could not imagine who would address such a letter to him and not include the name of his wife.

He stared at the handwriting. It was a woman's, and teasingly familiar. But the postmark meant nothing to him. He turned the envelope over, looking for clues. There were initials A.L. Who on earth was A.L.? Had the letter been sent to him by mistake? And yet there was something about that handwriting. He studied the generous scrawl again. And suddenly his heart began to beat painfully, and a pulse throbbed in his temple.

Adrienne! Adrienne Hollister the last time he saw her. But that was twenty years ago, and he could not expect her name to remain the same. She had married some Mr. L., and now Mr. L. was dead. And she wanted him to know. She was sending a challenge down the years. She was telling him she was free in a hand that was still firm and young.

Emotion swept over George as he fumbled with the flap of the envelope. Adrienne's face swam before his eyes. The mouth that was full and gently mocking, the delicate nose, the proud dark eyes. As clearly as though it were here and now, he heard the aching throb in her voice as she said good-bye. He saw her slim straight figure walk away, the head held high. He saw himself take one hesitant step toward her, then halt dead in his tracks as his mother's commanding voice made him turn his back on the beauty in which Adrienne walked.

'George, is that you?' It was Lottie's voice, and it had the same commanding ring as his mother's.

He started guiltily. 'I just came in. I'm here in the hall.'

'Well, dinner's on the table. It's six o'clock, you know.'

'I know,' he said apologetically. Sometimes he ran all the way from the subway so he wouldn't be a minute late. Dinner was put on the table to be eaten, Lottie always said. And she was right, of course. He hated his midday meal in town. You could never be sure how long the food had been standing.

But the letter impelled him toward the stairs. 'I'm going up to wash. Be down in a minute.'

'You can wash after dinner,' his wife said flatly. 'Your hands can wait but dinner can't.'

George put the envelope in his breast pocket. Yes, it was better to wait. He did not want to read Adrienne's letter hastily. After dinner he would shut himself in his room. He would be a changed man when he opened the door. He would turn his back on Lottie's voice as he had not turned his back on his mother's.

Lottie spread her napkin across her ample lap and turned her cheek for George's peck.

'Did you get your letter? Who's dead? Nobody I know, I guess. Must be a business acquaintance.'

He was relieved, and his kiss was warm. 'I just glanced at it. I'll read it later.'

She dismissed the subject as unimportant. 'Well, drink your soup while it's hot.'

He picked up his spoon and stared at his soup. He didn't want it. He was getting too fat. He was getting too flabby. Once he and Adrienne had laughed at fat people. Once he and Adrienne had laughed at Lottie when she puffed up a hill ahead of them.

'What's wrong with your soup?' Lottie said sharply.

'Nothing,' he answered. 'I just don't want it. I'm fat. I want to get thin.'

Lottie gave a little pitying laugh. 'You're forty-four,' she reminded him. 'You can't expect to be thin. You've got middle-age fat. You might as well get used to it.'

He pushed his plate away. 'That's easy for you to say. You've always been stout. I hate being heavy and slow and puffing like an engine.'

Lottie flushed. She put her spoon down as if her soup had suddenly lost its taste. Her mouth trembled a little.

'Do you hate it in me?'

The letter was snug against his breast. It was putting words into his mouth. It was making him bold and daring.

'Since you asked for it, Lottie, yes.'

She caught her breath, and her chair scratched along the floor as she struggled to her feet. She was puffing very hard and was painfully conscious of it.

For a moment George felt ashamed of himself. He was being cruel because Lottie wasn't Adrienne. It had nothing to do with her being fat. Yesterday she had been the same size, and yesterday he had not wanted to hurt her.

'George,' said Lottie unsteadily, 'did you dislike me so much when you married me?'

He rose, too. He was going to bring their world down with a crash. There was no use sitting in the ruins.

'I've never disliked you. I've just never loved you.'

Nothing happened. Their world was still standing. Lottie was, too. She had not fallen in a faint. She was just looking at him curiously.

'I've always known that. I thought you knew I knew it. I was twenty-nine. I was older than you, but I wanted to be married. No other man had asked me. I was never popular like Adrienne Hollister.'

He felt his scalp prickle, and the letter seemed to lie naked against his heart. He was certain that Lottie could see it.

'What made you bring up Adrienne Hollister?' he asked hoarsely.

'Because you were in love with her when you married me. Because she was made for love, and I was not.'

He sat down limply. He felt as if Lottie had knocked the wind out of him. All of these years she had known his heart was not hers, and she had not been dismayed by that knowledge.

'How did you know about Adrienne Hollister?' George asked thickly .

Lottie sat down and began to fill the dinner plates. 'Steak is no good when it's cold,' she said practically, and added, almost as an afterthought, 'Your mother told me.'

'What did she tell you?'

Lottie's mouth was full of steak. She swallowed and said reproachfully, 'Oh, George, let the dead lie.'

The aroma of the steak filled his nostrils. He could not keep his fork from exploring his plate. The steak cut like butter and melted down his throat. A sense of well-being began to pervade him. But he brought himself up sharp with the recollection of what Lottie had said about his mother. He said wearily, 'My mother came between Adrienne and me. My mother made me give her up.'

Lottie looked resigned. George was going to lay bare his heart. It was a pity he could not have waited until after dinner. But a man's ego popped up in the most unexpected places. If George was going to explore his soul, there was nothing to do but hear him out.

'Your mother knew best,' she said patiently.

'You'd think so,' George cried jealously. 'You got me. My mother pushed you in my way. She made me dependent on you. She made me believe you would be a better wife than Adrienne.'

'I was a better wife for you,' said Lottie quietly. George's head jerked up in protest. Lottie's smile was gently ironic. 'Because I am heavy and slow and stout. Your mother's shoes were a perfect fit. Adrienne would have swum in them.'

'I don't know what you mean,' George said stiffly.

Lottie passed George the plate of hot rolls. He carefully selected the largest two.

'Adrienne was head and shoulders above you.'

George stared at Lottie as if she had lost her mind. His open mouth closed on a bit of roll, and it turned to straw. He could not swallow it.

Lottie said evenly, 'That's what your mother told me.'

He found himself shrieking, 'That's a lie. You made it up. My mother never said that. I was her idol.'

Lottie bit into her own roll. Her face lit up with pleasure. 'Excellent, aren't they?'

'You can sit there and eat,' George cried wildly, 'after trying to destroy my memory of my mother. My happiness was her whole life. You can never make me believe otherwise.'

'Your happiness *was* her whole life. She would have sacrificed Adrienne to you if that would have made you happy. But she knew that it would not.'

George leaned forward. His fleshy cheeks quivered.

'Adrienne and I were made for each other. In a moment of weakness I let my mother persuade me that we were not. She told me that Adrienne did not belong in my world. That she would be restless and discontent. That she would destroy my way of life.' His voice was urgently imploring. 'You've twisted my mother's words. She meant that Adrienne lived in the clouds. That she would have been a poor housekeeper. She never meant that Adrienne was my superior.'

Lottie said agreeably, 'Yes, you can look at it like that.'

George got up and stalked to the door. He turned to deliver a parting shot. 'I've been your tame cat a long time. But don't forget a cat has claws.'

He marched upstairs to his room. He felt that he waddled a little, and it added to his sense of injury. He reached the landing and entered his room, closing his door with a bang. He crossed to his bed and sat down. His legs were suddenly water, and his hands did not belong to him. With ten numb fingers he opened the letter and spread it across his knees.

My dear Mr. Henty, he read, I am Adrienne Hollister Baxter. I am named for my mother whom you knew before her marriage. You may not know that she became a writer. She wrote under the name of A. H. Baxter.

My father has a mounting stack of requests for a biography about my mother. Father is Clinton Baxter of the publishing house of Baxter and Barrett.

I remember that Mother spoke of you very often. I believe that you gave her her inspiration to write. She often said if it had not been for you, she might never have become a writer.

You may remember many little anecdotes about my mother. I know that my father will be more than grateful for any material you may send him, if you have the time and inclination . . .

George read the letter to its end and quietly tore it into shreds. He shivered and crossed the room and put the minute bits into the wastebasket. He felt suddenly old and futile, and he needed reassuring.

He went downstairs and into the living room. Lottie was listening to the radio. On her comfortable lap was a box of candy. George sat down in his favorite chair. He stretched his feet toward the fireplace.

'Lottie,' he said, 'I apologize.'

'You didn't wait for your dessert,' said Lottie severely. 'I took a lot of pains with that pie. All this nonsense about being fat.'

'Am I all right as I am?' he asked earnestly.

'I like a good stout man,' said Lottie. 'Looks like his wife takes care of him.'

'My mother was right about Adrienne Hollister,' George said slowly. 'I've heard she became a writer. A home and husband are career enough for any woman. Adrienne would have made a very poor wife.'

FLUFF AND MR. RIPLEY

When Mr. Ripley began to stay late at the shop, because each new draft depleted the personnel, and those who were left had to double and triple their work, Mrs. Ripley decided not to believe her husband on the increasingly frequent occasions when he phoned to say that business was keeping him downtown.

Mrs. Ripley was forty-five and she did not wear her years with grace. She hated middle age more than she had ever hated anything in her life and did everything to disguise it. Her clothes were far too youthful, her voice was a poor imitation of a girl's, her friends were constantly changing because she sought the companionship of a woman years her junior, who laughed behind her back and soon tired of her.

When Mr. Ripley first married her she was plump and pretty and twenty. Mr. Ripley thought she would make an ideal wife and mother. Though he did not tell her so, he could see her in a wicker rocker with a round and dimpled baby in her arms, while he lay sprawled in the porch swing, reading the funnies to a three-year-old. The picture pleased him. He further embellished it with a nice old dog who would be stretched across the top step guarding his loved ones.

Mrs. Ripley hadn't wanted children. She had wept when her

husband, after a year of love and kisses, delicately suggested that it would be nice to start a family. She knew she would look adorable with a baby, like a little girl with a big doll. But the tiresome thing about babies was that they grew. You couldn't stick to twenty-five when your child turned ten. You couldn't stay under forty when your selfish child made you a grand-mother.

Mrs. Ripley never had a child, and Mr. Ripley hid his disappointment. He supposed some women were afraid of dying in childbirth, or of losing their figures, or of having to share their husband's love. If it was his bit of bad luck to be married to a woman with one of these fears, it was just a bit of bad luck and not a major tragedy. For his wife was really a child herself in all her charming ways. Watching her grow into maturity would be almost as much fun as watching a little girl's growth.

But Mrs. Ripley had not grown up, and with the years her determination to stay a wide-eyed child began to pall on Mr. Ripley. He grew lonely, because he grew tired of telling Mrs. Ripley that no, she hadn't gained a pound when it was plain that she had gained six; that yes, she still looked twenty, when, of course, she didn't; that certainly he wanted her to sit in his lap, she felt like a feather.

Mr. Ripley decided to buy himself a dog. He wanted companionship, and he wasn't getting it from Mrs. Ripley. He wanted a comfortable dog, not young, not frisky, not little and cute. He wanted a pal, who wouldn't preen before him, or climb into his lap.

Mr. Ripley found the dog he wanted, a gentle and dignified mastiff, out of puppyhood, who liked his new owner at once. He followed Mr. Ripley home from the kennel with no show-off tricks and no tiresome chitchat. Mrs. Ripley met them at the door and began to emit little squeals. She said she was afraid of that great big beast, and suppose he had fleas, and what did Mr. Ripley expect to do about him when he went to work?

Mr. Ripley kept Pal by his side for the rest of that day, so that Mrs. Ripley could get used to him gradually, and not be frightened by coming upon him unguarded. But Mrs. Ripley grew very jealous at seeing the two so inseparable. This, she imagined, was the way it would be until Pal rolled over and died. Long before nightfall she worked herself up into a temper tantrum, declaring she would not sleep under the same roof with a dangerous dog.

Mr. Ripley took his new friend back to the kennel. Walking home alone down the lonely road, he had a sense of loss so great that sometimes the road blurred before him.

The uneventful years passed. The war and the pressure of work gave Mr. Ripley the first real interest he had had in years.

He labored late at his shop, and Mrs. Ripley decided that he was deceiving her. With somebody young, of course, who did not dye her hair. Mrs. Ripley's jealousy of this unknown woman grew by leaps and bounds. And suddenly she had an overwhelming fear that her husband would ask her for a divorce and marry a girl who would give him a child.

She was desperate, and cast about in her mind for some way to keep her husband at home. Then she remembered Pal, and that day of her husband's devotion to him. Mr. Ripley was nearing fifty, many years her senior, Mrs. Ripley added hastily to herself. Surely at his age he was ready to settle down with a dog and a book. A dog would give him a new interest in his home and encourage him to stay in it.

Mrs. Ripley went shopping for a pet as a surprise for her husband. She settled on a month-old handful of fluff, because there was nothing about it suggestive of a big horrid dog that might bite. That afternoon she had a lot of fun making a charming ribbon-tied bed out of a clothes basket. When Mr. Ripley reached home late that night, basket and Fluff were ensconced on the window seat in the bedroom.

His mouth fell open. He stared at his wife, who had waked at his footsteps, and now sat up in her bed with her chin strap and curlers, looking very proud of her self.

'What's that over there?' Mr. Ripley asked almost harshly, hoping wildly that his wife would say someone had left a foundling on their doorstep.

'Go and see,' she urged contentedly.

Cautiously he approached the basket, walking on tiptoe, and feeling very big and awkward beside a small baby. He bent down to look and saw the sleeping puppy.

'It's a dog,' he said dully.

All of her latent maternalism roused to its defense. 'Well, what did you think it was?' she demanded sharply. 'I thought you were so crazy about dogs. You were mighty crazy about that old Pal. You just don't like Fluff because he's mine.'

The puppy waked at the sound of her strident voice and began to whimper. Mrs. Ripley jumped out of bed, streaked across the room, and cuddled the puppy in her arms.

Mr. Ripley was tired from the long day. He had the crazy feeling that his wife was making sport of him. This was her revenge for her evenings alone. This tiny white dog would never be a fine big fellow like Pal. This was a woman's pet that his wife had bought to show her contempt for him.

The lack of understanding between Mr. and Mrs. Ripley grew enormously in the next few weeks. Business continued to bring Mr. Ripley home very late, and Mrs. Ripley lavished the best of her love on Fluff. Mr. Ripley saw his wife's devotion to the little toy dog with sick eyes. He remembered how seriously his little sister had played house with her dolls, calling them her children, and pretending they were real. Fluff seemed symbolic of the whole unreality of his marriage.

One night he came home with a feeling of deep sadness. The week before, his secretary, Mrs. Heath, a gentle, unobtrusive woman, a widow in her forties, had told him she had lost her only child, a son dying in uniform in Sicily. This day another groundswell of grief compelled her to speak his name again. Today would have been his twenty-first birthday. What good was he dead, no wife ever wed, no children ever born.

Mrs. Heath had stayed after hours to work with Mr. Ripley, preferring to spend the evening away from home. At nine she and Mr. Ripley had left the office together. Mr. Ripley had watched her go in the opposite direction, and had had the impulse to follow her to keep her from brooding alone.

Mrs. Ripley's eyes were red-rimmed when she opened the door to her husband. They were swollen as if she had cried a long time. He came in quickly. 'What happened?' His mind, already oppressed by Mrs. Heath's grief, flew to his sister's boys, both overseas.

His entry started her tears again. She could not speak. He seized her shoulders and shook her hard.

'Tell me,' he demanded fiercely.

'Fluff,' she said between sobs. 'I took him to the hospital today to have his tail cut. He cried so when I left him, and he was so quiet and scared when it was over. I don't think I'll ever forgive myself. And Fluff may never forgive me either.'

The puppy came into view then. He was subdued, but very much alive. As a matter of fact he lifted his bandaged tail in greeting. 'I'll get you a bite and tell you all about it,' said Mrs. Ripley.

Mr. Ripley rubbed his hand across his forehead. 'Your dog lost his tail. Other women have lost their sons.' Suddenly he did not feel tired any more. 'I'm going out again. But before I go, I'll pack my bag. I'll send for it tomorrow.'

ODYSSEY OF AN EGG

Porky Tynes came out of the cheap movie house and stood for a moment under the marquee, staring at the lurid stills of the picture he had just seen. He wet his lips a little. It had been a swell show. Gangsters, and gats, and gun molls. Tough guys giving the works to little scared guys. Big shots running rackets, making millions.

Porky hitched his pants and lit a cigarette. Then he pulled his hat over one eye, thrust his legs apart, and drew his brows together in the menacing way the head guy had done in the movie. The passersby paid no attention. They scurried along the mean street like miserable rabbits. There wasn't one who looked as if he had guts enough to shoot a gun. Porky spat derisively. You had to be tough to get on in this world.

He sauntered slowly down the street. He had nowhere to go. His mother had given him two bits that morning to go look for a job. Said his old man was tired of supporting him. They had a nerve, them two. Did they think he liked living in their lousy three rooms? Did they think he wouldn't be gone in a minute if he ever got hold of a sweet hunk of dough?

Where was a guy going to get a job? It wasn't his fault he got kicked out of trade school before he could learn a trade. If it hadn't been for Polecat, that pushface principal would never have known which one of the guys was stealing his stinking tools.

Porky viciously kicked a tin can that a ragged kid was pulling along on a string. That ragged kid let out a yell and ran to show his cut hand to a burly man in a doorway. Porky walked away fast. No sense in getting in a fistfight over a lousy tin can.

The can whizzed down the street and got itself tangled in the trailing skirts of a shriveled old woman. Porky slowed down as he came abreast. He snickered. The old hag looked as if she had been hit by a hurricane. If she didn't fall flat on her face with fright, he'd be a son of a gun.

Porky speeded up again. If this old sister was going to fall, he wanted to be far, far away. Getting beat up – that is, giving a guy a beating over a sniveling kid and a bunch of old rags – was beneath Porky's dignity.

A hand clutched his arm. He stood stock-still. Perspiration came out on his forehead. He closed his eyes and could almost feel the burly man's fist connect with his chin.

'I feel awful faint, son.'

Porky opened his eyes and stared down at the frail veined hand on his arm. His glance slid up insolently to the ashen face. His lips lifted in a snarl. 'So, what's 'at to me?'

The old woman spoke with difficulty. 'Will you help me to my house, son? It ain't far.'

'What's in it for me?' said Porky disdainfully. The nerve of this ragpicker, asking favors of guys. She leaned on him heavily, but he was afraid to pull away. The guy back there might be watching him.

The old woman fumbled with her filthy handkerchief. 'There's a dime tied up in the corner, son. All I got in this world. You can take it.'

A lousy dime for carting an old dame down the block. Gingerly he extracted it. He could get a hot pup and a cup of java. Then he could go to another movie with the rest of the two bits his mother had given him.

'You don't got to lean so hard on a guy,' he complained. 'Folks'll think you're drunk.'

They shuffled off down the street, the old woman walking slowly and painfully, and Porky darting shamed glances around the street. Finally they halted before a run-down apartment house. The old woman spoke between gasps. 'I live in the basement. Here's the key.'

He took the soiled handkerchief again and helped her down the stairs. He was mad as hops. The old bag of bones had a grip on his arm that was like a death hold. He couldn't have gotten away without pasting her one. And if he did, she'd yell for the cops, and those lousy bums would conk him with their nightsticks.

He opened the unlocked outer door, and they entered the dark interior. With a pale wavering finger the old woman pointed into the gloom.

'It's there. My door. For God's sake, get me inside.'

He cursed, and felt his spine prickle with his dislike of the dark. He fumbled for the lock, found it, and inserted the key that dangled from the soiled handkerchief. The door swung open. This was better. Sunlight filtered through the drawn shade.

'Well, here y' are, sister,' he said ungallantly, thrusting the handkerchief into her hand. The toughness was back in his voice now. In a minute he'd be outside again, heading for a beanery. It wasn't a bad haul for a dime.

The old woman took a few feeble steps on her own. Porky turned to go. Jeez, what a lousy hole. He blew out his lips in contempt.

'Son,' came a desperate whisper, 'please – my heart medicine – over there.'

Porky saw red. What'd she want for a dime? A full-time flunky? He swung around to curse her.

She was staring straight at him with glassy eyes. Both hands clawed the rags that covered her chest, jerking and pulling with their failing strength as if they would yank out the stone that was her heart.

Porky stood rooted to the spot. The room was filled with the sickening sound of her tortured breathing. Porky's knees turned to water. The old dame was dying. What a spot to be in for a crumby dime.

She was falling! She was falling right toward him, her rags gaping open, and the rattle rasping out of her throat. Porky jumped to one side and felt the hair rise on his head. He'd never do another favor for anybody as long as he lived. What a lousy rotten trick to play on a guy.

The old woman lay at his feet. She was dead as a doornail. A kid could see that. Gingerly Porky skirted the body. His shoe struck something. He leaped a foot away. Cautiously he came forward again. Jeez, it was a wad of dough bulging inside a rubber band. He stooped, scrabbled up his find, and fled.

Reaching the street, Porky slowed down and tried to look nonchalant. The money weighed down his pocket. He was rich! He could tell his old lady where to get off. He could kick his old man where it would hurt most. He had the nerve, and now he had the money. He hitched his pants and spat triumphantly.

The money burned his fingers. He wished he knew how much it was. He paled. Maybe it was a dummy roll, a bill on top and nothing but paper underneath. He had to know now. He stared around wildly. Where could he go? His eye fell on the movie house. He could go in the gents room and see how he stood.

Porky reached the theater, averted his face, slipped his dime inside the cage, and scuttled through the lobby. The ticket seller and the ticket taker showed no signs of recognition. There was nothing about Porky's unprepossessing person to remember.

Porky went upstairs to the empty gents room and counted

the money. He was dizzy when he finished. There was five thousand dollars in one-hundred-dollar bills. He flopped in a sagging lounge chair and lit a cigarette with trembling hands. He was really in the money! He could hire a dozen henchmen and dope out a racket that would make him a million.

A million. He frowned and leaned forward, thinking hard. That screwy old dame, packing five grand. What kind of monkey business . . . His eyes grew crafty. She was one of them misers. There were always pieces in the paper about people like that, living in dumps, walking around in rags, and hiding their money in a hundred places.

He stood straight up with shock and chagrin. Maybe there was more where this lettuce came from. What kind of way was this to start being a big shot? Losing his head and running like a rabbit over a few lousy dollars. He should have stayed and searched the room. He cursed himself for a fool.

That old dame had played him for a sucker, all right. Giving him a dime and hugging five grand. The lousy dirty nerve of her. He was boiling mad. Little flecks of foam stood in the corners of his mouth. He crushed the cigarette under his heel.

He began to walk restlessly up and down. What to do now? He was too agitated to go past the ticket taker again. The guy might figure there was something up and call the cops. Someday he'd have a lot of fun drawing the bead on a rotten cop. Right now he'd better go sit through the show until he cooled off, and just keep his fingers crossed that nobody would find the old dame and beat him to the pickings.

Hunger attacked him as soon as he sat down. He should have brought a hot pup in with him. Or maybe he should go downstairs and get some candy out of the machine. No, the ticket taker might get wise to him. Someday he'd draw a bead on that guy, too. Minding other people's business. And that ticket seller. He'd get her up a dark alley some night and give her a reason to remember him.

The feature picture came on. Porky forgot his hunger and hunched forward, licking his lips a little. Yeh, this was the biz, all right. This was the way the big shots did it. Self-identification made him shiver with joy. He emitted a mouthful of lewd approval, and sneered at the bums who turned to stare at him. There wasn't a one in the lot he would use for a third-rate henchman.

The picture ended, and Porky went downstairs. The ticket taker had his back to him, but Porky cringed as he passed. You could never tell when a guy was going to turn and jump you. Or maybe the louse had turned his back as a signal to the cops. Porky ran through the lobby and did not stop until he was halfway down the block.

He stood puffing and panting outside of a lunchroom. The scent of frying food came through the ventilator. He felt faint with hunger. He ought to have a good feed. A couple of pork chops, and mashed with gravy, and some kind of gooey cake. You couldn't feel weak and faint for the kind of job he was going to pull. It took nerve to go fooling around a dead dame. Jeez, why did she have to die in the middle of the floor? He'd have to keep walking around her. Maybe he'd have to touch her! Maybe there was money in her shoe or in her stocking. The dirty rotten miser, hiding her money in places like that.

He had to have something solid under his belt. His stomach felt sick like it always did when he was hungry. Like when he was a kid and sneaked off to bed before supper, so he wouldn't be around when that parole rat came to squawk to his father. There were a dozen guys in this world he was going to put the finger on. He had the nerve, and now he had the money to hire a triggerman.

Porky started into the lunchroom, and his feet froze on the door-sill. What was he going to use for dough? It was crazy to pull out a wad of bills and peel off a century in a cheap joint like this. That lamebrain behind the counter wasn't used to big-money guys. He might get suspicious and call the cops.

Porky turned and went down the street. His shoulders drooped. He didn't want a hot dog. He wanted a meal in a restaurant. What a lousy world to live in. Guys minding other guys' business and calling the cops. He'd have to do the job on an empty stomach. But maybe it was better that way. That old dame didn't smell like no rose before. By now . . . Porky spat salt water. Well, afterwards he'd go where the swells lived and eat in a ritzy restaurant. Nobody there would blink an eye if he tipped the waiter the whole five G's.

The cellar stairs seemed endless as Porky slowly descended them. His mouth twitched, and his eyes were deep in his head with strain. Nobody was hanging around. They couldn't have discovered the body. If they had, the stoop would be full of gabby dames. Jeez, women gave him a pain. Just wait till he drove past his mother's door in a long shiny car. He'd buy a big horn and toot it in her face.

Porky looked toward the dead woman's window. The shade was still drawn. There wasn't a sound. He opened the outer door and slipped inside. The darkness terrified him again, and the dead silence. He leaned against the door for support and whimpered like a puppy.

He had to have a cigarette. He had to do something to steady his nerve. It might be a fool thing to strike a match, there might be a janitor somewhere in back, but he couldn't stand this creepiness closing in on him.

In panic he felt for a cigarette. It was pulp when it reached his mouth, but he did not know that. He took out his match safe, opened it, tore off a match, and felt the safe slip through the nerveless fingers of his left hand at the moment his shaky right hand stabbed at it.

With one wild lunge he reached the dead woman's door. There was daylight behind it. She was behind it, too, but there were a million more of her swirling around him in the dark.

He put his hand on the knob, and his heart stopped. What was the door doing closed? He couldn't remember closing it. Maybe he had, but he couldn't swear to it. As fast as he had gotten out of there, it didn't make sense he would shut a door.

Suppose the old skirt wasn't really dead? Suppose she screamed when she saw him? He hitched his pants with his free arm. He could take care of that. He had the nerve, and he had the muscle to croak a double-crossing old dame. He kicked the door open violently.

She lay as he had left her, now dimly outlined in the waning afternoon light. The dark outside was swarming with her, but this motionless thing he would have to pass, and touch, and put his back to made him want to yell for his mother, made him want to hide his head in her skirts.

'It ain't going to bite you, buddy. Come on in.'

The sound of a gruff male voice was like a shot in Porky's arm. Someone alive had made it. Porky was so humbly grateful that he wanted to cry. He stumbled across the threshold.

A man materialized from behind the door. He was a big man with gimlet eyes. One of his pockets bulged.

'I been praying for company. She ain't said "boo!" since I come.'

Porky eyed the man admiringly. Who was this tough-talking guy? He looked hard as nails. Jeez, what a triggerman he'd make. Maybe they could make a deal.

Porky hitched his pants. 'What's your racket, feller?'

The man smiled dourly and flipped back his lapel.

A dick, a dirty lousy dick. Porky was wild with frustration and fear.

'You got nothing on me,' he shouted. 'I don't know this old dame from a hole in the wall.'

'Believe it or not, you was waiting for a streetcar, huh?'

'No,' said Porky in a harried voice. 'It was like this, see. I see this old dame on the street, and she looks kind of sick, so I ast could I bring her home. So I bring her home, and she offers me a dime, see, but I don't take no money from no old dames. So I leave her, but she still looks awful sick, and I get to thinking about her, and I got a mother of my own, see, so I came back here. And that's how it was, so help me.'

'Talk sense,' said the detective wearily. 'Ain't you the one she went to meet?

'I already told you,' said Porky shrilly. 'Why would I be meeting a crumbly old dame?'

Without answering the detective searched Porky and drew out the wad of bills.

'Quit stalling, kid. You come here to see why she didn't show up.' He nodded toward the floor. 'That's why. I was trailing her and she give me the slip. Run like a deer. She was too old to kick up her heels like that. Her ticker stopped.'

'That's what I said,' Porky argued frantically. 'I see this old dame on the street, see, she looks awful sick, and she ast me to bring her home. She offers me a dime, and I don't take it. I don't take money from poor old dames. So, see, a guy that wouldn't take a dime that's give him wouldn't rob no poor old lady of a bunch of lettuce as big as that. I work for a big corporation, see, and I'm on my way to bank their dough. You're holding me up.'

'The banks close at three,' the detective said drily. 'And they ain't got no place to keep counterfeit money.'

Porky's jaw dropped. For a long second he tried to take it in. Then his whole body shook with helpless rage. 'Ain't it real?'

'Listen, squirt, I'm the one that asks the questions. Playing dumb ain't going to save your yellow hide. Come clean. I been trying to round up you guys for six months, but you been too slippery. I knew this old dame was the go-between, but she wasn't the fish I was trying to catch. I wanted the eels who been making this phony dough. I caught one or two, but I had to throw 'em back. You give me a break and walk in with the goods. Thanks, sucker. Now let's go see the chief. We can leave her. She ain't lonesome.'

The handcuffs snapped on Porky's wrist.

Porky collapsed against the detective. 'You got to believe me,' he wailed. 'It's all like I said. I ain't mixed up in no racket. I'm a good citizen, see. I been out looking for work all day. You can ast my mother. I wouldn't pull nothing crooked. I believe in guys obeying the law. A guy that wouldn't take a dime from a poor old dame ain't going to cheat the government.'

The detective jerked Porky from his knees. 'I been waiting two hours for this show, but I'm tired of the act already. Come on, big shot, let's go.'

Porky took one wavering step. Then the floor rose up and knocked him down.

The detective dragged him along like a sack of mail.

ABOUT A WOMAN NAMED NANCY

There was a woman named Nancy who lived in a house which was her whole life, or so it was said. It was a fine square house, noble beside the modest houses surrounding it. She kept it immaculate, polished, shining, not a smidgen of dust or dirt anywhere. Her lawn and flower beds looked as if they had come to life out of a garden catalog. There was not a weed showing, nor anywhere a tuft of grass that needed cutting, nor a fading bloom spoiling the beauty and symmetry of a flowering bush.

There was no birdbath on the lawn. Unwitting visitors had sometimes mentioned it. And Nancy's reply was firm. A birdbath would attract birds which would come to drink and linger and leave unpleasant droppings. The birds would attract cats who would streak across the lawn to do them mayhem. The cats would leave even more unpleasant droppings, adding the final injury of scuffing up a flower bed to conceal them.

On this Island where birds abound, where bird-watchers are uncountable, where birdseed is a household staple, she did not know one bird from another.

She had never owned a house until she came across this jewel and found herself able to finance it. Though to some the responsibility of owning a house is a nightmare, an albatross, a burden from dawn to dark, its bills more binding than a marriage contract, its upkeep everlasting, to Nancy a house of her own gave her the feeling of security that a long-gone husband never had.

I knew her, but not with any degree of intimacy. She was a year-round person as was I. That is a bond, and in time of need we knew we were here for each other. Her neighbors admired her industrious ways. She had a steady job. And for an hour or more before she left home, she worked in her yard. When she came home, tired though she must have been, she worked in her yard as long as there was light.

The neighbor women with babies almost always on the way and their husbands forever trying to stretch their pay to feed another mouth could not afford to have the concern for appearance that motivated her days. But instead of envy they felt secure in her solidity. However their fortunes shifted, hers remained unchanged.

She was a cook by profession and well paid, but she enjoyed most cooking for those who had nothing to give her but their thanks. She had stocked her kitchen with family-size pots and pans, and she regularly called some mother or older child to come and get some dish hot out of her oven. There was rarely a day that someone or more than one did not benefit from her bounty.

She had, of course, no time to visit people, and no inclination to waste time with idle callers. She was always doing something, and a knock on her door, or a hoot and holler from a car screeching to a halt when she was busy in her yard, interrupted her rigorous schedule that had every moment filled with her job, her house chores, and her yard chores from waking time to bedtime.

One day I was driving past, without, of course, honking my horn, when Nancy's door opened and a child, standing respectfully outside her door, held out her hands to receive the sizable dish that Nancy placed in them.

Nancy saw me, we exchanged greetings, and on some impulse she asked me if I would like to take home a piece of apple pie fresh out of her oven. I was pleased to accept. Apple pie is my favorite. She invited me in and we walked back to the immaculate kitchen through that beautifully kept house. On the table was a great oblong pan. I was totally bemused to see an oblong apple pie. I thought there was a standing rule that pies should be round. I took a piece home, ate it with pleasure, and would, in time, have forgotten it. But that day will remain in my mind forever. It was the last day I was to see Nancy whole and strong.

I began to hear that Nancy had come down with a cold that she couldn't shake off. She had tried everything that everybody recommended but nothing seemed to work. She finally tried a doctor who gave her some prescription to relieve her aches and pains, but they didn't. She had never had a cold that made her feel so bad.

I am terrified of the common cold. If you have a cold I won't go near you. When I was a child I had colds frequently and coughed all night. I thought maybe I was going to lose my breath and die. My mother said that people didn't die from coughing unless they were choking on a bone. The doctor said I would stop having colds when I was fifteen. When you are six or seven that seems light-years away. But he was right. Ever since my fifteenth birthday I've never had a cold of my own. That is to say, if you have a cold and cough in my face, I get sprayed with your germs, and your cold gets a grip on me.

I stayed away from Nancy. And it got to be very embarrassing because everybody was asking everybody, which, of course, included me, for an opinion about her condition. Was it one of those colds that had to wait on spring for a cure? When had I seen her last? How did she look to me? I deliberately made incoherent replies, and began to have the most awful feeling of guilt. A human being was my species, and I had turned my back.

One day I was so deep in thought about some personal concern that, in driving home, I took the shortcut through Nancy's street, a way that, for obvious reasons, I had been carefully avoiding. Suddenly, and then remorsefully, I was aware that I had driven past Nancy's house without a glance, and that she, for all I knew, might have been sitting by the window wishing for a visitor. Clearly I had no choice but to risk exposure to whatever might befall me than do her the unkindness of sailing past her door as if she could live or die for all it mattered to me.

I shifted gears, backed to her door, got out of my car and braced myself to stay for the obligatory twenty minutes at least, and not get the fidgets. I walked toward the porch stairs, and as soon as my foot touched the bottom step, I froze, the feeling, the knowing overwhelming me, that presence that grips me and will not let go, forcing me to face the hard fact of death in the offing.

I reached the top stair, walked across the porch, and in the Island way, knocked on the door, opened, called out my name, and waited for its approval. When Nancy called back 'Come on in,' the nature of her illness was now clear to me in the sound of her voice that seemed to well up from some limitless depth of pain.

I stayed some two or three hours or more, and I was full of breezy talk as if Nancy's world was the same as when I last saw it. It is my style in such situations. She was in bed in a downstairs room, and I said with mock reproach: 'I thought you'd be up and baking an apple pie. That's why I stopped by. I'll never forget the piece you gave me out of that long pan. It was the best I ever tasted. Whenever you feel up to it, call me, and I'll jump in my car and go get the makings.'

I asked her where she was hurting and she touched an area of her body where she supposed the cold had settled in some joint.

I thereupon told her a story, some of it true, some of it not, about a pain I had had once in some joint or other, which I thought would cure itself with home remedies. When it didn't I went to a doctor who promptly put me in the hospital for X rays and tests which showed up the cause and the cure became evident. Hospitals were havens.

Having pressed that point and, I hoped, impressed her with that point, I then pursued another. Didn't she have a friend named Connie, who was often between jobs or between husbands, and at such times showed up on the Island with some winnings from the numbers, and stayed and played until it was gone. Why not call her tonight to find out if she was free to come and stay for a while until she, Nancy, was back on her feet. I added that from my recollection of her, Connie just didn't seem the sort to say no to someone she liked.

I made a meal for Nancy. There was plenty of food in her refrigerator that she hadn't felt like fixing or eating. She ate what I gave her to please me more than because she wanted it.

But it made us both feel better that she had something hot in her stomach.

Now it was time for me to go. I had obligations at home. I stood by Nancy's bed, and my voice was very serious. I said, 'Nancy, I've kept you company a long time. I think you've enjoyed my being here. So now you must do something for me. You must promise me that if you feel one more pain too bad to bear you will pick up the telephone and call the ambulance. I'm writing down the number, and I'll leave it here beside you. Now I want you to say what I asked you to say. I beg you.'

And softly Nancy said, 'I promise.'

And I said, 'I'll come again tomorrow.'

I could not sleep that night. And the little sleep I had was troubled, jerking me awake. At half past six I got up for good, dressed, drank some coffee, and drove to Nancy's house. I had to know whether or not she had lived through the night. I tried the door and it was locked. I knocked on the door and it stayed mute. I called Nancy's name, and there was no answer. The stillness was overpowering.

I did not want to wake a neighbor at that early hour. And so I sat in my car, waiting for some stirring of life in some nearby house. There must be someone on that street who had some inkling of what I had to know.

Across the street a sleeping house came awake. A child's treble voice gave birth to the morning. A window shade shot up. Somebody coughed a routine morning cough. And presently the front door opened and a man in his bathrobe came out on his porch to pick up his newspaper that had landed on the porch instead of the sidewalk.

It was Harry, a fisherman, Nancy's good neighbor, who kept an eye out on her house whenever she was away. I got out of my car, crossed the street and said quietly, 'Good morning, Harry. I'm worried about Nancy. I saw her yesterday and didn't like her looks. So I had to come over to see how she looked today. But her door is locked, and she didn't answer when I called her name. There may be something wrong. Do you have the key?'

'What happened is she's in the hospital. I saw the ambulance and me and my wife went over. That was toward dark last night. Nancy was taking it calm. She said she called the ambulance herself. Maybe that cold turned to pneumonia.'

We exchanged a few more words, then I drove back home, and at a reasonable hour called the hospital. I was told that Nancy was undergoing tests and to come and see her later in the day.

In the late afternoon I visited Nancy. She was sitting up in bed and looking cheerful. She had never been a patient in a hospital before, and everything had made her feel happy. She thought the doctors and nurses were wonderful. She said she felt good. She felt, of course, safe in that place of healing which was better than feeling scared at home alone.

She was brimming over with good news and told me gratefully

that I had been right about hospitals. She was only sorry she had waited so long to find out for herself. The doctors had examined her inside and out and located the cause of her pain. In three weeks they would operate and she would be a new woman, or at least as good as she used to be. In the meantime they were sending her home in a day or two to build herself up to go under the knife.

Now, like Nancy, I felt good, too, maybe even better. I felt so good to have been wrong. My infallible intuition had been far from the mark. Maybe that knowing, that anguish of knowing was over. Maybe Nancy was going to outlive us all.

I asked her if she had called Connie. She said she had called her while she was waiting for the ambulance, and Connie had said for her to hang in there, she'd be on the Island the day after tomorrow. I asked her for Connie's telephone number if she knew it offhand or her address if she didn't. I wanted to call her and tell her I'd meet her ferry and help her with whatever needed doing.

When I left Nancy's room I went to the desk to see if there was someone who could give me instructions on how to prepare Nancy for her operation, what to eat, how much to exercise, if any, how much rest. The nurse looked a little uncomfortable, I thought, as if I was being intrusive. But in the same moment she said with relief, 'Here comes her doctor. You can speak to him.'

The doctor and I found a quiet corner at the end of the hall. I said that Nancy had told me about her coming operation, and had sounded glad. She only wished she could have it tomorrow instead of having to wait three weeks. But she knew she had to build up her strength. Three weeks was not a lifetime. She could wait.

The doctor said quietly, 'Her condition is inoperable. But she will die without ever knowing it. That is why I set that date. She will not live three weeks.'

I called Connie that night to make sure of the hour of her coming and to tell her the stark truth about Nancy's sickness. She arrived at the time planned, and we stopped at the hospital before going to Nancy's house to get Connie settled in.

We sat on either side of her bed, each trying to outdo the other in milking some outrageous story to the last ounce of laughter. We reach an age, beginning with our thirties, when acting becomes a natural part of our existence. Without it, in so many instances, we fail our fellow beings with gratuitous blunt truth that may hurt more than it helps.

At one time Nancy said she forgot she was in a hospital. She forgot she was going to have an operation. She did not envy us our wholeness. Her spirit, if not her body, took strength from it. We brought her home the next day along with the medication that, in her mind, would prime her for the operation. We knew it was to ease her dwindling days. As the first week ended and the second week began it was visibly clear that from then on, any day might be her last.

But Nancy stubbornly clung to life, holding on for several weeks longer, an exercise in willfulness beyond credibility. Every day her strength diminished and death stood ready to carry the burden of her body to some appointed place.

At such times she reached for our hands instead, making us help her out of bed, making us walk her up and down the room until the dying inside of her subsided, and she could sleep without the fear of never waking.

She was fighting for time for all the things she had put off to let her house come first. She had never even taken one second to break off a flower and tuck it in a little girl's tangle of hair. She had never telephoned anybody and said, 'Let's stop whatever we're doing and go for a walk on this lovely day.' I think she had never felt the joy of just being.

When we spoke in praise of her house, expecting to please her, she made a grim line of her mouth and turned her head away. She probably blamed it for causing her sickness, wearing down her resistance, and using up so much of her strength that she didn't know when she'd be ready for her operation.

One day when I had done some errands for her, she said, 'All I ever do is say thank you. I want to do more. Maybe there's something you've seen in my house that you'd like to have. Whatever you saw, I wish you'd take it.'

I said, 'I'd be delighted. I saw a small, square pan in your kitchen. Some day I want you to make me an apple pie in that square pan that's just the right size.'

She looked at me hard to see if I was teasing or if I really meant it. My face was serious. She said, 'I wish I could tell you when.'

'We'll keep our fingers crossed.'

That apple pie in that small, square pan became a routine between us. Time and again she would hint for me to tell her about the coming miracle of my finding her in the kitchen making a square apple pie.

Then, all in one day, it was over. It was the day the doctor made his routine visit and found Connie lying limp across a couch, with me standing over her, still in my coat, having just preceded him, and murmuring words of comfort to her for the anguish Nancy had just put her through with no one there to help her. Connie, alone, had had to walk Nancy up and down the room, a tour de force that she had somehow managed.

The doctor had been told of these excursions, but perhaps had not given thought to how devastating they must be to those involved, and on this particular occasion, to Connie, having to handle Nancy alone.

He called the hospital to prepare for Nancy's arrival. He asked if Connie and I could take her to the hospital. We could. And, of course, there was someone to receive her. The doctor had told Nancy he wanted to observe her in the hospital for a few days.

When we got back to Nancy's, Connie said, 'Do you mind if I get drunk?' I said with understanding, 'Go ahead,' knowing that having received my consent, she wouldn't, not wanting me to have to deal with it.

We sat around musing, sipping, telling each other about our misadventures, laughing a little hysterically. I don't know what Connie felt, but I somehow suspected that this was the end of the story. The script would not be replayed, Nancy coming home again, and Connie and I resuming our roles. Everything comes to an end, one way or another.

Sometime in the night Nancy died. I often wonder if she died calling Connie and me to come walk her. And nobody heard. It was long ago written in the stars that that was the way it would be.

THE ROOMER

She followed her roomer to the front porch and stood dispiritedly in the doorway of the small, two-story house, which stood a shabby block away from the railroad tracks.

Her roomer got into his little car, and she waved a listless goodbye. The wind whipped her skirts and sent a cold shiver down her spine. The air smelled of snow. It was time to get out her winter coat. The woman's sullen expression changed to one of half-frightened anticipation.

She re-entered the house and went upstairs to the cheerless back bedroom which she shared unwillingly with her husband. In nervous haste she began to unpack the worn cedar chest at the foot of the bed. At the bottom of the chest was the winter coat which she had bought at an August sale and hidden all these months. She was probably thirty, and when she was twenty, her hair had undoubtedly been shining black, her well-shaped mouth without petulance, and her big, brown eyes without the deep shadows of discontent.

She took off the coat, got a hanger from the closet, and went downstairs to the small, untended back yard. She hung the coat on the clothesline, and stood back and looked lovingly at it. Then her eyes filled with uneasiness. What would she tell her husband? How would she explain her possession of a sixty-dollar coat? She shrugged, and set her lips grimly. She would tell him the truth.

At noon she prepared her husband's tasteless lunch of warmed-up leftovers. There was a lamb chop far back in the icebox and a covered dish of strawberries. She would eat her own lunch later. For weeks now, ever since her coat was purchased, she had had these secret, special meals.

Her husband's key turned in the front door. His anxious voice called back to the kitchen, 'Hon, I'm home.'

He had said the same thing every day for a year, and for a year she had never bothered to answer. He came heavily down the hall and into the kitchen, his little apologetic smile turning up the corners of his flaccid mouth.

'Well, here I am,' he said bashfully. She saw no need to reply to that either. He went to the sink to wash his hands. 'Mike go to work?' Mike had not missed a day in the twelve months he had been their roomer. It was a foolish question. But she knew she had to acknowledge her husband's presence sometime. 'Yes,' she said.

'That's fine,' he said uncertainly. 'That's just fine.' He surveyed the unattractive table. 'This looks just fine, too,' he said hollowly.

She stood by the window. 'I got something to say to you.'

The pulse in his temple began to throb. His head slumped into his shoulders. 'Are you gonna dog me about my pay cut? You ain't let up all year. Mike's four dollars makes up the difference. We're no better off and no worse.'

'It ain't about your pay cut,' she said contemptuously. 'It's about that coat you promised me.'

'I ain't forgot my promise,' he said desperately. 'I'll see you get your coat. In two or three months.'

'I ain't gonna freeze no two or three months.' She drew a long breath. 'I got the coat already.'

For the first time he faced her, staring at her with an expression of tortured incomprehension.

'Quit kiddin',' he said through dry lips.

'Come see for yourself,' she said coldly.

He lumbered to the window. They stood together and gaped through the grimy curtains. Neither had ever believed it possible that she could possess a fine, fur-trimmed coat.

'How much it cost?' he asked bleakly.

'Sixty dollars,' she answered proudly.

The pulse in his temple beat like a hammer. Little beads of sweat formed on his forehead. He could not control the quivering of his mouth. After a while his words came slowly and even softly. 'I bet Mike give you the money.'

She looked at him with surprise and alarm. She had planned to tell him gradually, and now he had told her first. 'That's what I was going to tell you,' she said, and knew that it sounded weak.

He turned away abruptly and walked back to the table. For a moment he stared down unseeingly, then hurled the plates to the floor.

'I know how you and him eats,' he said thickly. 'I been seeing them fancy things in the icebox.'

She was terrified. She crossed to him swiftly. For the first time in years she clung to him. 'You got it all wrong,' she said hoarsely. 'Him and me never et together. Them things you seen in the icebox, it was me alone eatin' 'em. Mike's just my roomer. He ain't nothing to me. We ain't said two words to each other.'

He shook her off as if she were a worrisome puppy, and he an old and tired dog.

'He gave you the money,' he said inexorably. 'I've known about you and him all along. You turned me out of my bedroom. You give it to him. That back room ain't got no closet. The mattress ain't fit. You give him the best of everything.'

'Don't be a fool,' she cried despairingly. 'Was it my fault you got a cut? One of us had to do something about it. You was too scared to speak to your boss. I rented our bedroom to Mike. So what? It was good money.'

'Good money,' he said bitterly. 'Four dollars. A guy that can buy and sell us. You said he couldn't pay more than four dollars. You didn't fool me. You was getting plenty on the side.'

'Two dollars,' she sobbed, 'but not like you think. Mike doesn't know I'm alive.'

She was telling the truth, and he did not believe her. He snorted derisively. 'Why you think I call when I come in? I don't want to catch him and you together. You been treating me like I was dirt ever since he first set foot in this house. It's because he ain't dirt, and I ain't him.'

She said with tired defiance, 'It's because he's got get-up-and-go, and you ain't.'

The incoming local blew a derisive blast. The man jerked his head toward the sound. 'Get-up-and-go,' he said softly. 'Get-up-and-go.' He laughed in a crazy, exultant way. 'You think I ain't sick of our marriage? You think I don't want to work for myself and have a fling with my landlord's wife? Mike's plenty smart. And I ain't too dumb not to take his tip.' He turned and strode out of the kitchen.

She ran after him and past him and began to climb the stairs.

'Wait,' she panted. 'For God's sake wait. You don't have to believe me. Believe your own eyes.'

She raced up the stairs into Mike's room and tore open the top bureau drawer. The front door slammed. She ran to the window, jerked it up, and shouted her husband's name. He did not turn around. His rapid stride increased. She ran back to the open drawer, and after a moment's frantic search, snatched out a banded packet.

The sound of her sobbing filled the small house as she stumbled down the stairs. She reached the front door, flung it open, and unsteadily crossed the porch. Her straining eyes searched the empty street. She uttered a desolate cry. The outgoing train blew a mocking good-bye.

The packet of penciled scraps, bearing her scrawled acknowledgment of the weekly receipt of six dollars, fluttered away from her hand. The high wind carried them skyward.

THE MAPLE TREE

Liz Terrell and Betsy Comden were summer neighbors. Their friendly relationship did not extend into winter, except for an exchange of Christmas cards, because their common interests ended with their return to the city.

Liz and her husband, Clark, were a bright young couple, both busy with careers, she in the fashion world, he in advertising; and they and their New York circle of friends, most of them childless, as were Liz and Clark, moved under a compulsion of excitement and sophistication that was as natural to them as breathing.

Betsy and Steve were born and bred Bostonians, which is to say, they were nothing like New Yorkers. In their own group they were as popular as Liz and Clark were in theirs. They were parents of four delightful children. They had a comfortable income from Steve's law practice, and felt no compulsion whatever to live beyond it.

Before Liz decided to buy a summer cottage, she had never heard of the little Massachusetts town that charmed her so on sight. She had made her pick from a list of likely places, choosing it for the sleepy sound of its name.

Following through, she flew down one Saturday, and looked up a real estate agent. She found what she wanted, a lovely, sprawling house, which she could take care of herself with occasional local help.

The maple tree was what really decided Liz. She did not think she had ever seen a tree with more breathtaking grace and grandeur. She said so to the agent, and he agreed, though he was sorry to have to tell her that the tree was not on her property.

Her neighbors, the Comdens, he went on to say, had made the same mistake when they bought their cottage a few years earlier. It was the tree that had made up their minds for them, too, or at least Mrs. Comden's mind. But, fortunately, Mrs. Comden had not changed her mind when she found out that the tree was not hers, and he hoped Mrs. Terrell wouldn't either.

The confusion, he explained, was due to the fact that the tree stood alone on a very small lot. Because the Comden place and the soon-to-be-Terrell place were much larger in area, the small lot in between the two, barren of buildings, seemed part of one or the other properties.

Many years ago, there had been a house on the lot, with a sapling growing beside its front door. When the owner died, his estate had gone to a distant cousin, who made his home in California. The tax on the tiny house on the tiny lot was so trifling that the cousin preferred to pay it rather than sell the property.

Over the years the house deteriorated, while the tree grew apace. The cousin died, but his heir, out of habit, continued to pay the tax, which grew less as the house lost more of its value.

Now the house was gone, destroyed by time and the tree. The grass had grown over its wounds. The great tree commanded the lot, casting a wide circle of shade.

There was still an owner, presumably a very old man. But the agent assured Liz that she need not worry about having a neighbor any closer than the Comdens. The cost of uprooting so big a tree to build a house would be completely out of proportion to what the lot was worth. It was a safe assumption that the tree would outlast them all.

Liz bought her house. In June she and Clark flew down twice to see to the work they were having done. On her first visit Liz noticed that the grass had been cut on the lot where the tree stood. Her caretaker, Mr. Trueworthy, informed her that the Comdens, whose house he also kept an eye on during their nonresidence, had the grass cut with theirs so that their property would not have a stretch of unsightly wild growth beside it.

On their second visit Liz and Clark met the Comdens, who were also down for the weekend. They had a brief exchange of pleasantries, each thinking the other nice enough neighbors, but all of them too busy putting things to rights to make any further findings.

In July, Liz came to stay. She was not really on vacation until August when Clark's vacation began. But in July she could work as well at her desk in the country as in the city. She enjoyed having the house to herself, but she was pleased when Betsy Comden showed up a few days later.

Seeing that Betsy had driven down alone, Liz called over to ask if there was anything she could do.

'You can give me a cup of tea,' Betsy said gratefully. 'And let's drink it under the maple tree. I'll bring some chairs.'

Liz fixed a portable tray, wondering if she could include some martinis for herself, but decided not to. Afterward, she was glad. There was something very cozy about a cup of tea, though she couldn't remember the last time she'd had one.

Betsy said she always came down in July alone. She, too, liked the house to herself and doing as she pleased. The children were in camp in July. In August she sent for them, because by that time she missed them terribly, and Steve, who took his vacation in August, wanted the children with him.

They finished their tea, and both had things to do. They

rose. 'Let's leave the chairs,' Betsy said. 'May I bring you breakfast tomorrow? Not to pay for my tea, but because I want to.'

That was the way it began, and that was the way it went
through the cloudless month of July.

Over the weeks of that July, and through the two successive
summers their pleasure in each other's company, though deepened, did not leave the orbit of the maple tree. For in August,
the husbands came, and Betsy's children came. Liz had no children to play with Betsy's children. Betsy's husband was fiercely
athletic. Liz's husband lazed through August. They were each
bored at the sight of the other.

In August the tree kept the secret of the life that had centered on it in July.

There was something that Betsy had kept from Liz. At first
the matter had not entered her mind. When it did, she did not
know how to introduce it with the light touch she admired so
in Liz. And the matter was too delicate for heavy handling.

The truth was that when Betsy and Steve bought their property, and were told the story of the abutting lot, Steve had
asked the agent to give him priority if the owner ever decided
to sell.

At last the aging owner did. One day in the spring Steve
received a letter from the agent, advising him that the lot was
for sale, and naming a reasonable figure. Steve promptly sent a
check.

He wrote another letter to Mr. Trueworthy, asking him to
arrange for a carpenter to fence in the whole property. With the
new lot the house would be nicely centered, and a white picket
fence would set it off handsomely.

The day after school closed, Betsy packed her children off to
camp and left for the country the same afternoon. She was in a
fever to arrive before Liz, to explain the whys and wherefores of
the fence when Liz saw it for the first time.

Liz came. Betsy, hearing her car, rushed out to welcome her.

She took the shortcut across the lot, and then was stopped by the fence, embarrassment flooding her that she had forgotten to use the gate, and could only extend her hand in greeting.

'Oh, it's good to see you,' she said, but her voice sounded strained to her, and her hand felt hot in Liz's cold clasp.

'It's good to be back,' Liz said, avoiding any personal reference.

'We bought the lot,' Betsy said in a rush. 'We asked for preference before we knew you. And I didn't want to sound possessive by telling you. As for the fence, please forget it's there. Steve just thought a fence would be attractive.'

'It is,' said Liz, saying no more.

'I'll put the kettle on for tea, a large tea,' Betsy said too eagerly.

'I'll take a raincheck,' Liz said lightly. 'I couldn't eat a thing.'

'Then you'll be my guest for breakfast tomorrow?'

'I only want coffee. It isn't worth your bothering.'

Betsy took a step back. 'You've things to do. I mustn't keep you.'

'If you'll excuse me then,' Liz said, smiling a lovely, meaningless smile.

The fence had come between them and their understanding. They could only reach each other the long way round, and neither was sure the trip was worth making. There was only a tree at the end of it, and a tree is at best and at most a tree. Time is too precious to waste on it or under it.

They turned and walked out of each other's lives.

AN UNIMPORTANT MAN

He awoke to the dig of his wife's sharp elbow in the tender flesh of his side. He blinked for a moment bewilderedly and eased away from her. He glanced at the clock. It hadn't quite struck nine. He wondered, idly, if he had a clean collar to wear to church, and began to question wistfully whether he dared miss the church service just this once, and, the family having creakingly departed, patter about in his disreputable old bathrobe and slippers in the beautiful peace of aloneness.

He smiled. He was very hot and uncomfortable, but he was happy. He wanted, a little foolishly, to burst out laughing. He ached to express his joy. And for a moment he chortled softly with his head drawn under the sheet. But his wife stirred and groaned in her sleep, and he uncovered his head and lay quite still. He began to pray that she would not awaken to shatter the quiet with her shrill complaints. He sighed. He hated his wife. He rolled over gently and looked at her.

She lay on her back with her knees drawn up and her thick braids covering her narrow breasts. One thin arm hung over the edge of the bed, the other lay across her flat stomach. It struck him suddenly, looking down at her, that the bulge of her eyeballs seemed more prominent when her straight-lashed eyelids covered them. For the first time he noted how homely she looked asleep. Her face was unbelievably narrow. There were heavy bags beneath her eyes. The small, straight nose that had once intrigued him seemed pinched and too transparent. And with the increasing years of incompatibility the slender, sensitive curve of her lips had blended to a straight, stern line of bitterness.

She stirred again, and the long ropes of hair fell along her side. Her narrow bosom rose almost imperceptibly. He remembered with shamed surprise how he had told her, in the first, happy week of their marriage, that he would kiss her dry, young breasts to fullness. He remembered, too, the color that had rushed to her cheeks, and the instinctive lifting of her hands as if to ward off his lips.

With his own cheeks hot at the memory, he rolled to the edge of the bed. And then, as he lay there, his unseeing eyes blinking at the ceiling, a great swell of passion racked him. He shut his eyes. His flesh tingled. Sweat streamed from his pores, and his body itched with urging. Something was draining him of resistance. He almost heard a light, mocking laugh. Dark flesh sank warmly into his. Hot, thick, sensual lips burned his empty mouth. The phantom woman who lay in the grip of his arms was more terribly real than the passionless woman who lay every night by his side.

But after a moment of that sharp, beautiful agony he opened his eyes. The woman drifted out of his arms, and he drew a deep breath that was like a sigh. He wanted to get up and take a bath, but he hadn't the strength to rise.

He could hear his old mother coming down the narrow hall with her grandchild. They would be quarreling, of course, and the old woman would be shrill with ineffectual threats. He was sorry for his mother. These last years of her life were as full of toil and travail as the first. He was her only son, and it came to him, rather bitterly, that he had not been a good one. Bit by bit he had broken her valiant spirit, she who had given so much had received so pitifully little. There was ironic sadness, after the years of her teaching of independence, in her complete and unrewarded subservience.

He heard her voice rise. 'Mind now, Essie –'

And his first thought was 'I wish t' God she'd stop picking on that child. But the instant it formed in his mind, he felt a great surge of pity for his mother. And his lips framed an unexpected prayer: 'Oh, dear God, let me make it all up to her.'

He had a sudden vision of himself, in an oratorical pose – a Darrow for his race, eloquently pleading a black man's cause.

He was happy again. Little waves of joy rolled over him. But he had a panicky moment of doubt. After all of these years – bitter years of despairing failure – had he passed his bar exams at last? Rather sheepishly he pinched himself. It was beautifully true.

Well, by God, he had studied – and hard. He had felt somehow that if he failed again, it meant the end. The definite blotting out of the already flickering flame of ambition. He would never have had the courage to try once more.

He read the shingle swaying in the wind: 'Zebediah Jenkins, Attorney-at-Law.' His tongue rolled the morsel over his lips. Attorney Jenkins. It stood for achievement. It meant respect. Metaphorically he steadied himself on the first rung of the ladder.

But in that instant he heard again a light, mocking laugh. Wanda, somewhere in the hot sun, laughing . . . laughing . . . laughing . . . Calling him fool for his ambition when her arms were wide with love.

He hadn't, he decided, wanted to be a lawyer. He hadn't, he found with surprise, wanted to be anything. His only childhood ambition had been eventual marriage with Wanda. He had never seen beyond a two-room cabin.

He would always remember the night he had cried out his

love for Wanda. His mother had been doing last-minute things; and he had trailed after her, in hot protest, meanly refusing to help.

For Wanda, at dusk, with the wisdom of Eve, had bound him eternally to her with her darkly beautiful body. They had not made any promises. To both of them the North had seemed so far away they knew with bitter certainty they would never meet again. For Wanda it would forever suffice that she had been his first love.

In a rush of scarcely articulate words he had told it all to his mother.

He had not known that he was a sentimentalist. The years of her widowhood were to him a glorious record of sacrifice. He was just beginning to realize the purity of mother love. He knew a sudden sense of shame at his lust for Wanda. In a swift moment of refutation he hated her for what he could not then call her honesty. With a rather splendid gesture he offered his mother his future to mold it as she willed.

She was in the bathroom with Esther. He could hear the little girl gargling her throat, and his mother's impatient: 'That's 'nough, now. Jus' look at this floor.' And then a faint scuffle, and his mother again, 'You keep on, now. You jus' spoilin' for a spankin'.'

And Esther's bold, young voice – and he visioned her, arms akimbo – 'Yah, yah, yah! You just try it.'

Against his will he was envious of Esther. He couldn't imagine himself at ten talking back to his mother. 'Oh, my God!' he thought, and would have laughed if tears hadn't stung his lashes. He wanted passionately, this August morning, to lazily drift down a Southern stream with Wanda.

He decided – feeling, however, his betrayal of his mother – that he was proud of Esther's independence. He was glad, rather fiercely glad, that she knew enough to stand up to people. No one would ever – no one must ever – shape the course of

Esther's life. He would rather starve in the streets than drag his child back from the stars with his heavy hands on her skirts.

His mother was tapping on the bathroom door that opened into his bedroom. 'Min, y'all up? It's ha' past nine. I done started the coffee boilin'.'

Minnie blinked awake and started up on her sharp, pointed elbows. Her voice was thick. 'Who? Huh? Oh, that you, Miss Lily? Awright.'

She sat up then and hugged her thin knees, her mouth a wide, red cavern of interrupted sleep.

He told her pleasantly, 'It's a nice morning, Min.'

She regarded it imperturbably. 'Yeh,' she said.

He flung back the sheet and swung his legs over the side of the bed. He was boyishly eager. 'I could eat a house.'

'Seems to me,' she said with conscious meanness, 'you'd be sick and tiahed of the sight of food, cookin' in a white man's kitchen ev'ry day.'

All of the sparkle went out of his eyes. 'It hasn't been easy, Min.'

She felt a certain compunction. 'Well, it shouldn't be hard no longer. Things ought to brighten up in no time now, since you passed that bar exam.'

He was pathetically grateful. His words poured out eagerly. His nostrils dilated. His mustache quivered a little. He sat there, on the edge of the bed, in a humorous nightshirt that showed his thin legs.

'I guess you're right about that, Min. Guess this old ship's steered clear at last. Guess we'll know a little plain sailing now. I knew my God would answer my prayers.'

She snorted a little. 'If you'd done more on your own hook 'stead o' waitin' 'round for God to help you, you'd 'a' got on faster. That's the main trouble with all o' you niggers.'

He could not quite veil his annoyance, but his tone was very patient. 'I don't like to hear you talk like that, Min. I don't like it. *That's* the main trouble with us colored people – trying to act like white folks, mocking God. Let me tell you, Min, these white folks don't know nothin' 'bout slavery, and prejudice, and causeless hate. They've never had to go down on their knees and cry out to their God for deliverance. It's all right for them to talk like fools. But for us poor colored folks, it ain't!'

She was pale with vexation, but she had no adequate words to express her grievance. She said with childish irrelevancy, 'Why don't you go on an' take your bath? You ain't got your sign painted yet.'

He got to his feet and made an unexpected reply. 'But I'll have it done pretty soon.'

'You better see about gettin' an office,' she conceded. 'I see a nice place to let down on Tremont Street and I think there's three or four good-size rooms in back.'

'I'll see about it,' he answered, 'first thing tomorrow. But I'm not going to stay down on Tremont Street long. I've never wanted nothing but the best.'

He entered the bathroom then, his cheeks burning with resolute purpose. Above the running of the water he heard her swift retort, 'You'd oughta be content with anything, this late age.'

He tried to smile at his suddenly strained reflection in the glass above the bowl. 'I'm barely forty,' he told it definitely. 'All o' Ma's people live to be ninety.'

But there was no lessening of the pain in those mild brown eyes. He turned away dispiritedly and slumped into the tub. And it wasn't ludicrous, somehow, screwing about in the too-hot water.

He was hating Minnie and wishing passionately that he had never married her. The long, dark hair of his golden bride was the silken coil that had trapped him.

'If I had to do it again,' he thought with rueful humor, 'I wouldn't do it.'

*

All of the uneventful years prior to his marriage had been almost wholly devoted to an unhappy pursuit of what his mother sternly defined as independence. Even back in the South there had been daily lessons toward this end with the invalid Marse Jim, who was always faintly amused at the grim determination of his pupil.

He looked, as he squatted on the porch, his brown toes wriggling, as if the last thing in all the world he would have chosen for himself was a career. He should have been, thought Marse, swinging down a sunlit road, with a fishing rod over his shoulder and the image of a little black girl bright on his vacuous mind.

However, with praiseworthy courage he had shut one ear against the sensuous blandishments of spring in the South and let old Marse's droning voice pour into the other just sufficient knowledge to enter him in high school.

It was then his mother had gotten out the old cotton stocking that was heavy in her hand. 'The No'th,' she had said with something like awe, and her eyes had been like stars.

He was a shy, sullen boy of seventeen when he entered high school. The North had fallen so far short of his dream of it. Boston bewildered him. It was a bustling, unfriendly place where the young Irish hurled 'Nigger!' at you on every other corner. He dreaded the classroom, feeling his bigness and his blackness and vaguely resenting them. He thought, after the first few days, he would rather die than rise to his awkward feet and recite, in his hesitant Southern drawl, in that crowded, hostile room.

Thus he learned to bar it out of his consciousness by continuous and absorbing daydreams.

He spent seven years in that high school.

Zeb helped his mother after school in the house where she worked by the day. There was scarcely a moment, after he flung down his books, when there wasn't something to do. The house thronged with children and careless older people, and Miss Lily and Zeb did the thorough work of a competent staff for the salary of an underpaid cook.

It was funny, watching them both going about that delightful house, knowing their thoughts: 'This place ain't nothing to what we'll have some day.' They had, poor, tragic things, to live in the future.

Zeb graduated when he was twenty-three. Miss Lily went. Neither the building, nor the teachers, nor the parents awed her. She thrilled to everything. She thought her heart would burst with happiness. It was the one great moment of her life. She, too, like other Negro mothers, God knows why, had lived in the hope of this exalted hour. To her, as to so many others, that stereotyped stretch of paper was, for her son, the passport to a higher life.

She had not learned the pitiable wrongs of living for one's child.

Afterward there was the long-debated question of college. It was that which shook Zeb out of his apathy. He had looked down at his little gray mother and been suddenly honest and somewhat shamed. He had been overwhelmed with a strange sense of failure. He wasn't, he saw with brutal clarity, dependable. His future was too uncertain to risk the slim savings of his mother. For a moment he had a horrid foreboding that he would forever disappoint her. He decided then, dejectedly, to go out and get a job.

But they had compromised. Zeb, too, oddly eager, the fervor of Miss Lily inspiring him. He would work until he had saved enough to pay his own way to college.

He got the none-too-strenuous job of redcap in South Station.

It was there, two years later, on a Thursday afternoon, he met Minnie Means, a slim, shy girl like a lost white bird in the vastness of the station. Impersonally he had taken her proffered bag and led her to a cab, alone deploring the smallness of the expected tip.

At the door she halfway turned, apologetically slipping a thin dime into his hand. Her face all lovely confusion, she asked in a slow, soft whine, 'Look heah, Mister Redcap, could you please be so kin' as to tell me whar Ah could get a room 'round heah with a nice, quiet cullud famly?'

He gave the driver his own address with his heart pounding like a hammer.

In the days that swiftly followed, for the first time in his life, his mother's counsel could not guide him. Past and future were forgotten in the immediate beauty of Minnie. He would have rejected his hope of salvation for a single moment of complete possession. He was, however, honorable enough about his wooing. Two weeks later they slipped away and were quietly married.

In the blissful month that passed all too quickly, they had a perfectly riotous time on his two years' accumulated savings.

Thus it was four years later he had the small-salaried job of second cook in a self-service lunchroom, a little larger flat that his mother helped pay for, and an exemption from overseas service because of a dependent wife and child.

At first he had been glad he had escaped the draft. It was a white man's war. The President had said so. Well, let him fight it unaided by his darker brother. And why, Zeb reasoned, not without logic, should the black man avenge others' wrongs when he himself struggled in a maze of them?

And then one day he was caught in a cheering crowd that was watching a Negro regiment march by. In the first few moments he was stifled by the embarrassment he always felt at the sight of a concourse of colored people. And he felt a swift indignation that they should be grouped in a separate regiment. Even the war could not reveal them brothers under the skin. They were going, poor fools, ironically enough, to fight for justice.

But suddenly all of his bitterness was swept away in the beauty of a tall black boy, straight and fine and gloriously eager, marching sternly on because he was free and proud, and he wanted, a little bewilderedly, to do the right thing.

And in that instant Zeb wanted frantically to break into that line. He didn't want to go home to Minnie, and a fretful baby, and a mother whose reproachful eyes spoke her unsatisfied hopes. He wanted, with all of his heart, to redeem himself on the battlefield. To return to a proudly sad family with a Croix de Guerre and a wooden leg.

There was something, he found, watching that boy's splendid back, bigger than one's prejudice, bigger than one's President, to be fought for. And that, he saw, with his eyes squeezed hard against tears, was the country God saw fit to have one born in.

The next day he sneaked into a recruiting station on the Common and was kindly but firmly rejected because of his flat feet.

In 1919 he was thirty-two. And he didn't want to be. He was afraid of the advancing years. He had done nothing. He had gotten nowhere. All that remained were unfulfilled dreams.

It was then young Parker drifted into his life. Parker, the kitchen slavey, with his youth, and his courage, and the will to do. He hadn't a tenth the advantages Zeb had had. He was the illegitimate son of an intense dark woman and a worthless black man. But he had vowed, all of his unhappy, struggling years, to outreach their littleness.

In slack hours Zeb taught him the few things he had remembered, and later lent him the few books he had kept. Young Parker's eager brain absorbed like a sponge. In a year and a half he was ready for night high school. In two years he had finished with honors.

That was only the first lap, he told Zeb. And immediately he decided to go again to night school to study law. There were no visions in his eyes. They were bright with reality. He knew, this young Parker, what he wanted. God alone could have stood in the way of it.

Miss Lily talked with him eagerly. Her eyes were wet. Her voice was not quite steady. And instantly Zeb knew.

'Look here,' he had said, growing frightfully warm, 'say, guess I'll go along with you.'

Parker passed his exams at the end of the four-year term. He had known, of course, that he would. With little surprise from either, it had been Parker, during those four years, who was teacher and adviser. However, despite his tutelage, Zeb failed to pass. For the first time in her life, Miss Lily openly cried. For the first time, too, Zeb was sorrier for himself than for his mother.

With her tremulous pleas ringing in his ears, he obediently repeated the year, and again took his bar exams, feeling only a vague curiosity concerning the outcome. He dared not doubt his passing, but he somehow could not honestly believe he would. Perhaps it was a merciful indifference steeling him. For the second time he failed.

And then there was Miss Lily, bravely undismayed. 'Times was hard las' year, son. It was a struggle to make both ends meet. It would sorta have surprised me if you had gone and passed them exams, worryin' an' all like you was. Jus' you try again, son. God will hear my prayers.'

Zeb was thirty-nine the third year he repeated. He entered the class with dogged determination. He could not fail again. He knew that he would not. It wasn't egoism. It was only that he could not see beyond his failing. The hour must strike for him now. He read his Bible daily and prayed with childlike earnestness.

He had felt only an intense relief the morning the post brought the succinct letter informing him he had passed.

The family was at table when he entered the dining room. Miss Lily was pouring his coffee. 'Jus' set right down, son.'

He said expansively 'You look right bright, Ma . . . How's Essie?'

She screwed up her little eager face. 'Good mornin', Papa.'

He sat down at the head of the table and helped himself liberally to pork chops and hominy.

'You all certainly got a nice breakfast this morning, Min.'

But she wasn't pleased by his compliment. 'It must be cold now,' she told him. 'I never in my life saw a man so slow. I bin waitin' 'bout an hour to get in that bathroom. Looks like we never will be on time for church.'

She rose, dragging her kimono about her. 'Don't you spill nothin' on that dress now, Essie. Miss Lily, you oughtn't to of let her put it on until jus' time for church. She's a don't-care young one like her father. And, Zeb, no need o' you eatin' slow so's you won't be ready when we start. We're all goin' out o' this house together this mornin'.'

She left them visibly breathing sighs of relief.

'I declare,' said Miss Lily, finishing her biscuit, 'Minnie don't speak one pleasant word from one week to another.'

'You kinda fussy, too, Gramma,' Essie observed.

'Your pa,' said Miss Lily, hurt, 'never said a thing like that to me in all his life.'

She went on with her game of spooning the grounds in her milk-diluted coffee. 'Papa was scared of you, wasn't you, Papa? I ain't.'

He corrected her gently. 'Don't say *ain't*, dear. Papa wants you to grow up a lady. You never hear a lady using English like that.'

The eyes in her beautiful, little dark face glowed somberly at him. She had all of the youthful loveliness of her mother in brown. She was thin and nervous and passionately eager.

'But I don't want to be a lady, Papa – that kind. I don't want to go to college and learn things. It hurts my head, Papa, it does. That's why I'm glad,' she said with the honesty of children, 'you're going to be a lawyer, and buy a big house, and be rich an' ev'rything. Then I won't have to be smart and make money for you and Mama and Gramma. And I can just be whatever I want. And I guess I'll be a dancer.'

The word was anathema to Miss Lily. 'Not while they's strength in my body to keep you off the stage. You'll have your own dear mammy to bury if you keep that wil' idea in your head. Both o' our fam'lies is church-going people. None o' 'em's ever done nothin' bad.'

'Actresses ain't got the name they used to have, Ma,' Zeb interposed. 'There's good and bad women in all walks of life. And I don't b'lieve in stifling a child's natural impulse. Sow the seed and let it sprout unaided.'

'Choked by rank weeds,' said Miss Lily grimly. 'They never was a garden yit that didn't need a gardener.'

'But you can't force a flower that hangs its head to stare up at the sun, or a plant that lifts its face to the rain to bend toward the earth without,' he said coldly, 'breaking its stem.'

'Then I'd far rather see this chile dead,' she said quietly, 'than a half-naked dancer on the stage.'

'I think, Ma,' Zeb answered seriously, 'the one thing that matters is Essie's happiness.'

Miss Lily got to her feet. She stood above her son, this little, stooping old lady whose hands and lips were trembling. Nervously she smoothed her neat black gown and patted her soft, crinkly hair, while a torrent of eager words beat against her mouth.

'An' could Essie be happy livin' in sin? Could I say without shame my son's only chile is a dancer? Zeb, listen, son, I don't know how it'll be later on, but to us po' cullud people right now our chillen is all we got. They is our hope, an' our pride, an' our joy. They is our life. We live for them, and oh, son, we gladly die for them. An' all us po', strugglin' niggers want is to send our chillen to school, so's we can tell them white folks we slave for my chile's jus' as good as yours.'

She wet her dry lips and blinked her eyes free of tears. Her voice was sharp.

'Essie's a chile. She don't know what she wants. She jus' heard somebody talkin' 'bout dancin'. But we know, Zeb, we older ones.' Her voice dropped to soft pleading. 'Don' she bring in nothin' but ones and twos on her card? She's smart, Zeb. That gal's got a head on her shoulders. She's like me. I want her to do all I might 'a' done if I'd had her eddication. And, Zeb, if you died, or somep'n went wrong, I'd work these old fingers to the bone to sen' that gal to college.

'She's got some'n in her. I see that. This chile's got the power to be anything. She don't want to sit down and trade on her looks. They's too many good-looking girls in the gutter. Let your brain work for you, chile, not your face. You got to remember that always.'

Essie's eyes were on Miss Lily, wide, and serious, and intent. She was interested but unmoved. Grandmother was an old woman. Old people were fools.

Miss Lily went on. 'Do you think I ain't a proud woman today? My son's a lawyer. Miz Bemis' son's a lawyer, too. It means you're his equal. An' I'd tell her so in a minute. But when you was only a cook, you wasn't. You was a white man's servant. And young Fred Bemis was his own boss. Oh, son, nobody knows the anguish I bin through. Nobody knows how I've prayed to my Maker. If it'd taken a thousand years, I would 'a' waited and hoped. They ain't nothin' I've done for you I regret. They ain't a gray hair on my head, they ain't a line on my old face, they ain't a misery in my old bones that I ain't glad it's there, if it's meant the independence of my chile!'

She fled the room then, with her hand pressed hard against her lips, but both of them heard her sob.

It was Essie who broke the silence. 'I hate women, Papa,' she said dispassionately. 'They're sissies.'

And before he could frame a shocked reply, she had asked

him, off on another tangent, 'What is a sin, Papa? Isn't it lying and stealing and not helping blind people? Then how is dancing a sin?'

She was bewildering him, but he was suddenly very proud to be a parent. He saw himself at the outset of a 'talk' with his daughter, and he was immensely flattered. There had never before been this intimacy between them.

He had meant to answer, 'Because good women never go on the stage. And good women never sin.' But on the verge of it, he looked at her, and her eyes were too clear and honest and eager for him to put her off with a platitude. He must grope, rather blunderingly, toward her honesty.

'Dancing isn't a sin,' he told her, 'unless you make it one. There is no good, there is no evil in the world really. The good and the evil lie within you.'

He didn't quite believe that, and he half thought he had read it somewhere, but Essie seemed to understand.

She said quietly, 'Like Reverend Dill, huh, Papa, winning all that money on the numbers?'

He was just a little annoyed. 'You mustn't repeat things, Essie.'

But she ignored that. Her voice was confidential. 'Gramma doesn't know, does she, Papa? Dancin' can be beautiful. Maybe she thinks I mean just jazz, but dancin' can be other things, beautiful things, Papa. Like on your toes, and like birds and things. You – you know, Papa.'

He was beginning to. And he saw, suddenly, that his little daughter was growing up and learning to express the thoughts that had heretofore found chaotic release through symbols on scrap paper.

'When I was younger,' he said, 'I used to go a lot to theayters, and I've seen some real pretty dancing.'

'Like fairies in a wood, huh, Papa? Like – like thistle-blowing.'

He tasted his coffee and found it cold and set it down. He pushed back his plate and folded his napkin.

'Is your heart really set on dancing, dear? Tell you the truth, Papa sorta wishes there was something else you wanted more to do. But if there isn't, nothing could induce me to stand in your way.'

She smiled at him and stretched her slim fingers across the table to pat his hand.

'You're orful nice, Papa, this morning. Honest you are.'

He beamed his gratitude. He wanted to kiss that lovely hand, but he hadn't the courage. To him had now come the inevitable realization that his daughter was better than he was. He felt a certain awe of this exquisite child.

She said, 'You know why I really want to be a dancer, Papa?'

'It's the one thing you can do best,' he concluded, trying to help her reason.

'No' – her eyes were soft – 'Nonnie can beat me dancin'. It isn't that, Papa. It's something else.'

She was silent for a moment, and he sensed her struggle for expression. Her face was sharp with the pain of it. Her nails were dug in her palms.

'I don't know how to say it, Papa. I know it inside of me, but it won't come out. I told Gramma dancin' cause I didn't know how else to put it. I'd just as lief sing. I'd just as lief do anything' – she caught her breath – 'beautiful. That's what I mean, Papa. I – I just want to be something that's beautiful, I don't care what it is.'

With a sharp sigh he averted his eyes from the innocent glory of her face. 'It's hard,' he said gently, 'for colored girls to do things that are beautiful, like acting in plays, or singing in op'ra, or dancing in ballets.'

She got up then and came around to him, putting one foot on the rung of his chair. She rubbed her chin over his closely cropped head, and her long, dark curls fell over his face.

'Nothin's ever going to be hard for me, Papa,' she said with conviction. 'God didn't make me that way.'

They were late for church again. Old Mr. Myrick frowned at them as they entered. But Zeb didn't mind. Miss Lily hurried down the aisle to her accustomed seat in a front pew. Minnie rustled toward the beckoning Lize Jones, with the whispered admonition: 'Now don't you let me hear your voice, Essie.' Zeb and his daughter sank down gratefully in the back row.

He bent to her ear. 'If it makes you nervous, you just tell Papa, and we'll sneak out.'

She snuggled her hand through his arm. 'Nobody's screaming yet.'

He leaned back complacently, balancing his straw hat carefully on his knee. He would have liked to come early enough to join in the singing. However, he was glad he had missed the announcements. There might have been some stupid social to which Minnie would have dragged him. And, too, he had forgotten to stop at the corner store for peppermints to change a bill for collection.

Reverend Dill was exhorting. Zeb remembered what Essie had told him, and he was puzzled by the obvious sincerity of the man. His deep, rich voice was clear and strong. He chanted his words, striding the length of the platform, pounding the little table until the single rose trembled in the vase, one fist stuck in his pocket.

'You that are sinners had better repent. For no man knows the hour when the Son of Man cometh. And there shall be weeping and wailing and gnashing of teeth. O brothers, O sisters, get on board. Drop your burdens at the foot of Jesus. Drink at the fountain of His love.'

A woman's shrill wail shattered the echo of his thundering. 'Oh, praise God, my Redeemer! I bin washed in the blood of the Lamb!'

There was an answering rumble from Brother Wheelwright. 'Glory be to ma God!'

Zeb felt Essie's hot grip on his arm. He looked down at her and smiled reassuringly. 'It's all right, dear.'

Her sensitive little face was anxious. She snuggled closer to him and furtively peered up into the face of the old lady sitting next to her. She hoped she wasn't the sort that carried on. But her lips were moving. Essie's little heart began to beat rapidly. She wished they could have sat beside an indifferent young man.

Zeb was sorry for Essie. He knew that now she had forgotten the minister and his sermon, and that her whole being was trained toward the slightest sound. She was almost impatiently waiting for someone to sob or scream. He couldn't understand her terror. He had been brought up in the Baptist church, and he honestly thought there was no other faith that could take one to heaven as quickly. Neither his mother nor himself had ever felt the urge to give public vent to their feelings. But he didn't see any wrong in it. He was often deeply moved. There were moments, too, when he wished the Spirit might descend upon him that he might shout his praise for God in this sympathetic congregation.

Reverend Dill's voice was a wail now. 'Listen! Do you hear Jesus knocking at your heart? Open to Him, sinner. Don't let Him stand out there in the dark, fumbling for the latch. Lay your burdens on His breast. Come to Jesus! Oh, great Lord! See Him standing in the seat of Pilate. Come to Jesus! The King of Kings being stripped and scourged. Come to Jesus! The Lord of Heaven with a crown of thorns. Come to Jesus. See Him dragging up a weary road, bearing the heavy cross. Sinner, sinner, He died for you! Come to Jesus!

'They drove a nail in my Lord's hand. Come to Jesus! They drove a nail in my Lord's foot. Come to Jesus! Oh, see my Lord with blood streaming down His side, and His head bowed down with the sins of the world. Oh, hear His lonely cry, "My God, my God, why hast Thou forsaken me?" Brothers, sisters, He gave up the ghost and died. Come, come – get ye behind them, Satan! – come to Jesus!'

They were in a religious frenzy, this shouting, stamping congregation. There was a rush of weeping converts. Brother Wheelwright paced the aisle, clapping his hands, crying his praise, the tears streaming down his cheeks. The older women had risen to their feet, and they bent and swayed to a fervent chant. The universal gesture was a flinging up of arms, and then a sudden slump down in the pew, spent. The youngsters nudged each other, pointing out the noisier Christians, giggled. For a long five minutes there was noise and dreadful disorder in this house of God.

The old lady beside Essie had gotten to her feet, and her continuously outflung arms were perilously near the tip of Essie's nose. She twisted and turned, a little mad with her love for God in this moment. Her words were wild. 'Oh, my Redeemer, I bin saved! Shout for joy! Praised be His name . . .' The odor of sweat was sharp.

And suddenly Zeb, in a quiet exaltation, was swept from the heights by Essie's voice, shrill and choked in his ear. Only then was he conscious of her vise-like hold on his arm and the nearness of her shaking little body.

'Papa, Papa, I wanna go home. I'm gonna be sick,' she sobbed.

He gathered her up in his arms and flung out of the nave and raced with her down the aisle.

Later, weak and ill and tearful, she told him, her dark eyes black with bitterness, 'I hate good people, Papa. I hate ev'rybody who goes to church. I hate ev'rybody who makes me nervous.'

He somehow could not find the words to rebuke her.

Young Parker dropped in after dinner. He was on his way to

pay a social call in the neighborhood. And since it was the incorrect hour of seven, he had decided to look in on Zeb and congratulate him. Heretofore he had been so busy.

He looked very expensive and prosperous, and he prattled a good deal about a new Harmon he was thinking of buying, and he held the reluctant Essie on his knee and gave her a silver dollar.

They sat in the overcrowded parlor, that was cluttered with Sunday disorder. And Miss Lily and Minnie beamed at young Parker, and smoothed their stiff frocks, and murmured apologies. And Zeb kowtowed no less.

It was only Essie, slipping from his knee and going to stand sullenly by the window, who felt no pride in him. She was thinking that there were little beads of grease on his forehead, and his nostrils distended too much when he talked.

'I knew,' he was saying, 'you'd make it, old-timer. The sun do move, you know. And heaven knows, if there's one man who deserves success, that man is you. You've been the most faithful kind of a son and husband all your life.'

Miss Lily's eyes filled with grateful tears. 'There is a God, and He answered my prayers. I guess,' she went on with quaint pride, 'these old hands will have done their las' lick o' work after Zeb gets really settled.'

'I sorta think,' said Zeb, 'I'll take tomorrow mornin' off and go see 'bout that office you spoke of, Min. I'll be getting my certificate any day now. And I've already talked with two or three men who got cases they want me to handle.'

'Fine!' Parker was honestly glad. 'I say, that's good! And I got quite a few minor cases I'll be glad to switch to you. Anything for old times' sake.' He patted Zeb's knee.

Minnie smiled. 'You're a good man, Mr. Parker. You're goin' to make some nice girl happy some day.'

'I got her picked out,' said Parker, expanding. 'A real Sheba.'

'A Boston young lady?' Miss Lily asked.

Parker made a disparaging gesture. 'Go out of the North when you want to get married. She's a little Washington schoolma'am.'

'I've heard,' said Miss Lily, her lips very tight, ' 'bout them Washington schoolteachers.'

'Good Lord!' said Parker. 'She's a society girl. Five years ago she wouldn't have looked at me. Why, I'm getting into the cream of Washington society.'

'I wouldn't marry an old teacher,' cried Essie hotly. 'I wouldn't care who she was.'

'All nice colored girls are teachers,' Parker said coldly. 'They either do that or sit down on their parents. There's nothing else for a real nice girl to do.'

'Then I won't be a nice girl,' Essie screamed, 'and I won't be a crazy old teacher. I'm gonna be naughty all the rest of my life, so I can be a dancer.'

Minnie rose excitedly. 'I'll break ev'ry bone in your body. Idea you talkin' back to folks. An' talkin' like a fool 'bout dancin'. March right on out o' here an' don't come back. An' I'll take the switch to you later.'

Essie crossed to the door and opened it. She stood quite still for a moment, savagely surveying them.

'I wish,' she said slowly, 'children needn't be born. I wish a mother hen could hatch them. And then they wouldn't have parents and other people to boss them. And they wouldn't be scolded, and spanked, and put to bed without any supper. When I have my little baby, I'm gonna give her to the cat.'

She slammed the door then, and they heard her run swiftly down the hall.

'Jus' give me time,' Minnie called angrily, 'to come after you.'

Miss Lily rose, too. 'Seems a shame that chile's got to break up the Sabbath. Ain't a day goes by she don't need a spankin'. But Minnie's got the right idea. She's breakin' that gal's spirit young. And she'll only grow up to thank her.'

'It's too hot,' said Parker suddenly, 'to spank a child.'

'I can only hope,' answered Miss Lily, going, 'Minnie don' have one o' her spells.'

'I hope to God,' Zeb flung at the closed door, 'she does.'

There was a long pause. Parker was horribly embarrassed, and Zeb terribly ashamed. He had never wished ill to anyone before. Suddenly he decided, staring hard at a spot on the rug, that he loved his little daughter above everything in the world. He rather wished he had been a better parent.

'It's a quarter to,' said Parker, rising and pulling out a heavy watch. 'I got to be going, Zeb.'

'Sorry,' said Zeb, and got rather heavily to his feet. 'Have a nice time.'

'Oh, I guess I will.' Parker's tone was easy. 'The Flakes are dicties, you know. Real quiet and refined. All of 'em have been to college, even that old grandmother.'

'You're pretty swell,' Zeb told him, his mind still on Essie.

'No.' He was striving for honesty. Zeb was the only middle-class intimate he had. In this moment he wanted definitely to express his thoughts aloud to someone who didn't really matter. And he was fond of Zeb.

'I'm not a swell, really. I'm not sure I want to be. But I do mean to make a good marriage – for my children's sake. There are too few colored people who realize the importance of good blood. And it tells, Zeb. You can pick out a dicty anywhere, no matter if he's black with woolly hair.'

'I know,' said Zeb, but he wasn't interested. He had a vision of Essie, dry-eyed and unbending.

'And I'll make a big name for myself some day,' Parker went on. 'I mean to. I sorta feel that I've got to. Race pride, I guess. I wouldn't change my color to be President. And I want to go up and up and up. I want to go just as high as a white man – and then just a little higher.

'Look here,' he said, and shook Zeb by the shoulders, 'that's your chief trouble. You dream too much. Man alive! Wake up and get going, old-timer. Way down deep in me I sorta like music, but nobody's ever going to know it.'

But Zeb didn't answer. He had heard a faint thump as of some one heavily falling, and had suddenly aged ten years.

'Oh, my God,' he whispered, 'that's Min again. 'Nother spell, I guess. See you later, Parker.'

He opened the door and quietly waited until his guest had passed.

Minnie lay white and rigid under the sheet, with that weight on her heart, and her eyes that were wide with terror and pain on Zeb. They clung to him because she knew so long as they held to him, they looked on life. And Minnie was afraid to die. She was afraid of God. All of her life she had visioned Him as an immense Person who could rattle your sins off like a flash. And although she knew herself to be a really good woman, she was also well aware that a white sin counted just as much as a black one. She tried to recall an encouraging sermon Reverend Dill had preached a few Sundays past. But all she could hear was her own voice whispering dire threats to Essie for being so fidgety.

Suddenly she felt that she must talk. If death were imminent, there were so many things that must be said. For Zeb was a fool about everything.

She gave a sharp sigh and felt her body relax. She stirred and carefully shifted her position until she lay on her right side, staring up at her husband.

'Zeb.'

He sat very stiffly on an old dining-room chair at the head of the bed. He looked down at her without emotion. For the last fifteen minutes, with utter calmness, he had been carefully trying to decide whether or not he wished his wife had died during her spell.

'How are you feeling now, Min?'

'A little better,' she said, brushing a tangle of hair from her eyes.

'You got to be more careful, Min. You oughtn't to let things make you mad. Essie's a big girl now. She's too old to keep getting spankings.'

'That's why I'm afraid to die,' she fretted. 'God knows how you'd raise my chile. Essie's a headstrong young one what needs guidance.'

He made a helpless gesture. 'Wouldn't love do as well? You two'd get on better if you were more gently with Essie. It's only natural that she should have her own opinion 'bout things. I've talked a long time with that child.'

She flung him a vicious taunt. 'I ain't like you. I don't think people's perfect because they's pretty. Upholding that chile in her dancin'. Miss Lily told me. I'll beat it out of her if it kills me.'

His eyes were gleaming. 'It very nearly did.'

'An' I guess,' she said, 'you would 'a' bin glad. You and Essie. You're 'like as two peas, you two. Don' care nothin' 'bout eddication. Seems like ev'ry mornin' I jus' has to drive that young one to school.

'You're doin' the wrong thing, Zeb Jenkins, when you encourage that chile. Neither you all's got common sense 'nough to fill a keyhole. What could she ever make out o' her dancin'? Some rotten man would ruin her before she got out of the chorus.

'Zeb,' her voice was sharp with pain, 'you think I don' love my baby? Why, she's mine! How can you judge a mother's heart? I'd cut off my hand in a moment if I thought it would do her any good.'

She was sobbing weakly. Tears welled out of her eyes and ran obliquely into the damp tendrils of her hair. She seemed pitifully helpless.

'You bin to high school, Zeb. You got a lot of book learnin'.

I went as far as the third grade and then had to stop to take care of my mother's baby. Nobody but them what knows can realize what it means to be so ignorant. You bring them books and magazines here, and all I can understand is the pictures. When we go to plays, I don't know nothin' people is saying. I jus' like to sit and sleep in the movies. And when I hear those big bands playin' real high-tone music, it don' sound like nothin' to me but a whole lot of noise.'

She was whiter than the sheet in this moment of terrible honesty. Zeb was more moved than he had ever been before. For the second time that day he felt absolutely unworthy before these two who were so utterly unlike – his wife and his child.

Her voice was thin and high. 'I'd rather my chile died right now than grow up an ignorant woman like me. Listen, Zeb, dancin' ain't bad. Nothin' is bad. Sin is what you make it. If you was makin' a big lot o' money, I wouldn't min' Essie takin' up dancin'. I'd know no matter what came of it, her future would be secure.

'But, Zeb, we got to be honest. You ain't a young man. And, Zeb, you ain't a smart man. The only thing really 'bout your bein' a lawyer is it takes you out o' a white man's kitchen. I don't expect you to mak' hardly more than it takes to eddicate Essie.

'Zeb,' she raised herself on her elbow, her eyes burned into his, 'you got to promise that whether I live or die, you'll sen' my chile to college.'

But in that instant, very clearly, he heard Essie's voice, shrill and sharp in his ear: 'I don't want to go to college and learn things. It hurts my head, Papa. It does.'

'Min,' he said miserably, 'I can't. Honest to God, I can't.'

She fell back on the bed, and her hand fluttered to her heart. 'You might as well kill me, Zeb, as tell me that.'

He got to his feet and crossed to the window. He stared up at a cheerfully winking star. He wanted to cry.

'Zeb,' Minnie's weak voice beat upon him, 'you didn't mean that, Zeb. Oh no, Zeb.'

'Essie's got a right to decide her own future,' he cried jealously. 'I'd bin a better man today if my mother had let me live my own life.'

'You might 'a' bin slavin' in a cotton field. You might 'a' bin swingin' from a tree. And then, God knows, you would 'a' blamed your mother.'

He did not answer. He had no words to combat her truth. He stood quite still in this silent room, torn between his evident duty to his wife and his given promise to his child.

And standing there, sick in spirit, he remembered the years of his childhood, and his boyish, unshakable faith in God. So it was then, haltingly, he repeated an almost forgotten prayer.

'Oh, dear God, if it's right for Essie to go to college, by tomorrow please give me a sign. I humbly ask it in Jesus' name. Amen.'

He turned and came back to Minnie, and knelt by the bed.

'I sorta want to think it over, Min. I trust God to help me decide what's right. Sometime tomorrow I'll tell you sure. You go on to sleep now. You already sorta brought me 'round to your way o' thinking.'

She smiled, a tired, valiant smile that, oddly, lit her whole face, that transfigured her, for a glowing moment, with the hope of unselfish triumph.

'I trust God, too. I can rest easy, Zeb. I ain't worryin'.'

For the first time in a great many years he kissed her on her mouth.

A few minutes later he fell asleep with a half-smile on his lips.

He started awake at the postman's familiar ring. He had slept a good deal longer than he had meant to. But it was nice of Minnie not to have waked him. He guessed that she had long been up, pressing his one good business suit, baking hot biscuits for his breakfast.

He stretched luxuriously. He had slept soundly throughout the night, waking only once to listen contentedly to Minnie's regular breathing. But his dream had been a queer jumble. And on recalling it, he felt a vague alarm, a confused dread of the inexplicable.

He had fallen asleep presently to dream that Minnie had died, and his mother had laid her out, in her old kitchen dress, on the new plush sofa in the parlor. And he had taken Essie by the hand, and they had run out and away; but always, no matter how far they ran, they had found themselves back in that dreadful room. And then there was Essie, with her head neatly bandaged, sitting on old Marse's wide verandah, recklessly turning the leaves of a ponderous volume. While it seemed to him, helplessly watching her, the incessant rustling of the pages would drive him mad.

And last, he had stood in a courtroom, with a sheaf of papers in his hand, trying to prove to Parker, stern and unbelieving in the judge's seat, that he was a dicty. And in a swift moment it wasn't Parker sitting there but Wanda, with the little yellow dog they had buried long ago. And Wanda was crying because it was dead, though it lay on her lap joyously licking her hand. And suddenly it seemed to him that there were a million steps between them. And no matter how many he mounted, she forever remained inaccessible.

He heard Essie's sharp rap on the door. 'Papa, you wake? Can I come in? You got a letter this mornin'.'

'Stick it under the door,' he commanded. 'I ain't dressed.'

He got out of bed and shambled across the floor, a bit grotesquely comic in his shuffle toward fate.

As he bent to pick up the letter, he had the thought, 'This may be a kinda sign like I wanted.'

He opened it with fingers that trembled.

The words leaped out at him and burned upon his brain. 'Bar Committee . . . Dear Sir . . . regret to inform you . . . fraud discovered . . . all of the innocent with the guilty one . . . examinations must be retaken . . . unfortunate . . .' ('Oh, my God!')

He was never to remember how long he stood there, staring down at the open letter. He suffered every torture of the damned. Later he would have sworn he did not even breathe. He thought that he had died and gone to hell.

And it might have been a minute later, or an hour, that he found himself by the window, and presently heard his own hor-rified whisper, 'No, no, I can't. Oh, my God, I can't. Colored people don't do such things.'

He went and sat down on the edge of the bed and buried his stricken face in his hands.

He thought calmly, 'I better look like getting to work. You can't fool with these white folks.'

But rage swept down upon him. His throat was choked with hatred of himself.

'You fool!' he cried. 'You G—— d—— cook! You failure!'

He shook with the terrible fury of self-revilement.

Slowly, then, his eyes filled with tears. He was horribly wracked by violent sobs that presently left him washed clean of despair, knowing a certain, sad peace.

Thus he thought, absolutely without reproach, 'That was the sign I wanted.'

He understood now. He had been shocked to self-revealment. He must save Essie from the terrible fate that had all but crushed his spirit. And if she fought bitterly for release, God give him strength to hold her. She was too much like him, too much the idle dreamer. And he had wrongly encouraged her. It had taken this brutal adventure to show him. Well, he would spare Essie this moment. Suppose – oh, dear God! –

suppose that Essie had flung herself out of that window. All the loveliness of Esther in a crumpled, blood-soaked heap.

Essie was fond of him. Essie trusted him. He would straightly guide her toward the goal of independence his mother had vainly desired for him. After all, she had really no definite ambition. Except being something beautiful. Well, there was beauty in everything, and in nothing unless you found it.

He was proud of his child. She was so brilliant. Why, she was already a grade beyond her age, and leading her class. It would be, of course, an unpardonable sin to indulge her childish whim and neglect that glorious brain of hers that could sweep her to the stars.

Essie owed it to herself. Essie owed it to her mother. Above all, Essie owed it to her race. That was it. He saw it now: the inevitable truth that Essie must face and brand upon her heart.

The race was too young, its achievements too few, for whimsical indulgence. It must not matter whom you loved; it must not matter what you desired; it must not matter that it broke your heart, if sacrifice meant a forward step toward the freedom of our people.

He went down on his knees by the side of the bed. 'Oh, dear God,' he prayed, 'keep me well and strong, to work for my child and send her to college. Guide Essie's footsteps. Show her the truth. Help me teach her to love her face above ev'rything.'

TO MARKET, TO MARKET

Mrs. Carmody opened the oven door cautiously and stole a look at her cake. In ten minutes she could take it out. There was this and that last-minute thing to do, and dinner would be ready. Jim was the sort of man who wanted dinner served promptly at six. Five minutes later was saying perversely that he wasn't hungry, and no amount of coaxing would persuade him to do more than nibble. Otherwise he was an altogether enviable husband. Mrs. Carmody didn't mind indulging him to the extent of having dinner on the stroke of six.

Suddenly Mrs. Carmody looked stricken, and stared around wildly at the clock. It was a quarter to six, and there wasn't a slice of bread in the house. Seven-year-old Jimmy had come home from school with his customary request for a sandwich. There were three buddies outside waiting to play ball with him. She had made peanut butter sandwiches for the lot of them, and sternly reminded Jimmy that he would have to go to the store. He had straggled in at half past five with the sleeve of his new sweater raveled halfway up his arm. In the process of scolding and exhorting she hadn't remembered to remind him that he had an errand to do. Now he was earnestly being a good boy by practicing on the piano without having been told to do so.

Mrs. Carmody called him and got some change out of her apron pocket. Jimmy came in slowly, for he had just struck a sour note. He wondered if his mother wanted to tell him about it. She looked at him reproachfully, and he shifted his eyes and stared at his feet.

'Jimmy,' said Mrs. Carmody sadly, 'you forgot.'

'I know,' said Jimmy coldly. 'That's why I was practicing, to get it right.'

'I'm not talking about your practicing,' said Mrs. Carmody impatiently.

Jimmy looked hurt. Most of the time his mother acted as if learning to play the piano was the most important thing in life. Now she was talking as if he had been wasting his time in the parlor.

'What did I forget?' he said wearily.

'The bread,' said Mrs. Carmody triumphantly.

'Oh!' said Jimmy. 'I'll get it now.'

'And you be back here in ten minutes,' his mother threatened darkly. 'You know how your father wants dinner at six. You'd better be back before he comes in, or you'll catch it.'

Jimmy took the money and scooted out of the house. But on the front porch he paused and slowly and carefully walked the cracks. He started down the stairs, then stopped, and took all the steps in one splendid leap that sent him sprawling in a slightly bruised heap on his mother's pansy bed. He got up and limped toward the gate, and then he remembered he had money in his pocket. He took it out and counted it. A penny was missing. Guiltily he tiptoed back and dug around in the pansy bed. After a long time, he found it.

He went down the walk at a gallop. In the distance he could see the courthouse clock. He stared at it open-mouthed. Five minutes had fled. Full of remorse, he kept up his steady trot.

In the neighboring empty lot, a bobwhite called him to come and see. Once he had found a baby bobwhite and carried it back to its nest. Maybe this was a mother bird calling for help. Maybe another baby bobwhite was somewhere in distress. It wouldn't be right to just walk past when the neighborhood was full of cats.

He veered left and climbed a low fence. No forlorn fledgling peeped up at him. And his earnest approach sent the caroling bird careening toward heaven in graceful flight. He stared after it until it was out of sight, zooming his arms and shooting down airplanes with sputtering sounds from his mouth. Then he jumped the fence, and sternly admonished himself not to stop again.

Bandy Carver was coming up the street. He was coming straight at Jimmy. Jimmy shouted warningly, 'I ain't got time to fight today, Bandy Carver. I gotta do an errand.'

Bandy didn't swerve. Instead he looked very menacing and doubled his fists. Jimmy had told a perfidious friend that Bandy had curly hair like a girl's. Bandy had sworn to fight Jimmy Carmody the first time he saw him.

'I'll fight you tomorrow,' Jimmy promised. 'Back of the schoolhouse. Cross my heart.' Bandy Carver just came on.

Jimmy stole a quick look at the courthouse clock. Its minute hand was moving inexorably to five minutes of six. If he fought Bandy, he'd get home late. His father would whale the daylights out of him. He knew that Bandy would call him a coward, but he crossed to the other side of the street.

'Yah, yah, yah, fraidy-cat!' jeered Bandy and crossed to the other side, too. Stolidly Jimmy crossed back, with Bandy right behind him. They repeated this process a half dozen times, with Bandy hurling harsh imprecations and Jimmy repeating his promise to beat him to a pulp tomorrow.

Johnny Ames came around the corner and hailed them. They rushed to him and explained the situation. Johnny offered a solution. He would tell all the other kids about the fight tomorrow, and Jimmy would have to show up or be branded a coward.

This was quite agreeable to the parties concerned, and their parting was amiable. Jimmy continued on his way, with Johnny beside him advising him on prize-ring tactics. The store was in sight, but the town clock struck the hour of six, and Jimmy's heart pounded. Daddy was opening the door. He, Jimmy, was in for it.

And in that moment of bleak despair, Jimmy saw the shining marble, a big one, a beauty, anybody's property. But a split second later Johnny saw it, too, and both boys pounced upon it. Johnny emerged from the scramble with the marble in his hand.

'I'll fight you for it,' said Jimmy hotly.

'You can't,' Johnny said tauntingly. 'You gotta do an errand.'

Jimmy glanced at the clock again. He might as well be hung for a sheep as a lamb. 'Put up your dukes,' he said.

The two boys danced about the street, weaving and ducking, and hedging for the opportune moment to strike the knockout blow. A large, strange dog trotted up to inspect them. He sniffed the animosity in the air, and growled his disapproval.

'Go 'way, you,' Jimmy urged. The dog's growls deepened.

'He won't go 'way,' Jimmy quavered.

'Here, boy,' said Johnny, and flung the marble far and wide. The dog raced after it.

'Whew,' said Jimmy. 'You saved our lives.'

'Aw,' said Johnny deprecatingly. 'Well, I gotta go this way. See you back of the schoolhouse tomorrow.'

Jimmy made a flying leap into the store, snatched up a loaf of bread, dropped the money on the counter, turned on his heels in one swift motion, and covered the distance back home in four fleet minutes. His father was standing on the porch, looking like a thundercloud. Jimmy skidded to a stop.

'I guess I'm late,' he said.

'Your mother says you left this house at quarter to six. She expected you back in ten minutes.'

'Yes, sir,' Jimmy said.

'What kept you?' his father asked sternly.

Jimmy stared up at the unyielding face. 'Well,' he began, and recounted the many adventures of the brief journey. When he had finished, he drew a long breath. 'I guess,' he said timidly, 'you're too mad to eat.'

Jimmy saw a funny thing. He saw his father blush. Then his father said a funny thing. He said, 'I guess I was seven once.'

'Yes, sir,' said Jimmy politely.

'Let's go in,' said his father. 'I'm hungry as a bear. I hope you win tomorrow.'

SKETCHES AND
REMINISCENCES

RACHEL

When my mother died, we who had sparred with her over the years of our growth and maturity said with relief, 'Well, we won't have her intruding herself in our lives again.' Our saying it may have been a kind of swaggering, or maybe we were in shock, trying to hide what was really inside us.

My mother had often made the declaration that she was never going to die. She knew what was here, she would say with a laugh, but she didn't know what was there. Heaven was a long way from home. She was staying right here.

So we just accepted it as fact that she would be the death of us instead. When her own death came first, we didn't know what to make of it. There was a thinness in the air. There was silence where there had been sound and fury. There was no longer that beautiful and compelling voice bending us to her will against our own.

The house that I grew up in was four-storied, but we were an extended family, continually adding new members, and the perpetual joke was, if we lived in the Boston Museum, we'd still need one more room. Surrounded by all these different personalities, each one wanting to be first among equals, I knew I wanted to be a writer. Living with them was like living inside a story.

My mother was the dominant figure by the force of her vitality, and by the indisputable fact that she had the right to rule the roof that my father provided. She was a beautiful woman, and there was that day when I was grown, eighteen or so, ready to go off on my own, sure that I knew everything, that I said to her, 'Well, your beauty was certainly wasted on you. All you did with it was raise children and run your sisters' lives.'

My mother had done what she felt she had to do, knowing the risks, knowing there would be no rewards, but determined to build a foundation for the generations unborn. She had gathered us together so that the weakness of one would be balanced by her strength, and the loneliness of another eased by her laughter, and someone else's fears tempered by her fierce bravado, and the children treated alike, no matter what their degree of lovability, and her eye riveting mine if I tried to draw a distinction between myself and them.

We who had been the children under her command, and then the adults, still subject to her meddling in our intimate affairs, were finally bereaved, free of the departed, and in a rush to divorce ourselves from any resemblance to her influence.

When one of us said something that my mother might have said, and an outraged chorus shouted, 'You sound just like her,' the speaker, stung with shame and close to tears, shouted back, 'I do not!'

Then time passed. Whoever forgot to watch her language and echoed some sentiment culled from my mother responded to the catcalls with a cool 'So what?'

As time increased its pace, although there were diehards who would never relent, there were more of us shifting positions, examining our ambivalent feelings, wondering if the life force that had so overwhelmed our exercise of free will, and now no longer had to be reckoned with, was a greater loss than a relief.

When a newborn disciple recited my mother's sayings as if

they were gospel, the chiding came from a scattered chorus of uninspired voices.

Then there was the day when someone said with wonder, 'Have you noticed that those of us who sound just like her are the ones who laugh a lot, love children a lot, don't have any hang-ups about race or color, and never give up without trying?'

'Yes, I've noticed,' one of us answered, with the rest of us adding softly, 'Me too.'

I suppose that was the day and the hour of our acknowledgment that some part of her was forever embedded in our psyches, and we were not the worse for it.

But I still cannot put my finger on the why of her. What had she wanted, this beautiful woman? Did she get it? I would look at her face when it was shut away, and I would long to offer her a penny for her thoughts. But I knew she would laugh and say, 'I was just thinking it's time to start dinner,' or something equally far from her yearning heart.

I don't think she ever realized how often she made the remark, 'Speech was given man to hide his thoughts.' At such times I would say to myself, 'She will die with her secrets.' I had guessed a few, but they had been only surface deep, easy to flush out. I know that the rest went with her on her flight to heaven.

FOND MEMORIES OF A BLACK CHILDHOOD

We were always stared at. Whenever we went outside the neighborhood that knew us, we were inspected like specimens under glass. My mother prepared us. As she marched us down our front stairs, she would say what our smiles were on tiptoe to hear, 'Come on, children, let's go out and drive the white folks crazy.'

She said it without rancor, and she said it in that outrageous way to make us laugh. She was easing our entry into a world that outranked us and outnumbered us. If she could not help us see ourselves with the humor, however wry, that gives the heart its grace, she would never have forgiven herself for letting our spirits be crushed before we had learned to sheathe them with pride.

When the Ipswich Street trolley screeched to a halt at our car stop, we scrambled aboard and sat in a row on the long seat at one end of the trolley that must have been designed for mothers with broods to keep together. We were thereby in full view. For the rest of that trolley ride into town, we were, in our infinite variety, a total divertissement.

Even my mother on occasion called our family a motley crew. We did not have pointed heads. We were simply a family that ranged in color from the blond child to me, a whim of

God's that had gone on over so many generations that we had long since grown accustomed to accepting whatever gift we got. In a world where order is preferred, we were not uniform.

That my mother appeared to highlight the differences by dressing the blond child and me alike did not seem odd to me then, and is now too long ago to seem any odder than anything else that happened in my family. Whether she did it to further confound outsiders or because she was genuinely charmed by pairing the fairest and darkest was no more a cosmic prank on her part than on his.

We were a tribal family, living under a shared roof because that was the way we liked it. My mother was chief mother because nobody challenged her. Her oldest sister, who should have been chief mother, had raised so many of my grandmother's batches of babies that by the time we came along, she had seen enough children to have seen them all, and none of us, including her own, had anything special to delight her.

We gave her the honor that was due her as the senior sister. She carried herself above reproach. She never told lies and was a true Christian. She went to church rain or shine and visited the sick. She read the Bible and could quote it. She gave counsel when asked for it, and was never wrong. We were all in awe of her, even my irreverent mother. She was the soul of starched dignity. We often felt unworthy beside her. We were right to feel unworthy. She would not sit at table with us because we ate too much and upset her digestion. My mother had to take a tray to her in the parlor. If we went to the movies together, she would sit in a different row, so that she would not have to be part of all that candy crunching and reading the titles aloud.

When it was time to go away for the summer and my mother packed a shoebox with sandwiches which we steadily ate between South Station and Woods Hole, that was the time my aunt could have said, 'Off with their heads,' without thinking twice.

We were black Bostonians on a train full of white ones. Because we were obviously going the same way, laden as we were with all the equipment of a long holiday, children, luggage, last-minute things stuffed in paper bags, a protesting cat in a carton, in addition to the usual battery of disbelieving eyes, we were being subjected to intense speculation as to what people with our unimpressive ancestry were doing on a train that was carrying people with real credentials to a summer sojourn that was theirs by right of birth.

We were among the first blacks to vacation on Martha's Vineyard. It is not unlikely that the Island, in particular Oak Bluffs, had a larger number of vacationing blacks than any other section of the country.

There were probably twelve cottage owners. To us it was an agreeable number. There were enough of us to put down roots, to stake our claim to a summer place, so that the children who came after us would take for granted a style of living that we were learning in stages.

The early blacks were all Bostonians, which is to say they were neither arrogant nor obsequious, they neither overacted nor played ostrich. Though the word was unknown then, in today's connotation they were 'cool.' It was a common condition of black Bostonians. They were taught very young to take the white man in stride or drown in their own despair. Their survival was proved by their presence on the Island in pursuit of the same goal of happiness.

Every day, the young mothers took their children to a lovely stretch of beach and scattered along it in little pools. They made a point of not bunching together. They did not want the whites to think they knew their place.

There was not much exchange except smiles between the new and the old, no more was needed. Bostonians do not rush into relationships. Sometimes the children took their shovels and pails and built castles together. It was a pretty scene. The blacks in all their beautiful colors, pink and gold and brown and ebony. The whites in summer's bronze.

The days were full. There were berries to pick, a morning's adventure. There were band concerts for an evening's stroll. There were invitations to lemonade and cookies and whist. There was always an afternoon boat to meet, not so much to see who was getting off, but to see and talk to whatever friends had come for that same purpose.

For some years, the black Bostonians, growing in modest numbers, had this idyll to themselves. The flaws were put in perspective because no place is perfection.

And then came the black New Yorkers. They had found a fair land where equality was a working phrase. They joyously tested it. They behaved like New Yorkers because they were not Bostonians. There is nobody like a Bostonian except a man who is one.

The New Yorkers did not talk in low voices. They talked in happy voices. They carried baskets of food to the beach to make the day last. They carried liquor of the best brands. They grouped together in an ever increasing circle because what was the sense of sitting apart?

Their women wore diamonds when the few Bostonians who owned any had left theirs at home. They wore paint and powder when in Boston only a sporting woman bedecked her face in such bold attire. Their dresses were cut low. They wore high heels on sandy roads.

I had a young aunt who would duck behind a hedge and put us children on watch while she rubbed her nose with a chamois when we told her it was shiny. We did not think her performance was unusual. It was the New Yorkers who seemed bizarre, who always seemed to be showing off wherever they gathered together.

The New Yorkers were moving with the times. They had come from a city where they had to shout to be heard. It was a city that offered much, judgeships, professorships, appointments to boards, stardom on stage and more. Whoever wanted them had to push. The New Yorkers wanted them. They were achievers. They worked hard and they played hard.

They would unwind in another generation. They would come to the Island to relax not to posture. They would come to acknowledge that the Bostonians had a certain excellence that was as solid an achievement as money.

But in the meantime they lost the beach for the Bostonians. That beach like no other, that tranquil spot at that tranquil end of the Island. All one summer the Bostonians saw it coming like a wave they could not roll back. It came the next summer. The beach became a private club, with a gate that only dogs could crawl under, and a sign that said, 'For members only.'

You lose some, and by the same token, you win some. The world was not lost, just a piece of it. And in the intervening years more has been gained than was ever forfeited, more has been fought for and won, more doors have opened as fewer have closed.

Harry T. Burleigh, the composer, who left a priceless legacy in his long research of Negro spirituals—those shouts of grace and suffering and redemption that might have perished forever if he had not given his gifts to preserving them – he was the first to bring back glad tidings of the Island's fair land to his New York friends, who had always thought of Massachusetts as a nice place to come from, but not to go to unless bound and gagged.

Mr. Burleigh had come to stay at Shearer Cottage in the Highlands, a quiet boardinghouse operated by Boston friends, who had recommended the seclusion of the lovely wooded area, where New York's busy lights seemed as remote as the Island stars seemed near.

He was very good to the children of his friends. There were seven or eight of us who were his special favorites. He gave us money every time he saw us. We did not know any better than to spend it in one place. With abundant indulgence he would give us some more to spend in another. He rented cars and took us on tours of the Island. He told us about his trips abroad. To be with him was a learning experience.

There is a snapshot of him in a family album. Under the snapshot, in the handwriting of that aunt who could take us or leave us, there is the caption: 'H.T.B., the children's friend.' He was rich and well known in important circles at the time. There were a dozen glowing captions that would have applied. I think it is a tribute to him – and perhaps to my aunt – that she chose this simple inscription.

Mr. Burleigh's summers were spent working as well as sunning. Every weekday morning he went to a church in Vineyard Haven where he had use of the piano. Many of the spirituals sung around the world were given arrangements within God's hearing in an Island church.

In the course of time Mr. Burleigh grew to regret the increasing number of New Yorkers who brought their joyous living to his corner of the Highlands. He had extolled this sacred spot, and they were taking over. Who can say they did not share his vision? They simply expressed it in a different way.

Adam Clayton Powell came to summer at Shearer Cottage when he was a boy. He came with his father. His mother stayed home. Adam came to our house to play every day, and every day Adam's father came to ask my mother if his son was somewhere around. We were sorry for Adam that a boy as big as he was had a father who was always following him around. I can see that great tall man, who looked so like Adam was to grow up to look, striding up the road to ask my mother in his mellifluous preacher's voice if she had seen his boy. He would hold her in conversation, and she would turn as pink as a rose. He seemed to make her nervous, and we didn't know why. Sometimes he would come twice a day to see if Adam had lost his way between our house and Shearer Cottage. He never did, but all that summer his father couldn't rest until he had seen for himself.

Judge Watson – the first black man elected to a judgeship in New York City – his wife, and their young children spent several summers on the Island. They were a splendid family. The younger members still return to see the friends of their childhood. They have all achieved much. Barbara Watson is Assistant Secretary of State for Security and Consular Affairs, and the first woman to attain such rank. Grace Watson directs an HEW program for volunteers in education that encompasses nearly two million teaching aides across the country. Douglas Watson is an aeronautical engineer and Chief Project Officer with Republic Aircraft in Jamaica, L. I. James is a judge in the U.S. Customs Court in Manhattan.

Though all of their titles are impressive, they have not changed. Like all who have come to the Island in the years of their innocence, something here has touched them with sweetness and simplicity.

The summer wound down in September. Labor Day came, cottages emptied. Ours stayed open. We were always late returning to school. My mother could not bear to leave. Fall was so lovely. Winter would be so long to wait to see an Oak Bluffs sky again.

We lingered for those magic days until my father wrote, as he wrote every year, 'Come on home, there are no more flowers to pick.'

Then we packed our shoebox with sandwiches and left.

THE GIFT

When I was ten years old I was accepted by the Girls' Latin School as a suitable candidate for admission to the sixth class, the level from which one progressed to the pinnacle of the first class. The average age of sixth-class students was twelve, which has a more impressive sound than ten. I was worried by that age gap which was compounded by the fact that I was small for my age, and maybe looked as young as nine, an absurd situation for a student who, I had been told, was addressed by her teachers as 'Miss.'

I asked my mother if my classmates would make fun of me. In my lower school, attended by both boys and girls, the boys had made fun of me because I was colored. With them name-calling had been routine. In the Brahmin Boston of that day, boys of their simple background needed a scapegoat for their self-esteem.

My mother's reassuring answer was that people of proper background never made fun of other people because of conditions over which they had no control, like being ten, like being small for ten, like being colored. I must never forget, she reminded me, as she frequently reminded me, that I was my father's daughter. He had survived the condition of slavery. I would never face an endurance test more difficult than that.

So I went to the Latin School on opening day, holding my head erect, hearing myself formally addressed by my teachers, and not for a moment feeling that the title crowned my head unbecomingly. Then it was lunchtime and I made my way down the long hall to the lunchroom, never having even seen a school lunchroom before, or paid for a meal by myself before, but determined to treat it as an everyday occurrence, and not spill anything.

Two presumably first-class young women, tall and perfect in appearance, saw me, stopped dead in their tracks, enchanted by my difference, their faces spread with smiles. They rushed toward me, pulling me back and forth between them, one of them saying, she's my baby, the other one saying, no, she's mine.

In that comic tug and pull the title my teachers had conferred on me in my passage from childhood lost all meaning. I was stunned and speechless. Then I wriggled, found my voice and said urgently, 'Beg your pardon. I'm not a baby. I'm not really as little as I look. I'm ten years old.'

At that, to my surprise, instead of sobering, they burst out laughing and walked away doubled over with mirth, the sound of which lingered with me for the rest of the day.

That encounter made me feel a great unease about another matter which I had never let surface, knowing my mother knew the truth of it, but not yet sure I was ready to surrender my chosen belief to her reality. Nevertheless I wanted to avoid a misstep and stand on firm ground in front of the twelve-year-olds in my class. I could no longer put off facing the truth about Santa Claus.

If ten seems too old not to know whether Santa Claus is real or not, that period in America's history was called the age of innocence for the general population, at least for those who had never had to struggle with want. I was one of those so blessed.

When my mother said that my father was Santa Claus, I wasn't demolished. I know I felt sad, but I think I felt relieved.

Now I could talk to my classmates about Christmas without skirting around the edges. That I was shedding the last vestige of my childhood was not traumatic, considering that in return I saw my father in a special light.

Slavery ended when he was seven. His mother, who had been a cook, found hire in a boardinghouse, my father sharing her quarters, and shining shoes, running errands for the boarders, and putting his pennies and nickels and occasional dimes in a cigar box except for a small sum he paid an indigent townsman to teach him to read and write and figure sums. The latter became one of my father's indispensable skills.

When he was eight or so, he went to the open market with the boardinghouse owner to carry her baskets when they were laden, and watched her pick and choose, heard her haggle over prices, listened to the market talk of the men. The Christmas that he was ten he knew what he wanted. He wanted a business of his own. He got out his cigar box with his savings, and asked his mother how much she had in savings. He told her, this ten-year-old man-boy, that he wanted to go into business for himself, he wanted a boardinghouse of his own. If he could borrow her money and services, he promised that he would make her rich in return.

I am told that he did, that they had a boardinghouse and a restaurant in Richmond, Virginia, that my grandmother learned to wear silk.

My father moved on, as men seeking wider opportunities do. I don't think it ever occurred to him that his race and former condition of servitude might be handicaps. They were not. He came North to Springfield and apprenticed himself to a wholesale buyer of fruits and vegetables. When he had learned the art of trading, he opened two stores, one a retail fruit store, the other an ice cream parlor, catering to those who could afford to eat fruit every day, to whom an ice cream parlor was a pleasant place to dally.

My father's dream was to be a wholesale merchant of fruits and vegetables in the venerable Boston Market. And so he was. His place of business was on South Market Street just opposite Faneuil Hall, and I will cherish forever the sound of the great dray horses' hooves on the cobblestones as I waited, with my hand in my mother's, to cross the street to my father's store, with its big banana rooms, and the big store cat that thought small children were varmints to attack.

My father was a generation older than my mother. Yet I cannot imagine either one married to anyone else. I cannot imagine belonging to anybody else. On the Christmas of my father's tenth birthday he prepared my own coming of age in my tenth year on Christmas Day. Then I knew the gifts he had given me were endurance and strength of will. The tangible gifts were just extras.

THE PURSE

The Christmas that I was six my father's banker, Mr. Lowell Bancroft, gave me six five-dollar gold pieces in a lovely little brocaded purse that swung from my wrist on a drawstring. I was not impressed with the gold pieces. I was a simple-minded child who did not care for money because I did not care for candy. When you are a child one is related to the other. Six five-dollar gold pieces were beyond the bounds of any familiar reality.

When my mother saw the contents of my purse, she said that Mr. Bancroft was a fool. What could a child do with all that money but lose it? My father said that I could bank it and watch it grow. My mother said Mr. Bancroft hadn't given me much of a gift if I had to put it back in his bank and watch it grow for him.

She reached for my purse and said coaxingly, 'Let me keep it for you until I can take you downtown and show you how to spend it sensibly. You can start saving when you're old enough to decide for yourself.'

I was not a balky child, and never about money, which my mother regularly fleeced from me whenever my father gave me a piece of change from his pocket. But this time I jerked my arm away. If she had thought to say, 'You keep the purse and give me the gold pieces,' I would have been glad to oblige. It was only the purse that I was being mulish about. I knew that one of my aunts was taking us children out later. I wanted to show off my splendid purse to all the people I passed. What I didn't know was that a purse hanging loosely from a child's forgetful arm was just waiting to slide off.

As a rule my father did not interfere with my mother's commands to the children. She had long since taught him that she was our boss. She believed that children belonged wholly to women. It forever annoyed her that only one woman in history could really substantiate that claim. She always felt that immaculate conception should have come down through the ages.

My father said gently, 'Christmas is for children. Let her have her way today. You can have your way tomorrow. It'll please Mr. Bancroft when I tell him she loved his present so much she wouldn't let go of it.'

'I get tired of hearing about Mr. Bancroft,' said my mother, who got tired of hearing about rich people who had more lovely money than they could ever spend. What good did it do her to have Mr. Bancroft give a simple-minded child thirty dollars in gold if that child's father gave her an open invitation to lose it. My mother was pretty sure that if she went to Mr. Bancroft on bended knee and begged him to lend her as little as ten dollars, he'd call a bank holiday so he wouldn't have to.

Mr. Bancroft's money was not that sanctified. He was always lending it to my father. But my father had collateral, and all my mother had was what my father gave her, which was never enough for her unending spring of needs.

I never saw Mr. Bancroft. To me he was just a name that my father spoke with pride and respect. He was my father's banker. At least that was the phrase my mother always used, in a voice tinged with sighing because my father's money disappeared into Mr. Bancroft's bank, and all she had access to were the leavings.

Mr. Bancroft gave me presents as a gesture of affectionate regard for my father. He was a Boston blueblood, born to everything that my father was not. I suppose he admired my father for never seeming to know that he was born the wrong color to succeed.

My father was a wholesaler in the Boston Market, the only black man who had ever been a wholesaler in that traditionally rich company of old firms and old names. His produce business, its lettering, 'Imported and Domestic Fruits and Vegetables, Bananas a Specialty,' was just opposite Faneuil Hall. To Mr. Bancroft that was a stupendous climb for a slave-born man who had only a few snatched hours of the rudiments of learning, and had taught himself to write in a Spencerian hand, to read whatever was set before him, to talk with a totally literate tongue, and most of all, perhaps most importantly of all, to figure like a wizard.

When he rattled off figures to his bookkeeper, he was adding them up in his head faster than she could put them down on paper. He loved figures. I often felt that he would have been a mathematics professor if life had offered him a college education. I am probably wrong. The reason my father was a wholesaler was because he knew he wanted to be a buyer and seller when he was ten years old – just three years out of slavery – and he never veered from his goal.

That was why he married late in middle life. He hadn't meant to get married at all. In the beginning he was too busy turning himself into a businessman to think about marriage. After he became a solid businessman and had some dollars in his pocket, he was terribly afraid that every woman he met had designs on his money.

Then he met my mother. She was poor as a church mouse, and she hated him on sight. She hated the gold tooth he flaunted in the middle of his mouth to show the world he was rich enough to have his own tooth yanked out and a flashy gold one set in to spotlight his smile. She hated his diamond stick-pin because diamonds should only be worn by ladies. She hated his self-assurance. He was old enough to be her father, and he had no right to act as if it didn't make any difference. Above all, she hated the way he looked at her, as if he had fallen in love at first sight.

My mother was a beauty, and it was always more of a bother to her than a blessing. She walked at six months and talked at nine. She was spirited, fearless, sassy, and smart. Her older brothers made her their mascot and rode her around on their shoulders. From that bold height her gold-colored, pink-cheeked beauty was like a banner.

People with nothing better to do stopped dead in their tracks to talk baby talk to her. They wasted her brothers' precious playing time by getting in the way of their rush to the secret places where they kept their boyhood joy, a wonderful region of whooping and hollering, from which they had better return by chore time or get a good licking.

My uncles sought revenge on these usurpers of time, and used my all too willing mother as their patsy. They taught her every cuss word that had ever been invented. When well-intentioned souls came toward her, my mother let out a string of curses that could curl a sailor's hair. She didn't know what she was saying, but from her brothers' snickers, from the faces falling apart in front of her, she very well knew she was saying something she shouldn't.

When these outraged souls broke their necks to tell my grandmother, Mama had a green switch waiting for my mother's return. My mother got at least one licking a day from the time she was two until she stopped being a tomboy at twelve. She always said that Mama lived on her behind, but she had enough fun to make up for it.

Half of her lickings were for tearing the lace on her drawers. Mama had more children than any house around. When you have that many children noseybodies mind your business, wondering how you can feed so many mouths, how you can clothe so many growing bodies, and where you can find the time to bring them up in the fear of God, which is where my mother's cussing didn't help.

The sum of my grandmother's pride was the lace that decorated her little girls' drawers in those days when little girls wore long-legged drawers that showed beneath their dresses. The lace that my grandmother made by hand and sewed on all those homemade drawers was her way of showing those noseybodies who minded her business that nobody went in want at her house, not for bread, not for meat, not for lace on their britches.

One of my mother's worst lickings was the one she got for bringing home cold biscuit and bacon rind that some misguided soul had given her because she was one of all those hungry children Mama had to feed.

Mama could feed her children better than cold biscuit and bacon rind, and she didn't want my dumbhead mother accepting hog scraps like that was what she ate at home. But how were noseybodies to know any different if my mother, always ready with her fists, always ready to take a dare, was as ragged and dirty as anybody's orphan as soon as Mama turned her back and she could sneak away?

How often that torn lace hanging from my mother's dirt-streaked drawers put shame in Mama's pride. How often Mama had to take a switch to the seat of that shame. She could not know that down the years my mother would tell it over and over, her eyes alight with the wonder of it, how Mama found time out of bits and pieces of her overburdened hours to transform her love into handmade lace.

My mother's massive atonement was taken out on us. She told us early in our lives that we weren't going to worry her to death the way she worried Mama to death. Every word that Mama had preached to her she practiced on us. She wore us out with keeping us clean. How often she snatched us up from our tidy play on her spotless floor and changed our unoffending drawers in memory of Mama. She who had been a heathen from dawn to dark made us behave around the clock.

But in keeping with her character, she was often bored by our predictable behavior. She would come into our orderly play area with its coloring books, its blunted scissors, its toy piano, its dollhouse and other pallid playthings, and she would look at us with a kind of disbelief that we were contentedly playing in such pitiful surroundings.

Standing in the doorway, the telltale pink in her cheeks giving her gloating away, she would tell us one of her stories, maybe the one about the time she stole Papa's big gun and made up a game called 'Run, children, run, you massa's drunk and got a gun.' She was only six and Papa's hunting gun was bigger than she was. Mama's children scattered like scared chickens, with my mother running after them, that big old gun bumping along beside her. Everybody was yelling and screaming, half in fun, half in fright.

By accident that gun went off. It knocked my mother off her feet, but in a moment she scrambled up and scooted under the porch. The other children were hiding, too, from the hail of bullets they thought were whizzing at them.

Mama came to the door. For a moment she just stood there, staring at that big smoking gun in the yard, her face pale as ashes. She said an anguished prayer to God. Then she began the roll call of her children, all those names, all those children, each one so dear to her, even my mother, that one child less, though it might have eased her burden, would have broken her heart.

It took a long time to call those names, starting with Bubber at the top and ending at the bottom with the walking baby. She called every name except my mother's. She was saving that for last.

One by one Mama's children came out from their hiding places saying, 'Yes'm, here's me,' and turning up for her inspection. Her eyes darted up and down the line, looking for blood. They were all alive, and nobody had a limb shot off.

Then she called my mother in a voice that reached under that porch and scooped my mother out like sand in a shovel. Mama didn't even bother to ask who else in that lineup had stolen Papa's gun. She just lit into my poor mother as if all her other children had halos on their heads. My mother so often said that when she was a child she got everybody's beating. But mostly, I think she got her own.

Sometimes I think how young Mama was when her children started coming. She was sixteen, maybe that's why she made herself so strict, letting her voice boom like a deep-toned bell, being so almighty handy with that switch. She was trying so hard to act as if she had been grown a long time back. She was trying so hard to act as if she was born to be the boss and not take sass.

She was born a slave, bound to obedience as soon as she was old enough to say, 'Yes, mistis, yes, massa,' with a beating waiting in the barn for any show of wishing she had a say of her own.

Then there was a war, and then there was a cessation of war, and for a moment of time, my grandmother was free, jumping up and down on an old stump, the master's red hair in her bouncing braids, shouting, 'I'se free, I'se free,' not quite knowing what it truly meant, but knowing the sound was sweet to hear.

All too soon she was bound again. For at fifteen she was bound in marriage to my nineteen-year-old grandfather, whose beauty my mother's beauty couldn't hold a candle to, though a family saying is that my mother tried to look like Papa. Then Mama was bound forever by her batches of babies, her girlhood over before it was ever experienced. Between the time that she walked the wide road away from the circumscribed world of the plantation and the time that child raising engulfed her, she had such a little time to look at the larger world and make wishes.

But she made wishes for her children, some of them as passionate as prayers. She wished for them to be born without blemish. She wished for them to thrive at her breast. She wished for God to bless her table with enough to go around, and perhaps an extra portion for whoever wanted more, so that hunger would not stunt their bodies or slow their minds, and they could live in a harsh white world with the strength and the wit to survive.

In some miraculous way so many of Mama's wishes came true including her deep-down wish for a Christmas doll for whichever little daughter had turned seven.

This was Mama's leftover longing from the Christmas of her slave childhood when she hid behind the parlor door, and watched her master's little daughters playing with their Christmas dolls that looked as real as babies.

Mama had rag dolls, and clothespin dolls, and such, but Mama never had a doll that looked like real. The morning her first girl baby was born Mama made herself a vow that every girl child she gave birth to would have a real true doll to treasure.

For a month before her special Christmas my mother never told a lie, or cussed or tore her drawers, or came home bloody, or did anything bad enough to change the mind of God or Santa Claus or whoever was in charge of giving dolls to colored children. For a month my mother was as nearly perfect as she would never be again.

And then came Christmas morning, and the moment in that morning when my mother saw a real true doll propped beside the fireplace, a real true china doll with real hair and real eyes that opened and shut. With her heart pounding my mother looked shyly at Mama, and Mama said, 'See what Santa Claus brought you. She's holding out her arms to you. Go pick her up and love her.'

All that day my mother loved that doll with a tenderness Mama didn't know was in her. She was possessed with love for it. The doll looked so real. She looked so alive, maybe she was alive, Santa Claus could do anything.

My mother began to believe it with all her might. She thought she could feel her doll's heart beat. She thought she could hear her breathe. She thought she could feel her body turn to flesh.

The suspense became unbearable. There came a moment toward dusk of that Christmas day when my mother had to know.

She carried her doll outdoors where she could be by herself. She knew what she had to do. She had to see if her doll had brains. If her doll had brains, it had to be real. Only real people had brains.

In her highly excited state my mother was trembling uncontrollably. As she struck her doll's head against the step, she only meant to give a light tap to make a little crack just big enough to see if there were any brains inside.

My mother's aim was all too true, her hand was all too heavy. That doll's head broke into a hundred pieces. In one split second there was no head at all, just my mother wildly screaming, and Mama coming running and seeing my mother with a headless doll in her hand before the day was over.

The look that passed between them was one of hopelessness. Mama's heart was breaking because my mother was beyond redemption. My mother's heart was breaking because her doll was dead, and she had killed it. She got a licking, of course, but she didn't feel it. She was too numb to feel Mama's crying hand.

Though none of us walked when we were six months old or talked when we were nine months old, we showed sufficient signs of intelligence to keep her from cracking our heads to see if we had any brains.

On my mother's side we were a tribal family, happiest under a shared roof. Our house, though big, was never big enough for our permanent or passing kin. The family saying was that if we lived in the Boston Museum, which was the biggest building we knew about, we'd still want one more room.

My mother had more brothers and sisters than she or they could ever count. I remember the arguments that were part of every try. Even before my mother and her sisters really got started – her brothers never bothered – they stopped to squabble.

Somebody would say that Mama had twenty-one children. Someone else would protest indignantly that Mama only had eighteen. Everybody would begin to take sides, with each side feeling it was upholding Mama's honor, either by defending her right to bear twenty-one babies or by refusing to brand her with this dumfounding distinction.

Finally my mother would command, 'Get the chairs, get the chairs.' The sisters would line up the chairs in two facing rows, both rows chafing to start the rundown of Mama's children, and settle the matter once and for all.

An older sister, as was befitting, would start calling the names of Mama's babies in the order of their birth: Bubber, Daughter, Robert, Carrie . . . But at some point along the line a scornful voice would rudely interject that her sister had left out Scipio, Mama's baby that died between Robert and Carrie.

This second speaker would be challenged by a third, who insisted that Scipio didn't come along in Mama's first batch of babies. He didn't come along until midway in Mama's second batch. It was Mama's baby girl Jessie that lived and died between Robert and Carrie. This statement drew the outrage of a fourth contestant, who retorted that Mama never had a baby girl named Jessie. She lost a baby boy named Jessie.

The ball went back and forth. An argument would rise, subside. The name count would begin again, and again an irate voice would take over. Everybody had a turn at starting the count. But nobody ever got to finish it. Even those sisters on the same side would start disputing with each other about the color of a dead baby's hair. One by one they hollered each other down.

Oh, so many times I wished that somebody would get to finish that count without being hollered down, that somebody would be allowed to get it right. But always the count was cut off until there was nobody left to try.

A wounded silence would engulf the sisters, draining their joy in being together until my mother could think of something funny to bring them back to laughing and loving, like one of her stories about Rena Robinson, who was so fat that once around Rena Robinson was twice around Central Park.

Maybe only Mama could have told the total of her children, letting the lost ones lie on her lips a little longer than the living, remembering their struggling breath against her rejected breast, from which they had no strength to draw sustenance. But that she gave so many children vigorous life in that harsh time and place was the comfort that eased her weariness.

Sending her children to school was my grandmother's greatest miracle, an enduring monument to her memory. That she who could neither read nor write, and could so easily have said that such adornments were of poor use to black folks whose hands could learn faster than their heads, that she could aspire to open the doors of their minds was the miracle that made the generations that came after her more than mind creatures.

The incredible part of it was that she paid their way. Free schooling for blacks had not been invented. But beginning to spread across the state was a scattering of private academies, established by gentlewomen from the North, mostly New England spinsters of means and selflessness, whose abolitionist background was their impetus.

The tuition was little more than a token imposed to give pride and purpose and value to those parents and children who were participants. However small the sum, when it had to be multiplied over and over, it added up to a sizable sacrifice.

Papa had his regular job in the factory and in growing season a job in the fields before the factory whistle. All year round he stretched his working day beyond all normal limits, doing odd jobs of any description. He was known for and sought for his great strength and his indifference to danger. He could do alone for one man's pay what two other men would take longer to do.

My mother lived in backcountry. School was twelve miles going and coming. She skipped and ran and leaped for joy all the way.

Her first day at school the teacher wrote something called the alphabet in bold and beautiful letters on a blackboard. My mother practically learned them in one gulp. She loved the feel of them marching in her mind. It was the most magical day in her life. She couldn't wait to get home and stand before Mama, and sing the song of revelation from A to Z.

When she learned to spell *cat*, she was in a fever to learn to spell *dog*. When she learned to count to ten, there was no stopping her rush to reach twenty. When she knew the exaltation of reading whole sentences, and stood before Mama, reading aloud from her first reader, she held in her hands the lifeline that would link the generations.

When my mother was big enough, eleven or so, she found little jobs before and after school to help out. For one, she carried covered dishes between two widowed sisters who sent each other daily delights from their tables each with the hope of enticing the other to come and live where the eating was best. For another, she helped a crusty old cook with the supper chores that kept her on her hurting arches past the shouting point of pain. She lent her young shoulder to the feeble hand of an old sir on his nightly walk with his old dog who knew no better than to expect an old habit to continue forever. She made beds, and got fired for falling asleep in one of them. She only meant to see how a feather bed felt, and the next thing she knew she was being shaken awake.

The most she earned for any job was twenty-five cents a week. But if she was lucky enough to have a job before school and one after, that was fifty cents a week to drop in Mama's lap for Mama to make do the work of a great big dollar.

Those noseybodies who had always predicted that my mother's beauty would bring proud Mama sorrow and shame saw my mother bud into her teens and sat back to watch and wait.

They were disappointed. On the day the first admiring male crossed my mother's path she was so unglued by this innocent encounter that she ran and hid for hours.

She was fourteen or fifteen, homebound on a windy day that was whipping the color high in her cheeks. Her oldest brother, Bubber, was coming toward her walking with a young black man whom she'd never seen before. When they drew abreast, she said, 'Hey, Bubber,' and kept on walking, not wanting to embarrass him by making him stop to talk to somebody who was nobody but a sister.

As she sailed past she heard the stranger let out a hoot like he'd seen a sight he couldn't believe, then say to her brother on a burst of crazy laughter, 'My God, Bubber, what a beauty.'

Nobody that grown had ever made such braying fun of her. She burst into tears and broke into a run. She who never cried couldn't stop crying. She who never ran from anything didn't stop running until she reached home.

She tiptoed in and felt along the high shelf for Papa's looking glass that had to be kept out of reach of careless hands. She took it down and tiptoed out.

Still unnoticed, she flew across the yard and found a hiding place in the comforting clutter of the barn. When she could bear to look, she lifted the looking glass and stared at her face.

Just as she knew it would, a gold-colored face stared back, and she remembered all the times she had had to fight darker kids for calling her yaller punkins, as if yaller was the ugliest color in the world.

And just as she dreaded, on top of all that yaller was all that pink, which my mother's family called 'high color.' She supposed those two bright colors together made her look like a painted circus clown for Bubber's ole fool friends to laugh at. She put down the glass, doubled her fists, and beat her face in a fury of self-hatred. For the first time in her life she was conscious of her looks, and the feeling was too new and enormous to control.

Nobody in my mother's family had ever told her that she was beautiful. Families never do. If they've got any sense they tell you to mind your manners, watch your temper, tell the truth, don't sass back, share with your sisters, comb your hair, keep yourself clean, and serve God. They figure that beauty is only skin deep anyway. And the Christian virtues come first.

My mother took her hurt feelings to her teacher. There was nobody else. Mama would only have told her she was making a mountain out of a molehill, and if she couldn't take teasing, she was going to have a sorry life.

As she poured her embellished tale into Miss Tewksbury's sympathizing ear, my mother gradually became alarmed at Miss Tewksbury's clucks and sighs. She soon had the feeling that Mama's molehill might have been a better bargain. Miss Tewksbury was imagining my mother in flight from a full-scale assault.

Even more distressing was Miss Tewksbury's obscure answer to her burning question about her looks. Miss Tewksbury said that looks were not important. It was character that gave people grace. She hoped that my mother would always run from any man who called her beautiful. Such a man was not looking for character. He was looking for something else. Her brother's presence in the woods may have saved her from only heaven knew what. There were too many woods in the sultry South.

That's how it was that my mother came North. Miss Tewksbury arranged it. When her teaching assignment was over, her conscience would not let her leave without advising Mama about my mother's brush with danger. Beauty was a mixed blessing.

Mama had heard it all before from noseybodies and turned a deaf ear. But Miss Tewksbury was an educated woman with a face full of kindness and concern. Mama had to listen with respectful silence and say 'yes' to whatever she was expected to say 'yes' to because to say otherwise would have made her sound like she didn't care what became of my mother.

So it was that my sixteen-year-old mother stood with Mama alongside the tracks where the Jim Crow train would stop, Mama letting her go to see if the world would let her in, my mother dressed in her homemade best, wearing her first real hat, one hand holding the neatly tied bundle of her belongings, and the ticket that Miss Tewksbury had sent her, the other holding her napkin-covered basket of vittles that was going to have to last her until she got where she was going two days away.

My mother saw the train coming down the track, heard its mournful whistle – some I take, and some I leave – and felt Mama ease her basket from her and take her freed hand. Mama began to sing soft and low, just for the two of them to hear, long-meter singing, as close to crying as singing can come. In a moment my mother joined in. May the Lord watch between me and thee while we are absent one from another . . . Their town was only a whistle stop. The train took my mother and left her childhood to be remembered forever.

My mother never saw Mama alive again. It was common occurrence in those days of black migration. It takes money to go home. If you have enough money to go home, you mail it home to help out.

Those six five-dollar gold pieces in that blue brocaded purse that slipped unnoticed from my vain arm somewhere between the trolley stop and back was money that was needed down home to help somebody who needed help.

When money is hard to come by, and money down home is hard to come by, a child with a father who lets her throw money away had better listen to her mother, who knows how much it costs to be poor, and how much thirty gold dollars would help defray that cost.

THE SUN PARLOR

This is a tale with a moral. I will try not to tax your attention too long. But I have to go way back to begin because it begins with my childhood. It is about houses and children, and which came first.

There were four of us children, well-schooled in good manners, well-behaved almost all of the time, and obedient to the commands of grown-ups, the power people who could make or break us.

We lived in a beautiful house. The reason I knew that is because all my mother's friends said so, and brought their other friends to see it. On the day appointed for the tour, which included inspection of every room on every floor, my mother would gather us around her and say in her gentlest voice, 'I'm sorry, children, but Mrs. So-and-so is coming today and bringing a friend to see our house. You children keep clean and play quietly while they're here. It's not a real visit. They won't stay long. It'll be over before you can say Jack Robinson.'

Most often a first-time caller, having lavished praise on everything she saw, including us, proceeded out without any further remarks. But there were others who, when they saw four children good as gold, did not see beyond their size, and asked my mother in outspoken horror, 'How can you bear to let children loose in a lovely house like this?'

Every time it happened we were terrified. What would happen to us if my mother decided her house was too good for us and she hated the sight of us? What would we do, where would we go, would we starve?

My mother looked at our stricken faces, and her own face softened and her eyes filled with love. Then she would say to her inquisitor, though she did not say it rudely, 'The children don't belong to the house. The house belongs to the children. No room says, *Do not enter.*'

I did not know I could ever forget those sentiments. But once, to my lasting regret, I did. With the passage of years I took my place with grown-ups, and there was another generation, among them the little girl, Sis, who was my mother's treasure. The summer she was eight was the one time I forgot that a child is not subordinate to a house.

We had a cottage in the Highlands of Oak Bluffs of unimpressive size and appearance. My mother loved it for its easy care. It couldn't even stand in the shade of our city house, and there certainly were no special rules for children. No one had ever looked aghast at a child on its premises.

Except me, the summer I painted the sun parlor. I am not a painter, but I am a perfectionist. I threw my whole soul into the project, and worked with such diligence and painstaking care that when the uncounted hours ended I felt that I had painted the Sistine Chapel.

School vacation began, and Sis arrived for the long holiday, the car pulling up at the edge of the brick walk, and Sis streaking into the house for a round of hugs, then turning to tear upstairs to take off her travel clothes and put on her play clothes, and suddenly her flying feet braking to a stop in front of the sun parlor, its open door inviting inspection.

She who was always in motion, she who never took time for

a second look at anything, or cared whether her bed was smooth or crumpled, or noticed what was on her plate as long as it was something to eat – she, in the awakening that came when she was eight, in her first awareness of something outside herself, stood in the doorway of the sun parlor, her face filled with the joy of her discovery, and said in a voice on the edge of tears, 'It's the most beautiful room I ever saw in my whole life.'

I did not hear her. I did not really hear her. I did not recognize the magnitude of that moment. I let it sink to some low level of my subconscious. All I saw was that her foot was poised to cross the threshold of my chapel.

I let out a little cry of pain. 'Sis,' I said, 'please don't go in the sun parlor. There's nothing in there to interest a child. It's not a place for children to play in. It's a place for grown-ups to sit in. Go and change. Summer is outside waiting for you to come and play wherever you please.'

In a little while the sounds of Sis's soaring laughter were mingling with the happy sounds of other vacationing children. They kept any doubt I might have had from surfacing. Sis was surely more herself running free than squirming on a chair in the sun parlor.

All the same I monitored that room, looking for smudges and streaks, scanning the floor for signs of scuffing. The room bore no scars, and Sis showed no trace of frustration.

The summer flowed. My friends admired the room, though they did it without superlatives. To them it was a room I had talked about redoing for a long time. Now I had done it. So much for that.

The summer waned, and Sis went home for school's reopening, as did the other summer children, taking so much life and laughter with them that the ensuing days recovered slowly.

Then my mother's sister, my favorite aunt, arrived from New York for her usual stay at summer's end. She looked ten years younger than her actual years. She seemed to bounce with energy, as if she had gone through some process of rejuvenation. We asked her for the secret.

There was no way for us to know in the brimful days that followed that there really was a secret she was keeping from us. She had had a heart attack some months before, and she had been ordered to follow a strict set of rules: plenty of rest during the day, early to bed at night, take her medicine faithfully, carefully watch her diet.

She was my mother's younger sister. My mother had been her babysitter. She didn't want my mother to know that she was back to being a baby again, needing to be watched over, having to be put down for a nap, having to be spoon-fed pap. She kept herself busy around the clock, walking, lifting, sitting up late, eating her favorite foods and forgetting her medicine.

And then one day standing over the stove involved in the making of a meal that a master chef might envy, she collapsed, and the doctor was called, and the doctor called the ambulance.

She was in the hospital ten days. When she was ready to come home to convalesce, we turned the sun parlor into a sickroom, for the stairs to the upper story were forbidden to her. At night we who, when she slept upstairs, would talk family talk back and forth from our beds far into the night, without her we were now quiet, not wanting our voices to wake her if she was asleep, knowing her recovery depended on rest and quiet.

But at night she slept fitfully. The sleeping house and separation from the flock were unbearable. She was afraid of the sun parlor, seeing it as an abnormal offshoot from the main part of the house, its seven long windows giving access to so many imagined terrors. She did not know if we would hear her if she called. She did not know if she would ever get well.

She did not get well. She went back to the hospital, and for our sakes was brave in her last days, comforting us more than we comforted her.

When it was over, we took the sickbed away and restored the sun parlor to its natural look. But it did not look natural. The sadness resisted the sun's cajoling. It had settled in every corner. The seven long windows streaming light did not help. I closed the door and locked it.

My mother saw the closed door and the key in my hand. She said as a simple statement of fact, 'A little girl wanted to love that room, and you wouldn't let her. We learn so many lessons as we go through life.'

'I know that now,' I said. 'I wish I had known it then.'

Another summer came, and with it Sis. The sun parlor door was open again, the room full of light with the sadness trying to hide itself whenever she passed. I did not know how to say to her, 'You can go in the sun parlor if you want to.' I did not know whether she knew it had been a sickroom, and might say, 'Take your sun parlor and you-know-what,' though in less succinct phrasing. I did not know if she yet knew that nothing can be the same once it has been different.

Other summers passed, older family members died, and mine became the oldest generation. I was living on the Island year-round in the winterized cottage. The sun parlor was just another everyday room, its seven long windows reduced to three of standard size, most of the furniture replaced for sturdier sitting.

Sis was married, a mother, coming to visit when she could – coming, I think, to look for bits and pieces of my mother in me, wanting to see her ways, hear her words through me.

It was a year ago that I asked her the question that had been on my mind, it seems, forever. A dozen times I had bitten it off my tongue because I did not know what she might answer.

'Sis,' I said, 'do you remember the summer I painted the sun parlor and acted as if I thought more of it than I thought of you? I'm not asking you to forgive me. All I want to know is if sometimes my mother said to you when I went out, "She's gone."'

My mother always referred to me as 'she' when she was annoyed with me. '"She said she'd be gone awhile. You go play in that sun parlor if you want to. There's nothing in there you can hurt. Nothing in that room is worth as much as a child."'

I saw her lips beginning to part. And I felt my heart trembling.

'I don't want to know the answer. Please don't tell me the answer. I had to ask the question. It's enough for me that you listened.'

She smiled.

REMEMBRANCE

When I was a child of four or five, listening to the conversation of my mother and her sisters, I would sometimes intrude on their territory with a solemnly stated opinion that would jerk their heads in my direction, then send them into roars of uncontrollable laughter. I do not now remember anything I said. But the first adult who caught her breath would speak for them all and say, 'That's no child. That's a little sawed-off woman.'

That was to become a self-fulfilling prophecy. I have shrunk in size, a natural concomitant of my advanced years. That my enthusiasm for life and for people of all races and nations has not diminished is sufficient consolation.

In the year that I was five, perhaps because of my precocity, my mother took me to see the greatest evangelist of his time, Billy Sunday. My mother was not really a churchgoer, she did not assume a mantle of righteousness, and knowing that, her sisters made their faces severe and tried to dissuade her from taking so small a child to a large auditorium that was bound to be crowded beyond its capacity. But my mother stubbornly said that she wanted me to have that experience. She wanted me to remember that I had seen the great Billy Sunday.

I have never forgotten. We went early so that we could have

a seat down front, and I could see everything. An earlier service was still in progress. We stood just a few feet away from a large side door that led directly to the front rows. People began to pile up behind us, more people piled up behind them, then more and more people until there was a restless army – and probably none as small as me – packed together like sardines.

Suddenly the side door began to open, not inward but outward. Presumably other doors in other sections of the building had people inside and out trying to exit and enter at the same time. For there was now madness. And presently ambulances came clanging. There were cries of pain. And I heard my mother say to a man whose back was toward her, 'Mister, for God's sake, pick up my child before she gets crushed.' In a sorrowing voice, because he heard the anguish in my mother's, he said, 'Lady, I can't. I'm squeezed in so tight I can't even turn around.' Perhaps at that time I went into shock. Because all I remember after that is quietly sitting in the auditorium beside my mother, seeming to show no sign of distress, and looking at and listening to Billy Sunday with my mind a perfect blank.

But from that day and for years thereafter, I was terrified of evangelists. When television became a household habit I could not look at or listen to them without trembling. The emotion I had not shown on that terrible day always surfaced. Now I can stand the sight of an overzealous preacher, but I still cannot stand the sound of them. To me they stir up their followers and make them act crazy, flinging their arms around and going into fainting spells, the process becoming an anticipated ritual.

It was in that same year, as I recall, that my undaunted mother took me to see the moving picture version of *Uncle Tom's Cabin*. In my safe world I knew nothing of slavery, not even the word. She wanted *Uncle Tom's Cabin*, pictures on a silver screen, to prepare me for the truth of slavery and its heritage.

We went to the movies. I knew about movies. They were

stories told with pictures. We went often, and had lively discussions on the way home. The motion picture began, and we were both absorbed. I had never seen a movie before about white people and black people and their interplay. The white people looked happy and the black people looked sad. The white people looked rich and the black people looked poor.

Then there came a scene when a white man whipped Uncle Tom, and Uncle Tom just stood and took the beating. And I was suddenly aware that my mother was crying softly. Gently I patted her knee. It is still very vivid to me. I said softly, 'Don't cry. It's not real. It's make-believe. No man would beat another man. You said only children fight because they don't know any better.'

When we were walking home, she could have told me, 'I was crying because it was real.' Perhaps she decided I was not ready to be told. I was not yet ready to bear the burden of my heritage. In this week I have watched the television series *Eyes on the Prize*, a documentary about the racial unrest of the sixties. And I have wept as my mother wept because it was real.

AN ADVENTURE IN
MOSCOW

The Moiseyev Dance Company of Moscow was on tour in this country, and it brought to my mind a bittersweet memory of the world-renowned Bolshoi Ballet and the evening in Moscow that I spent in the company of its dancers, an enchanted evening that was to end in my humiliation and a torrent of tears. Though the other young Americans with whom I had come to Russia were present, by some mysterious process I had been selected to be the center of attention.

It was very flattering and I was in a state of euphoria until the filmmaker Sergei Eisenstein, the host of this gathering, who, in this period of the 1930s, was acknowledged the film-maker without equal across the world, said to me in the kindest, coaxing voice, 'Will you dance for me?'

A little amused by the question, I said politely and pleas-antly, 'I don't dance.'

Still quietly, still gently, he asked me again to dance. Again I murmured a refusal. The exchange went on for fifteen minutes or more, though it seemed like a day and a night to me, and perhaps to him.

Finally, his face and voice full of wrath, his patience com-pletely exhausted, he rose to his feet and bellowed at me in a voice like God's, 'I am the great Sergei Eisenstein, and you *will* dance for me.'

It was then that I burst into tears and fled from the room. I had never danced alone in my life. In my childhood I had learned to dance – little boys and little girls awkwardly clutching each other – under the calming eye of a dance teacher. It was one of the expected parlor accomplishments, designed to make all proper children feel at ease in social situations. I knew no dance steps that would fit the exigency that I was quite literally facing. There was only one way out. And I took it.

I flung myself down the stairs, half hoping I would break my neck and never have to see the sun rise on Moscow again. There were steps racing behind me, and as I reached the outer door, four young male dancers of the corps de ballet caught up with me, their eyes full of sympathy for my tears.

We walked five abreast with locked arms. They did not speak English; I have a tin ear and spoke no Russian. We did not talk, but we sang Russian songs all the way to my hotel, they lustily singing the words, I joyously da-da-da-ing along with them, my tears dried, my heart mended, the evening restored.

I had come to Russia with a group of twenty-one young black Americans, the youngest just turned twenty-one, the oldest, I think, hardly more than twenty-five, to make a movie about the black condition in America. The film company Mesrephom had invited bona fide black actors to come to Russia, but all of them had declined. Though jobs on the stage or screen were scant for black actors, the paper rubles that Russia offered them would not buy them a cup of coffee when they returned to America.

The offer was going begging until it sifted down to a group of adventuresome spirits, among them Langston Hughes, prose writer and poet, and Henry Lee Moon, who wrote fairly regularly for *The New York Times* and thought the experience would make good copy. They asked me to come along because they liked me. I liked the idea because I liked them.

The nineteenth-century Russian writers were my gods of good writing, Fyodor Dostoyevsky becoming my master when I was fourteen and made my discovery of what the word *genius* meant in the very first book of his that I read. Russia had become communist, a state of being that for me was not the solution to man's dilemma, but having learned from the Russian writers that salvation lay in the soul, I was glad to leave New York for a time and re-examine my own soul.

We arrived in Russia, were greeted warmly, were well fed and well housed. Langston, as our resident writer, was asked to read the script and give his opinion. The script had been written by a Russian, and the writing fell far short of the intent. It was Langston's assignment to rewrite it, a task which he undertook with reluctance, and despair that it would ever come out right.

During that waiting period one of the pleasures planned for us was the meeting with Sergei Eisenstein. And until that moment of disaster I had been, to all appearances, the most popular person at the party. Every dancer of the ballet asked me to dance with him. I never sat down once. I felt as light as a feather. My pride in myself was monumental. Then came the moment when one by one the other couples left the floor, leaving my partner and me to whirl about the room alone.

Suddenly my partner slowed, stopped, eased me out of his arms, kissed my hand, and left me standing alone on the floor, the center of an endless expanse of Russian eyes. I stood there frozen to the spot. There was thunderous applause, meant, I suppose, to be encouraging. When Sergei Eisenstein thought I was sufficiently encouraged, he asked me to dance. The rest, of course, has already been recorded.

The next day some sorrowful member of my group tried to explain that what had been planned as a mild joke on me to unsettle my natural reserve had gotten out of hand. Word of dancing achievements – I couldn't even tap – was passed from mouth to mouth until it got way out of bounds, and I became an event, the reigning jazz dancer in America, known in every major city. But I had one fault. I was so excessively modest when not onstage that I would never dance offstage when asked. Indeed I would deny that I could dance. I had to be coaxed to a tiresome degree, though in the end it was worth it.

It was not worth it to Sergei Eisenstein. I never asked who had thought up the joke. Had it been someone I trusted, it would have hurt me too much. Had it been someone I was so-so about, it would have made our proximity intolerable to me.

Two weeks later I received an invitation to a dinner party. I did not know, or I could not place, the people who invited me. But it was not unusual to be invited to a party by people who wanted to know an American better and polish their English.

I found my hosts and their guests charming and worldly. It was a lovely gathering. At one point I happened to glance at the dinner table. I saw my place card, and the place card nearest it bore the name of Sergei Eisenstein.

I could not embarrass myself again by running out of the room. Instead I prepared myself to meet my enemy. In Russia it is said that five shots of vodka drunk one after the other will help you achieve anything.

I drank my five vodkas, with everybody laughing and cheering and calling me a true Russian. I was young. I was healthy. I didn't blink an eye. I must admit that to this day I don't know how I did it.

There was an excited murmur. Sergei Eisenstein had entered. Unconsciously I think the guests formed two lines with Eisenstein walking between them, being greeted on each side with the honor that was due his genius. I deliberately stood at the end of the line, and when he reached me my five vodkas gave me courage to say in clearest tone, 'Ah, the great Eisenstein has arrived,' and make a very low bow.

He reached for my hand, kissed it, and said, 'I want to beg

your pardon. I know now that a joke was played on you. I am sorry I was made a part of it. Will you forgive me?'

I remember saying in what came out as a childish voice, 'You didn't believe me. And I never tell lies.' (And in those days I didn't.) Then I gave him a smile that swelled straight from my heart.

I'm certain it was he who asked his hosts to invite me to their party, and to seat me beside him for one of the most memorable evenings of my life. He had brought stills, wonderful stills, of his current pictures, and we sat together while I marveled. I know that I was fortunate to be in his presence. I am not unmindful.

We never made the movie. It had become general knowledge that a movie on the black condition in America was being planned. America had not yet recognized Russia. And an American engineer who was building a great dam for them vowed that if Russia went on with the movie, he would bring his own work to a stop, and advise the President to postpone or withhold recognition.

There was much sabotage in Russia in those years when she was reaching for the stature of a world power. One did not have to be a communist to work in Russia. Russia desperately needed the skills of skilled foreigners. Germans, Americans, Englishmen, Frenchmen were invited for their skills, not their sympathies with the communist cause, and with the hope that they would complete a project instead of sabotaging it. Russian suspicion of foreigners may have started in those highly crucial years. And outsiders' suspicion of Russia may have started in those years, too. It is true that when one had something to say, it was better to say it outdoors.

THE CART

One morning in the summer that my nephew Bud was seven and here on school holiday, he went walking in the nearby woods and came across a wooden box. A wooden box has many possibilities, though at that moment Bud could not think of one. Nevertheless he brought it home as being too important a find to leave behind. He felt confident that my mother, who, in his unsophisticated judgment knew everything, would tell him what to do with his discovery.

It was her voice, rising from the region of the side yard, that waked me. My mother often engaged in overstatement. She was doing so now.

'You want to know what to do with a wooden box? I'm sure you're the only boy in the world who's ever asked that question. Every boy in the world knows the answer.'

His voice was humble. 'Do I have to guess or will you tell me?'

'You'd probably give me a dozen wrong guesses. It will save my time to tell you straight out. Every other boy in the world would make a cart.'

Every boy but himself could make such a miracle come to pass. He said in self-defense, 'A cart has to have wheels and stuff. I haven't got any wheels and stuff.'

'I can see that as well as you can.'

His voice was inquiring, not brash. 'So?'

'So we take the next step.'

'What next step?'

'We go find some.'

'Where?'

'I know where. Come on.'

In the side yard there was silence now. My mother and Bud had gone to whatever hideaway place where the wheels would materialize. After a while I heard them returning and the sound of something being rolled across the lawn. Curiosity compelled me out of bed, into my robe, and down the stairs. Then, walking quietly into a room that overlooked the side yard, I could see the enterprise in progress. My mother and that boy and an assortment of tools were wrestling with the wheels of my aunt's wheelchair.

The year before, my mother's sister Carrie had suffered a stroke and taken to a wheelchair. When my mother got tired of seeing her let a wheelchair control her existence, she took it out from under her, handed her a cane and told her to get going. And indeed the cane would fit her into places that her wheelchair could not, and give her more freedom of movement.

When the splendid wheels had been wrenched away, both of them stood back for a moment, my mother to take stock, the boy to glow.

'All right,' said my mother, 'let's start.'

'Where do I start?'

'With your common sense.'

For the time it took them to turn a wooden box into a moving vehicle, my mother never stopped admonishing the boy for picking up the wrong tool, for asking what she called 'fool questions,' for taking ten minutes to do what should have taken ten seconds. She rarely lifted a finger to help him. She made him do it all himself, do and undo until he got it right.

My mother's face was deep pink with impatience, a clear indication that her pressure was rising. The boy's face was a deeper pink as he fought to hold back his tears over what my mother was constantly telling him was a 'fool mistake.'

A half-dozen times I started to rap on the window to attract my mother's attention and make a fiery speech about all that great to-do about a wooden box. As soon as I could dress, I would take the boy downtown and buy him a red cart. Every little boy in the world was entitled to a store-bought cart.

But time and again something stayed my hand, some feeling that I had no right to take part, that I must be a silent witness, and no more. Finally it was over. My mother said, 'Well, boy, it's done, and you did it yourself. Always remember you made it yourself. Go try it out, and don't kill yourself.'

A look passed between them that I could not fathom. I turned away and went upstairs.

For the rest of that summer, Bud was the golden boy of the neighborhood. No other boy had a moving vehicle made by his own hands. Everybody wanted a ride. Going to the beach took second place.

Then the summer was over. It was time for the round of goodbyes. Bud's best friend, Eddie, said that he was going to get a bicycle for Christmas. Bud said joyfully that he was, too.

But when I met Bud at the boat he got off without a bicycle. I didn't go into the why of it. His parents had married young. They could not always keep their promises. I did not want him running behind Eddie's bike like an orphan. We stopped at the bicycle store and bought what I could afford. As far as Bud was concerned there was nothing more he could want.

For the most part, the little cart stayed snug in its nesting place, on occasion surfacing when some younger child asked to play with it, and my mother giving firm instructions about its return before sundown.

She would grumble to me, 'That's Bud's cart.' I would reply,

'He'll never play with it again. Why don't you give it to the next nice child who asks for it.'

She would say grimly, 'Over my dead body.'

Bud entered his teens, then his mid-teens, no longer coming to stay all summer, but working for an uncle in the city, and coming weekends when he could. He and my mother would sit together on the back porch and talk, that communication between an older generation and one much younger.

A young mother, a charming new friend, whose summer cottage was some distance away from mine, asked if her children could play with the cart for the few remaining weeks that they were here. Her children had seen my neighbor's children playing with it and had been entranced. I said of course, without adding the burdensome imposition that they bring it back every sundown.

Fall came, the young mother left, and the cart went with her. She wrote me an endearing little note and sent me a handsome present, explaining that her children were in tears when she told them they must take the cart back. They wouldn't stop crying until she put it in her station wagon. She would bring it back next summer, and she wished me a good winter.

That was the winter my mother died. I wrote Bud's mother that I didn't want him to come. I wanted him to remember her strong and well and full of talk and laughter.

But I was haunted by that cart. I do not really know why. Through the rest of that winter, the feeling of guilt recurred. Bud had not mentioned the cart to me in years. But I could not forget the morning he made it and their remembered faces.

He came that summer. He came on a late boat, and there was a party to go to. He was in and then out of the house. He did not mention my mother, and I sensed it was because he could not.

The next morning he left the house before I waked. He loved to take an early swim, to have the beach to himself, with his thoughts turning inward. He came back. I was on the back porch. I think now he must have looked for his cart, and had not found it. He said to me very quietly, 'Where is my cart?'

I had read it in books, but had never believed it, and had certainly never experienced it. My heart lurched. There really is such a feeling. I wanted to make a full confession. 'I lent it to somebody who didn't bring it back.' Now I wanted absolution.

'That's okay,' he said, the way he used to say it when he was a little boy, and he didn't want you to know how much he was hurting.

'Do you remember the morning you made that cart? She never forgot it. We talked about it often and always in a loving way.'

'Nobody else had ever helped me make anything. It was one of the happiest days in my life.'

He had remembered the good part and forgotten the rest, which is the dictate of wisdom.

ELEPHANT'S DANCE

In 1925 he came hopefully from the West Coast. He was twenty-five, and the Negro literary 'renaissance' was in its full swing. He wanted to get on the crowded lift and not get off till it skyrocketed him, and such others as had his ballast of self-assurance and talent, to a fixed place in the stars. He died on Welfare Island ten years later, with none of his dreams of greatness fulfilled. Yet the name of Wallace Thurman is more typical of that epoch than the one or two more enduring names that survived the period.

He was Wallie to his friends, and his sycophants were legion. He could 'dish it out' and there was no tongue that could return it. Perhaps if Harlem had produced his disillusion in drink, under his leadership something better might have come out of that period than the hysterical hosannas that faded on the subsequently stilly night.

Thurman was a slight man, nearly black, with the most agreeable smile in Harlem and a rich, infectious laugh. His voice was without accent, deep and resonant; it was the most memorable thing about him, welling up out of his too frail body and wasting its richness in unprintable recountings.

Oscar and Beulah Thurman had been responsible for his birth in Salt Lake City, Utah, on a hot August day in 1902.

They were a mismated pair and indifferent parents. He was soon turned over to his maternal grandmother, who raised him and gave him as much love as was left to an aging woman who had been drained by her own brood.

Thurman had come into the world the unwanted shade of black. He was not his mother's pride and joy, and his undesirability was made apparent to him. In his book *The Blacker the Berry*, the dedication reads: 'To Beulah, the goose who laid the not-so-golden egg.'

He was determined to be a success, and through inclination chose the spectacular field of writing. His father was rapidly rolling downhill, and his mother was adding little to the family luster by her uncertain occupation in another city. In Thurman's mind, to the handicap of color was added the tremendous task of overriding his heritage.

He read about the goings-on in New York, where Negroes and whites were mingling socially to discuss that elephant's dance, Negro writing, remarkable not so much because it was writing, but because it was Negro writing.

He was twenty-three, and had just received his Bachelor of Arts degree from the University of California, where he had gone after four gainful years at the University of Utah.

He was writing a column called 'Inklings' in *The Pacific Defender*, a Negro paper, doing pieces of topical interest on mildly controversial subjects, when wind of the 'renaissance' blew West. He got very excited about it and was young enough to feel inspired. There in New York people like Carl Van Vechten, Fannie Hurst, H. L. Mencken, the Van Dorens, and others equally well known were talking shop with newly arrived young Negroes no older and maybe no wiser than himself. Their things were being published and hailed as masterpieces. Contests were in progress, and hotels heretofore closed to Negroes were hired for the award presentations.

Calling on the young Negro college graduates who were his

contemporaries, Thurman tried to organize a literary group in Los Angeles. His friends, however, had not followed the Eastern activities with his interest. He tried to be a movement all by himself, and started a paper, which he personally financed. It failed, but he had a lot of fun doing it. After this abortive attempt to revolutionize the West, Thurman headed East.

Countee Cullen, Langston Hughes, Zora Neale Hurston, Bruce Nugent, Rudolph Fisher, Jean Toomer, Eric Walrond were the new names. Thurman was later to say of Cullen, '[He] looms forth as the premier poet. There is a great possibility of his running dry, that is of exhausting his fund of inspiration.' And of Hughes, '[He] is by far the most original of the poetic group, if not a conscious craftsman. His potential worth is unpredictable and immeasurable.' Jean Toomer, Thurman felt, was the only Negro writer who had the elements of greatness. Toomer, however, has written little since his memorable *Cane*, and is far removed from Negro living.

A few older writers, Jessie Fauset, James Weldon Johnson, Walter White, Claude McKay, had preceded the renaissance. Although they were writers to be reckoned with, their age and activities set them apart from this younger group whose high spirits kept it on a continual round of gaieties. When the dawn came up like thunder, the new luminaries were still ablaze. Thurman fitted patly into this gayer crowd. Only Cullen, remote in his lyricism from the primal earthiness which Thurman extolled, looked at him askance.

There were a brief three months after his arrival when Thurman had no job and very little money. He said of that period, 'I knew only one person in New York, and I wandered around for two or three months. Then I got a newspaper job, but the newspaper failed. Then I landed on the *Messenger* [Negro magazine now defunct, then under the capable editorship of A. Philip Randolph]. Then I was offered a job on *The World Tomorrow*, as circulation manager.'

The intermittent periods of unemployment did not matter, for that was the great sponge era; you ate at anyone's meal-time, and conveniently got too tight to go home at your host's bedtime. There were other means of survival. Downtown whites were more than generous. You opened your hand; it closed over a five spot. Or you invited a crowd of people to your studio, charged them admission, got your bootlegger to trust you for a gallon or two of gin, sold it at fifteen cents a paper cup, and cleared enough from the evening's proceedings to pay your back rent and your bootlegger. There was usually sufficient money left to lay in a week's supply of liquor and some crackers and sardines.

Thurman had settled in a private house, whose owner, a Negro woman realtor, thereupon turned it into a haven for the serious as well as for the pseudo litterateur. She was greatly attracted to Thurman because he was educated and knew with growing intimacy the Negro writers whose names had heretofore been only a bright legend to her. Thurman's room with kitchenette, which his landlady called a studio, became the gathering point for whoever had the price of a pound of bologna or could contribute toward a jug of gin.

The landlady acquired the habit of dropping in, which had its advantages, since her sociability made it hard for her to be un-social about the rent. She soon confessed her literary aspirations, however, and brought in her manuscripts expressly for approval. When an escaping splutter from Thurman released the pent-up laughter of the others, she was deeply wounded. Then and now a race-conscious woman, she cooled toward Thurman when his widening circle began to include unknown whites who were seen too often and at too odd hours coming in and out of the house. Thurman found another furnished room.

Later this landlady provided comic relief in his novel *Infants of the Spring*. When she recognized her likeness, she was loud in her reproaches. Voicing her feelings in the Negro press, she stated that should Thurman ever dare cross her path, she would yank him into her house, put him to bed until he sobered – she swore he would be drunk as always – and spend a satisfying morning telling him exactly what she thought of him. They did not meet, which was a pity, for each was genuinely fond of the other.

Thurman's first job on the Negro periodical *The Looking Glass* lasted long enough for the appearance of his review of *The New Negro*, Alain Locke's analysis of the flourishing period. Of this book Thurman wrote, 'In it [*The New Negro*] are exemplified all of the virtues and all of the faults of this new movement, even to a hint of its speciousness. Many have wondered what this Negro literary renaissance has accomplished other than providing white publishers with a new source of revenue, affording the white intellectuals with a 'different' fad and bringing a half a dozen Negro artists out of obscurity.'

He was acquiring cynicism already and biting the hand that was feeding him. To him there were only one or two whites who did not patronize. The rest were exploiters, and since they were the important people, one must either wrap a handkerchief around one's head or steadily insult them. This last, which was Thurman's way, they found amusing, for they considered the Negro a childish creature not to be taken seriously. Thurman was a bad boy and therefore doubly endearing. Where the others were sometimes too docile, he was full of delightful surprises.

His attitude was no deterrent to job-getting and, although he continued to sponge on his friends, he was rarely unemployed. It was his way to carry a check for days, invite a succession of friends out for the evening, show them the check and bewail his inability to identify himself to the waiter. His guests would pay the bill. Since he was always stimulating, neither party was the loser. He rarely tried this trick with his own young friends. Instead he would invite a string of them to join him as his guests, and an unsuspecting downtowner would foot the bill for

the lot of them. The fall guy would expand with simple kindness while Thurman and his coterie went into peals of laughter
which he imagined were peculiar to Negroes after a hearty
meal.

Thurman was writing steadily, but just as steadily his life was
growing more hectic, and his philosophy more confused. It was
his nature to pull the pedestal out from under the plaster gods
of other people .

He hated Negro society, and since dark skins have never
been the fashion among Negro upper classes, the feeling was
occasionally mutual. In *The Blacker the Berry* the dark-skinned
heroine suffered many of the humiliations he would not have
admitted having suffered himself. The book's intent is satirical,
but because of angry overemphasis it becomes a diatribe. He
makes his black heroine more than a little unsympathetic, and
color screams from every page. He appears in the book as
Truman Walter, describing himself as 'a small, slender, dark
youth with an infectious smile and small features.' It is an accu-
rate description, and the only complimentary one of a black
person in the book. To the social group which he despised the
book was not revelatory, for Thurman was never humble or
apologetic, and he laughed very hard when things hurt him
most.

Negro society was taking itself very seriously in those days.
Carl Van Vechten's *Nigger Heaven* was thought to be a documentary record of the way its wheels went round, and Harlem
had become a mecca for the thrill-seekers. Downtowners sought
any means to gain entree to uptown parties. Van Vechten could
hardly lead the throng, for his unfortunate choice of title for his
book, the exotic types he had portrayed as typifying Negro society, the whole exposé, caused a quick successive slamming of
doors by all but the few close friends from whom he had drawn
his chief characters.

Harlem, however, had had a taste of white patronage and

had found it sweet to the palate. There was no party given which did not have its quota of white guests. The artists were the liaison group. They were not exactly an exemplary lot, but they knew the downtowners. A carefully worded note from a Harlem hostess, requesting them to bring a friend, color unimportant, would be correctly interpreted.

It was Thurman's delight to take a whole entourage of whites, some of them sleazy, to these parties. He earned the enmity of many hostesses by his companions' silly behavior and his own inability not to pass out and be carried bodily from a party. The conservative group disinherited him. Though he despised them for their insularity and their spring of privileged whites, still he allowed himself to personalize their changed attitude and to believe it was his black skin that had made him déclassé. He mocked their manners and their bastard beginnings, and divorced himself completely from a conventional way of life.

It was during this period that he first read Thomas Mann's *Magic Mountain*. Comparing as best he could the decaying European culture which Mann depicted and the confusion of life among the Negro upper classes, he urged his followers to read the book carefully. His enthusiasm bore fruit, and it was not long before his intimate friends, and those who received the suggestion secondhand, were walking through the streets and going to call with copies of *The Magic Mountain* under their arms.

Negro leadership was vested in the upper classes and Thurman could see little hope for the future from his observation of the imitative behavior of the men and women of this class. His social renunciation of them was quickly followed by intellectual renunciation, crystallized for the first time. He was equally hard on the nationalists and miscegenists, but he had no personal theory which he could substitute for those which he rejected.

Thurman's life and emotions were increasingly complex. He

began to surround himself with a queer assortment of blacks and whites of the lost generation. They clung to him like leeches, and although he saw them clearly and could evaluate them in a half dozen brutal words, he chose to allow them to waste the valuable hours of his ripening maturity. In his book *Infants of the Spring* which tells their sad mad story, Thurman, who was admittedly the prototype of the hero, spoke in character when he wrote, 'I cannot bear to associate with the ordinary run of people. I have to surround myself with individuals, unusual individuals, who for the most part are more than a trifle insane. Unless buttressed by stimulating personalities I am lost, no matter how despicable or foolish those personalities may appear in retrospect. They are the life of me . . . I am forced to surround myself with case studies in order not completely to curdle and sour.'

His way of living was almost wholly on the tawdry side. His friends were no longer confined to his writing colleagues. The profitless conversations and philosophical discussions which resulted in nothing constructive had finally wearied him. Now he held open house for the precious young men who were his new satellites, and had no privacy except in the rare moments of rage when he turned them out of his room, thoroughly castigated himself, and wrote for an uninterrupted stretch of forty-eight hours. Occasionally, too, he escaped to the suburban home of a married friend, and lived in peace and normalcy until a writing job was finished.

In the suburban home his sanity returned, and he always came back to the city with a sense of something lost. There was a child in that suburban haven whom Thurman loved. He wanted a child and was afraid that he had wasted his energy and would never be a father. He wanted to be thoroughly male and was afraid that he was not. He looked about his narrowing circle, and of the few women on the fringe of that group, there was none whom he would have wed.

Suddenly in the summer of 1928 he married. It was precipitous and provided a comic morsel for his entourage for months. Inevitably, he chose the first fresh face that pierced the thick fog of his horizon. The marriage was ill-fated from the start. Thurman uprooted himself and went housekeeping with his bride and her mother. His wife had been a teacher of business in a Negro college. Lately arrived in New York, she was thoroughly unfamiliar with bohemianism. Other women, however, were marrying artists and firmly entrenching themselves in Negro society. Thurman's possibilities were realizable enough to make him a desirable husband.

The marriage lasted about six months. Thurman had long wanted to be a father, but he had not taken into consideration that he must first be a husband. When he did, it was too late to unlearn his oft-repeated philosophy of doing everything once before he died. Habits had taken hold of him that heretofore he would not have admitted were habits. He missed the drinking sessions, the all-night talk fests, the queer assortment of queer people, and the general disregard for established customs.

Under the announcement of his marriage in his scrapbook is penned, 'Proof that even the best of us have weak moments.' That was braggadocio. With the failure of his marriage Thurman, for the first time, became uncertain of himself. Scandalous things were said about the disunion. Nothing was salvaged out of the nightmarish months. The people who aligned themselves with Thurman were the people to whom nothing was scandalous. To them he was not the marrying kind. This proved it. The disastrous interlude was over and better forgotten.

His wife had left his home the night before his collaborated play, *Harlem*, opened on Broadway. On opening night, he went around to the flat of some friends with his tie and collar in his hand. He was sober but too shaken to manipulate his collar or to tie his bowknot. He had wanted his wife to share in what he hoped would be his triumph, or to go out with him and get drunk in the event of a cold reception. That she could desert him at a crucial hour did not make him see that she was as much a failure as a writer's wife as he was as a conventional husband.

She took very seriously the embarrassment of the breakup and went through a period of utter instability. Later she made a complete about-face, replaced her old gods, and became an active worker in the labor field.

With *Harlem* already in the back of his mind, Thurman had gone into the Theatre Guild's Negro drama, *Porgy*, in the hope of learning the rudiments of stagecraft. His was a walk-on part, and his salary was sixteen-fifty weekly. He fought vigorously for an increase in pay for the supers. The fight was won one week before he quit the company to sit in at the rehearsals of *Harlem*. Some months later his own cast made capital of this fight when it waged a similar one of its own.

Thurman collaborated with William Jordan Rapp on *Harlem*, which was a vivid cross section of lower-middle-class life. The play ran with fair success in New York and Chicago. He and Rapp had met at Macfadden Publications, where both were employed.

While working at Macfadden's at Broadway and Sixty-third Street, Thurman would visit nearby friends on Sixty-sixth Street. It became a regular routine, for he was free from Macfadden's by lunchtime. Over a table of odds and ends, occasionally augmented by his own contributions of a bottle half full of bathtub gin, for he was fond of these friends, he would laughingly give detailed synopses of the more lurid stories that were polished by his pen. Then he would settle down to a fantastic tale of his own, and, growing fascinated by his own fabrication, would ask for pad and pencil. Later the completed story would appear with some such pathetic caption as 'I Was a Child-Bride.'

Thurman's chief interest was magazine editing. The idea of a well-established magazine kept him hopeful when his ghost-writing and hack writing would have plunged him into deepest despair. Had he found sustained support for a literary publication, it is probable that he would have given up creative writing, which was not his proved forte, for critical analysis, in which his judgment was sound.

Under his guidance the young writing crowd had launched two literary magazines. The first, *Fire*, so christened by Zora Neale Hurston, appeared in 1926. Thurman outlined the magazine's aims when he said, '[It] is a declaration of independence directed at certain cliques of blacks and whites who would shape our destinies. It is also a reply to the accusation we make ourselves that the present art boom is a mere fizzle. We seek to sift it down and preserve those elements in it worth preserving. And again it is a revolt against the conventional type of contemporary Negro magazine, pulsing with propaganda but devoid of art.' When queried as to whether or not he felt there was a distinctly Negro art, his answer was, 'No, not a definite, distinctly Negro art. But because of the differences in the Negro's background, there will be differences in what he writes and paints. There is bound to be a Negro note, but not a Negro art.'

The first issue of *Fire* cost a dollar a copy, and the several hundred copies were sold immediately. They were sold, however, to the friends and well-wishers of the editorial staff, whose members included Langston Hughes, Zora Neale Hurston, Aaron Douglas, and others less well known. Much of the material was oversensational. Where the friends of this group could regard these outpourings with indulgence, the wide audience which the magazine needed for its support rejected them because they were too far removed from ordinary, conventional experience. Thurman, as chief editor, had mistaken the shadow for the substance, and after its initial appearance, *Fire* was extinguished.

After a two-year interval, *Harlem*, subtitled *A Forum of Negro Life*, appeared. With a creditable sum at his disposal, Thurman unwisely decided to run the magazine on a large scale. He rented an office on Seventh Avenue, installed a telephone, and called in several young writers without commitments to help with the business of running the magazine. Carfare, cigarettes, occasional meals, and loans rapidly depleted their capital.

Aware now that any successful magazine must of necessity draw its support from a wide audience rather than from a select group, *Harlem* was less esoteric than *Fire* had been, and its appeal was broader. It was twenty-five cents a copy, and included older writers among its contributors. While the magazine was not lacking in favorable response from readers, expenses increased disproportionately with returns on distribution. After the second issue, *Harlem* folded.

The late Elisabeth Marbury was one of the few whites who met with Thurman's wholehearted approval. He met her one afternoon when he went with a group of writing friends to her home in Sutton Place. She received them like Queen Victoria on her throne, and Thurman was not amused. She was more nearly genuine than anyone he had lately met, and her tongue was as sharp as his. She liked Thurman best – though he made no effort to outshine the others – and wanted a hand in his writing career. She believed enough in his talent to advance him a generous sum to keep him in food and rent while he completed a novel. The novel was *Infants of the Spring*. His tribute is that she is nowhere in its pages.

In this novel is summed up Thurman's disillusion with the New York years. He writes of a typical party, '. . . the drunken revelry began to sicken him. The insanity of the party, the insanity of its implications, threatened his own sanity. It is going to be necessary, he thought, to have another emancipation to deliver the emancipated Negro from a new kind of slavery.'

Infants of the Spring was published when Thurman was thirty-two years old, two years before his untimely death. He knew now very definitely that he did not have the elements of genius. He did not even know whether or not he was a first-rate writer. He had begun to ponder the one-book appearance of Negro writers, and wondered if it was 'the result of some deep-rooted complex or merely indicative of a lack of talent.'

The truth was that for the most part the young writers of the period were not ready for publication. Thurman's two novels give evidence of this immaturity and incomplete experience. At that time publishers were vying with each other to bring out Negro books. Zora Neale Hurston, now an established novelist, had written a half dozen creditable short stories. Publishers pressed her for a full-length manuscript. She stoutly maintained that she was not ready to affix her name to a novel. Her contemporaries, including Thurman, insisted that she was simply lazy, and predicted that she would peter out as a writer.

Thurman knew that the traditional attitude of white America, despite its shift in emphasis during the period, was still such as to discourage by overpraise and specious evaluation any honest Negro writer's productive impulses. Yet he allowed himself to be exploited, and has left as heritage two imperfect books.

In 1933 he was chief editor of the editorial staff at the Macaulay Company. Through the publishers he met their lawyer-brother, A. A. Furman, and with him began his second collaboration, this time on a novel titled *Interne*. It was Furman's first novel and Thurman's last printed work. The book had little to offer save its sensational exposé of conditions on Welfare Island. It was cheap and poorly written. The characters were white, and of a class about which Thurman could know very little. There were many who did not believe he had a hand in writing this book, but his scrapbook gives evidence of material collected. He visited Welfare Island and for the first time in his New York years was shocked and horrified. He came away loud and bitter in his denunciation, and with the avowal never to set foot again in the place.

Furman introduced him to Bryan Foy, who had lately arrived from Hollywood, where he had been engaged in the making of class 'B' pictures. Thurman's work with Macfadden Publications had taught him what a large part of the public wanted. He was editor of Macaulay's, successfully turning out 'popular' fiction. These facts, with Thurman's congeniality, sold him to Foy. They talked about a contract over dinner in a downtown restaurant. It amused Thurman very much that, although John Barrymore's profile was on prominent display at a nearby table, it was he who was the object of all the ogling.

He left New York in February of 1934 with a contract from Foy Productions, Ltd., in his pocket. His first scenario was *High School Girl*, which had a fair run at the Astor. His second was *Tomorrow's Children*, a film on sterilization which was generally banned in New York. The story sessions in Hollywood were mad, and Thurman's nerves were shot. He hated the long-drawn-out, senseless discussions. On one occasion he became acutely ill through sheer physical revolt at the insane antics of his colleagues.

It was June when a doctor on the West Coast cautioned him about his health. He was losing weight and a cold he had caught one night on the beach persisted. He and the joy-seekers with whom he had quickly become allied would bathe and imbibe and, more often than not, fall asleep on the beach in their wet bathing suits and wake hours later in a chilly dawn.

Thurman knew that he had tuberculosis, but refused to consider living by rules for the rest of what might be a long dull life. Having been advised that he must give up all indulgences, he reasoned that death might come quickly if he didn't. Twice before he had attempted melodramatic suicides, and they had been fun rather than funereal. This time there would be no human hand to snatch him back from a theatrical finish.

He flew to New York, determined that his end should be spectacular. He arrived on a hot summer day in a flamboyant Hollywoodian costume and sounded an alarm on Seventh Avenue. He rounded up his friends, laughed more loudly than he ever had before, told unprintable tales of the cinema city, and refused to be left alone for a minute.

He was frightened and determined not to admit it. He got drunk, and stayed drunk, and talked very much and laughed very much, and would not face himself alone, nor sleep alone, nor say one serious thing.

One day he found himself faced with a solitary hour. After a tortured fifteen minutes which liquor could not lull, he climbed out uncertainly onto the fire escape and mounted the steps to the upstairs flat of a friend. She was not at home, and he knew that she would not be, but her window was open.

He went in, found that he did not feel so lonely among less familiar things, flung himself down on the unmade divan, tossed for a bit, and slept. When the friend returned she was neither surprised nor startled. She made him hot milk, which he drank with a grimace, and did not send him packing until he was satisfied that his unlocked door had been entered by the ghouls that gathered nightly for the death watch.

Suddenly he collapsed. Later, he found himself recovered from unconsciousness, and not dead. On a hot July first he lay in the incurable ward on Welfare Island. For six long months he lay there. They were the bitterest months of his life. Death was to be drawn out, and that last riotous month was only making it harder. He was too weak for anything but contemplation, and his thoughts, turning inward, probed little but waste. His friends fell away. Only a few visited irregularly. Only two continued faithful to the harrowing end in late December.

It was these two schoolteacher friends who were notified of his death. It was they who buried him. On Christmas Eve his wasted body lay in a Harlem funeral parlor. His family had telegraphed their inability to come East. His former wife, who learned of his death on the day of his burial, came hastily to his rites in a red coat.

So Thurman lived and died, leaving no memorable record of his writing, but remaining as the most symbolic figure of the literary 'renaissance' in Harlem. His death caused the first break in the ranks of the 'New Negro.' Assembled at the funeral in solemn silence, older, hardly wiser, they were reminded for the first time of their lack of immortality.

A DAY LOST IS A DAY
GONE FOREVER

There came a day in these later years of my life when I entered the hospital as an inpatient for the first time, with an operation scheduled for the next morning. Once various forms were signed, I was separated from my free will, led down the corridors into a room which was now to be the boundary of my existence, told to surrender my clothes, handed that comic invention, the hospital gown, and sent to bed in broad daylight like a child being stripped of her privileges.

In this unflattering way so ended my charmed existence of never having anything wrong with me that required a surgeon's knife. I trusted the surgeon's skills. His reputation confirmed his excellence. When we met in his office for the first time, there was a mutual liking. When his examination corroborated my doctor's opinion that surgery was advisable, I accepted the wisdom of that. The operation was said to be routine. There was no foreseeable reason for anything to go wrong.

Nevertheless there was an undercurrent of fear in me that I did not let show. It was not the surgery that I dreaded. It was the anesthesia, the settling into a long sleep with no fixed limitation. Suppose I couldn't wake up. Suppose my vital signs diminished. There, like my mother before me, I would lie between two worlds, the one I knew and fiercely treasured, and one in whose ranks I had no wish to be included.

It seemed to me that I was awake all night, remembering my mother and the hours of her dying, and knowing that, in my state of surrender, I too would have no strength to break death's hold. And for me there would be no unseen force to reach out in resurrection.

I must have slept a little, for the nurse had to wake me to prepare me for the stretcher, which was presently rolling me along the busy corridors to the operating area. It felt very strange to be exposed to so many disinterested eyes.

On my arrival a doctor appeared and introduced himself to me as my anesthetist. Both of us made graceful small talk to ease this sudden intimacy of strangers. Then he was ready to put me under. I closed my eyes and tried to blot out of my mind the recurring image of my mother that had so unsettled my night. Then suddenly I was enveloped in nothingness and the remembering stopped.

My operation was a success from start to suture. I wakened in due time, back in my room, not even remembering at first that I had ever left it. For there was no aftermath of pain, no feeling that death had stood close by. It had not been my bitter inheritance to suffer my mother's unrelenting sleep that propelled her hour by doomed hour toward the hell of dying for no reason that made sense.

The hospital had gone on alert. The good doctors and the good nurses were rushing back and forth, trying everything their training had taught them to make my mother live.

Until the day before her operation when she was signed in at the hospital, my mother, like me, had never been an inpatient. If she thought about hospitals at all, I suspect she thought of them as way stops for the elderly on their way to heaven. And she was in no hurry. She had a love affair with life. There was nothing more beautiful to her than a child, a flower, a summer's day, a friend. On the other hand heaven was an unknown risk.

The change in the pattern of her days came on an innocent winter morning when she was in the backyard feeding the birds. In a moment of inattention she tripped over a stone and fell. She picked herself up, continued to scatter seed for the birds who fed on the ground, then filled the hanging feeders for those birds who preferred to feast above ground and not have to be on constant watch for the neighborhood cats.

When she returned to the house, wisdom told her to call her doctor. The jolt of her fall had loosened a pain inside her more intense than the soreness of her surface bruises. I think she had felt warnings of that pain before, but not to that extent of hurting, and she had pushed it out of her mind, testing the theory that mind could overcome matter.

The doctor came and examined her. He knew her essential strength of mind and body. He did not mince words. He told her he was going to admit her to the hospital immediately for an operation that all signs seemed to indicate was imperative. It was all so sudden that I forgot, as did she, a tale that she had told me more than once about a frightening experience she had gone through when she was eighteen. To us both my mother in her sixties was so far distant from that girl in Springfield that she did not enter our thinking.

It was only when my mother was in the agony of dying and her death began to invade my own body, turning my flesh to ice, that I remembered the story.

When my mother was eighteen, with radiant health and a head full of dreams of a long and happy life, a tooth began to give her trouble. When home remedies were of no help and the pain persisted, she made an appointment with a dentist, who, upon examination, advised her that the tooth should be extracted.

She had no concern except the hope that it would cost no more than she had in her purse. When she was seated in the chair ether was administered, her eyes closed, the numbness set in, and the extraction began and ended as expected. So it appeared until the dentist began to talk to my mother and she didn't answer.

He raised his voice and said, 'You can open your eyes now, it's all over. If you feel a bit groggy just sit awhile. It will soon pass.'

Somewhere deep the words took root for later remembering though she could give no conscious sign of having heard. The dentist began to feel uneasy. He called her name sharply, but she did not respond. He opened a window, but the rush of air did not rouse her. He even tried lightly slapping her face, but still no reaction.

Time passed, and she did not stir. More time passed, and she went on sleeping. He did not want to call a colleague or a doctor and have them speculate on what he had done wrong. But he did not want to regret not having called them. It was a real dilemma.

Mercifully my mother waked, her strong, young body refusing to let her die with so much living undone. She snapped back into being, the pallor fading in her cheeks, the color rising, her hands no longer cold to the touch.

When my mother had her operation, she was, of course, put under ether, the anesthetic then in general use. Throughout her operation I sat in the waiting room with my good neighbor, Robert, whose blood was my mother's type as mine was not. In those years there was no blood bank in the hospital.

Robert, by nature a quiet man, a Yankee of generations of Yankees, did not expect me to make small talk. To keep a confident expression on my face, to smile in a reassuring way whenever our eyes met was the price I had to pay for being an adult. And Robert's being there when there were a dozen other things he had to do was the price he had to pay for being a caring person.

At last I saw my mother being wheeled out of the operating room. The surgeon came toward me smiling and was very pleased to tell me that the operation had been a complete success. In answer to my question about going to see my mother, he advised me that it was better to wait until the next day. When she waked, she would be tired and perhaps disoriented. It would be less strain for both of us if I gave her until tomorrow to get back to being herself.

Robert and I left the hospital; he was relieved for me and glad to have my good news to pass on to his wife, I expressing my gratitude for the comfort his presence had given me. We parted, he to go back to work, I to go home and do some walk-about chores to help me unwind.

But I could not erase the picture of my mother being wheeled down the corridor, her face without color, her body so still. She, who never wanted me to catch her sleeping ever since she overheard me say when I was five that mothers stayed awake all night to watch over their children, she was now rolling past me in a faraway world of her own, indifferent to my presence.

I went about the rest of the day trying to do some writing, but not really able to focus on anything that needed my full attention. I was really waiting for night to come and go, and morning to follow, so that my mother would be herself again in the world that she, as a child, had rushed outside to meet in the country morning, flinging her arms wide to gather every tree, every bird, every flower, every living thing around her in her fierce embrace.

Night came, and I was glad to go upstairs and get in bed with a book undemanding of my closest attention, and lull myself to sleep with the rhythm of its words. Just as I was beginning to drift into forgetfulness, my feet began to get cold. I rubbed them together in the hope that they would warm each other. Instead the cold began to creep up my legs.

I got up to check the house. Perhaps I had forgotten to lock the front door and it had blown open, or maybe a window had blown out, or the heating system had fouled itself up. But I found nothing at fault, and nothing was cold to my touch.

I went back to bed, and under the warm covers the cold continued to creep up my legs like no cold I had ever experienced. I had spent a winter in Moscow, where for a week the temperature was twenty-eight degrees below zero. I had cheerfully walked its streets while my American companions ran from tram to hotel with tears streaming down their cheeks.

This cold was beyond that. This cold now, creeping up my legs, now reaching my knees, was like death. And suddenly I knew that my mother was dying, and her dying was invading my body as a cry for help. I did not move from my bed. I did not move at all. But I never fought so hard in my life, commanding the cold to leave my body, and thus to leave hers.

I do not know how long it took before I began to feel it move, my knees no longer cold, my legs beginning to warm, and finally my feet free of their encasement of ice.

I jumped up and ran downstairs to the telephone. I called the hospital. A young woman answered. When I told her who I was and asked how my mother was, she gasped and dropped the telephone. The waiting for her to pick it up again was one of the longest waiting periods in my life. Finally she did, then said in a painful voice, 'I'll let you speak to your mother's doctor,' and put down the telephone again before I could respond.

How long I waited for the doctor to come to the telephone I do not know. In such situations one has no conception of time. Finally he came. I heard his voice, and I will remember it as long as I live. He sounded as if he had run a long race, a long, almost unendurable race. His voice was steeped in exhaustion. But he had won. He said, 'Your mother was dying. But she's all right now. Come and see for yourself tomorrow.

When I reached my mother's door, I could not bear to look.

I did not know that until my mother told me later that I came to the door, backed away, came to the door again and again backed away, and did not make it to her bedside until the third try.

I suppose it was because I did not know what she was going to look like. I did not know what the toll had been in bringing her back to life. But she was sitting up in bed, her eyes bright, her cheeks like pink roses, and her voice full of animation. She was in fact herself.

'How do you feel?' I asked.

'Fine,' she said. 'And just look at that beautiful sun. It was snowing this morning when I had my operation. And it's already stopped.'

I said gently, 'You had your operation yesterday morning. And after it you slept a lot.'

She said softly, 'Then I lost a day. At my age I can't afford to lose a day.'

'The whirlwind that you are, you'll make it up.'

Now in these years I am very aware of time. Now I know, too, that a day lost is a day gone forever. When I am wasteful of time, I do not forgive myself.

THE LEGEND OF OAK
BLUFFS

I t was once called Squash Meadow, this down-Island town, a
fine dimension of accommodating land, rich for farming,
with fields of native squash for Indian hands to harvest
when fall nudged the nodding earth toward its winter sleep.

It was the English who named the fertile tract Squash
Meadow, and the pond that nourished it Squash Meadow Pond,
'squash' distilled from the longer Algonquin word for it. Those
names are now buried in archives, the freshwater pond long
opened to the sea and called Lake Anthony, Squash Meadow
turned into a town of steamboat landings, gingerbread cottages,
and summer children on flying horses, whirling round and
round in the realm of forever remembering.

The Englishman who fathered the birth of Squash Meadow
was Thomas Mayhew of Watertown, a merchant by trade,
knowing a bargain when he saw one. He bought Martha's
Vineyard, Nantucket, and the Elizabeth Islands from two
Englishmen with royal grants for fifty pounds. To Mayhew the
land that would sustain a man best seemed to be Martha's
Vineyard, the name itself – for it was always so named – a guar-
antee of enduring benignity. His son, Thomas, Jr., and a group
of his friends bought their farm and forest tools and hunting
guns, and shaped a settlement out of the eastern end of the

island, calling it Great Harbour, and, in time, Edgartown.

In 1642 John Daggett, also English-born and a Watertown neighbor of Mayhew who was now taking part in the island adventure, purchased from Mayhew the five hundred acres of farmland known as Squash Meadow. Sometime thereafter his son, Joseph, having turned twenty and taken an Indian bride, felt ready to add another notch to his manhood with the stewardship of the Squash Meadow property.

Joseph became the first white man to build in Oak Bluffs, his squat, square house hard wrestled from oak and pine. He stayed on Squash Farm until the land was proud, his house was tight, his children flourishing. There was a new settlement called Takemmy, later to be the township of Tisbury. Joseph itched to move on to new ground, to feel its soil, to test its streams. His father had died and Squash Meadow was his inheritance. The choice was his to keep or sell. He sold it in several parcels. Among the new owners was one Simeon Butler, whose parcel included the beautiful grove that one day would be called the Camp Ground, a place whose future would be determined by religion.

The colony's established church was the Congregational Church in Great Harbour until 1795, when an evangelist named Jesse Lee, the father of New England Methodism, came to spread the new faith to a small gathering that numbered more curious than converts. But the scraggly meetings continued, sometimes in a borrowed house. Eventually week-long meetings were held on the grove during summer months and the numbers continued to grow. There were families who came two weeks before the meetings got under way and stayed two weeks after the closing, writing the association in advance of their coming to secure a favorite location beside familiar neighbors who were making the same request. Their children looked forward to playing together, to wading in the lake, to climbing trees, to eating together camp style outdoors.

Grown-ups and children alike began to look forward to escaping the city heat for a month or so on a breezeswept island, mixing prayer and innocent pleasure. These were the first summer people, though they would have been startled by that appellation. They had never taken vacations, as had few Americans, and they did not yet know they were doing it now.

With the association's permission the regulars began to build small board structures, not yet resembling the gingerbread cottages, but at least they could tell one board structure from another by some individual touch.

The gingerbread cottages began to be built around 1860, the cottages being owned by the families who built them, but the land, then and now, leased from the association for one hundred years. The association had received its charter from the Massachusetts legislature that year.

In that same period of time a huge amphitheater of sail cloth containing three thousand yards of canvas was erected in the center of the grove. In 1870 it was replaced by the huge iron tabernacle that was a wonder in its day.

The Baptists were the second-largest denomination on the Vineyard. They had come as missionaries to convert the Indians, then added the white population as souls in need of proselytizing. The Baptists did not meet the same resistance from the missionary Mayhews as had the Methodists, which may have been an indication that their raids on the Congregationalists did not yield the same harvest.

The success of the Methodist camp meeting emboldened the Baptists to approach the Methodists to suggest a summer coalition, the grove to be shared, the ministers alternated. The Methodists preferred to keep a good thing to themselves.

The Vineyard Grove Company was one of many real estate ventures. Boardinghouses and eating places began to border the Camp Ground to serve the onslaught of visitors coming not so much to seek a spiritual place in God's grace but to seek a summer place in his garden.

A group of wealthy mainland men purchased the land between the Camp Ground and the sea, and incorporated themselves into the Oak Bluffs Land and Wharf Company. They called that area Oak Bluffs, and laid out streets and avenues and lovely parks. Somewhere along this point the Camp Ground Association enclosed its thirty-six acres behind a seven-foot-high picket fence to separate the sacred from the noisy hordes of the secular.

There were now three prosperous summer settlements: the Camp Ground; the Highlands, its Baptist Temple the center-piece of a circle of cottages, continuously extending; and Oak Bluffs, with its waterfront of magnificent cottages, its elaborate hotels, its main street shops.

The tax money flowing into Edgartown was considerable, with the county seat complacently accepting it and doing nothing to deserve it. Oak Bluffs' nearest neighbor, Tisbury, was not more than a mile away, but the only access was by boat, a slow and inconvenient arrangement. Edgartown refused to build a bridge between the towns. But after much debate, petitioners presented a bill to the Massachusetts General Court compelling the county commissioners to build the bridge. Edgartown fought the petition, lost, and the bridge was built.

In the 1880s the first Portuguese settlement burgeoned in Oak Bluffs on rich land planted for market gardening. The area in which they lived was bound by Dukes County Avenue and County Road, and Vineyard Avenue and School Street.

The summer cottagers bought everything the Portuguese planting brought forth, as did the hotel, the boardinghouses, the restaurants. A prized crop was flowers. There was a feast of flowers. The summer people packed their porches and parlors. It seemed to be a summer pastime to see how many flower baskets and vases could squeeze into a given space.

There were spring and summer jobs for every able Portuguese, road work, opening cottages, readying lawns and yards, meeting the many boats, and carrying baggage to nearby houses or hotels. Women did housework, and there were those who did fine hand laundry. The summer ladies would ride through the Portuguese enclave looking for a sign that said 'Fine Hand Laundry.' Those were the years when starched clothes were a mark of distinction.

The summer people were Republican and reluctant to hire anyone who was not. They had no hesitation in asking a job-seeker about his politics. The Portuguese understood the question's intent. They did not want the summer jobs slammed shut in their faces, and winter's hunger to howl at their door. They said they were Republican, and in the next voter registration made sure that they were so inscribed. The town and the Island are still Republican.

Manuel De Bettencourt – that surname still prevails in its many branches – had been one of the first to own land in the Portuguese settlement. In many ways he was the liaison between the English and the Portuguese cultures, neither at odds with the other, both loosely joined in a pragmatic union of mutual need.

Manuel and Anna, his wife, had managed everything except a gift in the name of God. It troubled them. They and the others from the Azores who had settled on this bountiful land had much to be thankful for, and no sacred place in which to give thanks together. In their very own house, in their rarely used parlor, they made room for that sacred place. Manuel wrote to his former parish in New Bedford, asking with proper humility if there was some mainland priest who would come to say Mass whatever Sunday he could spare the time.

And so it was that every two weeks a priest arrived from the mainland. Then there began to be a feeling of loss, of double loss on the alternate Sundays. Like a rising chorus, talk of building a church began in a muted way, then soared to a crescendo. Quickly the talk turned into tithes. A building fund was started, swelled. A Catholic manservant purchased a building lot just around the corner from Manuel's house and donated the lot to the cause.

In a miracle of time the church was built and called the Sacred Heart. Across the street there was soon to be the Sacred Heart Rectory and the joyous affirmation of a priest in residence. The old church is now the Sacred Heart Parish Hall. A larger, more centrally located church is Our Lady Star of the Sea, its congregation, year-round and summer, of every social stratum, with an easy mingling of races.

The twenties were in giant-size bloom on the Island. Summer money fell like rain on all the towns, especially the down-Island towns, and notably Oak Bluffs, with its accessibility to steamboat landings, with its carriages and automobiles for hire, its Tivoli dance hall, its moving-picture houses, its bandstand in the park, and the Methodist Tabernacle, no longer a hotbed of fiery evangelists, but still an impressive place of assembly, with important guest speakers on a latitude of topics, and musical performances with gifted artists, and the magical, lantern-lit Illumination Night, as unique an experience as can be had.

Then it was 1929, and the stock market crash, and on its heels, the Depression. And for the decade following the crash Oak Bluffs suffered a lingering sickness of meager summers. It was the town hardest hit because it was the town whose summer business had been its only business. The great houses stood empty, too large to run without servants, and too few, if any, families who could still afford a staff. The hotels and shops that struggled to stay open were barely staying alive. 'For Sale' signs were everywhere, and there were no buyers. Those half-empty steamers discharged from their decks only those summer arrivals whose cottages had been family-owned into the fourth generation. They could not deny these fourth-generation children their birthright to an island summer and break the chain of privilege.

The non-WASPs were of such slight numerical strength that they had never come close to rocking the boat. Nor had they tried. They had kept a low profile, especially the little pockets of vacationing black Bostonians. It was a fine accomplishment for these early comers to the Island to own summer cottages, whatever their size, whatever their lack of inside conveniences. Kerosene lamps cast a lovely soft light. The backyard pump poured water sweeter than any from an indoor faucet.

That they could afford a cottage at all, that a black man could send his wife and children on a summer vacation was a clear indication that he had made a profitable place for himself in the white world, vaulting whatever color bar stood in his way. His motivations were a fierce sense of family and a proud acknowledgment of his role as its head.

In the Depression years there were enough of them established as summer residents to constitute a definable colony, devoutly committed to a yearly return at whatever sacrifice of winter's priorities, with whatever pared amount of vacation money, and with the most careful piecing together of summer clothes.

They were among that legion that adds adherents every summer, those who find the Island irresistible, and have to set foot on its waiting shore, and sift the white sand in a cupped hand, and smell that salt tang of the sea. This is the rite that purges them of all evil.

The genesis of the black colony was no more than a dozen families. From that group of cottagers the colony made slow but pervasive growth, drawing its component parts of acceptable people from Boston, New York, Philadelphia, Washington, and a scattering of other certifiable cities, excluding the Deep South cities because of an obsessive fear that the Deep South people might bring their attitudes of uncertainty to a place where blacks did not hang back to let the whites go first.

With Pearl Harbor, prosperity zoomed from high-rise to hovel, money became a common commodity, and those who had never had a cent to spare could look beyond the landlord's outstretched hand. New economic classes emerged and rapidly became aware that there were people in established classes who lived lives of more variety than city streets and subway benches. The new partakers of prosperity did not know what a day in the country looked like but now had the means to find out.

Oak Bluffs received its share of seekers of the good life. And the good life had many definitions. It was a time of experimentation, of trial and error, an occasional triumph, adjustment or disengagement, observed behavior abided by or rejected.

There were blacks who tried the Island once, and came no more. They were done in by the fog, and the creepy feeling, and the foghorn making mournful sounds all night. And the beaches, the whole place surrounded by beaches. When you've seen one, the others don't look any different. And the woods. When you've seen one tree, you've seen the rest of the forest. A dirt road goes nowhere. What do you do for excitement? Dullsville.

But the others found more than they ever hoped that they would find. A place where they could stand to full size. The town was right for them, and the time of their coming was right for the town. The wave of whites washed across the whole Island, but the blacks settled where the way had been charted.

They made a massive imprint. They bought the big neglected houses, and other long-empty cottages, lifted their sagging facades, put in new plumbing and wiring, scrubbed and polished and painted. The more improvements they made, the more they paid in taxes and increased the town's returns.

In the early eighties the old guard, the originals, are only remainders, a vanishing though unvanquished group, once labeled the Forty; forty women serenely secure who, with their husbands, were on everybody's party lists, those big August parties when the husbands who could afford a longer stay than a weekend took a two-week vacation which, as time passed and incomes doubled, would extend to the standard month.

In the main they were always a professional group, a pattern of people whose occupations in the fields of white predominance demanded a confident self-image, which enlarged their worldliness and gave strong support to their observation that summer vacations were the color of green money. Black money, Jewish money, Irish money here were just as green as high-and-mighty money, though maybe not as old and honorable or as carefully used.

In the upper strata of black families, loyalty, and, almost concomitantly, group loyalty are chiseled into their earliest consciousness. If these loyalties were once regional, it was because the automobile had not yet become a national necessity, nor was plane travel a common practice. Now from anywhere to everywhere is only a matter of hours. On the Island, in particular Oak Bluffs, the bonding of blacks comes into sharpest focus.

There are some who think that these blacks sprang full-grown from the earth into preordained postures of success. No, their advantage was that their forebears came out of slavery with a fierce will to make up for lost time, and few descendants have let that momentum slacken.

Oak Bluffs is an archetype of the art of people living together where their similarities are points of contact and their differences are intriguing regions to explore. Almost everyone, summer or year-round resident, has friends of every race and every level of experience. The few and fragile summer strongholds of resistance still remaining are now anachronisms. If the best is yet to come, the present will blend with it beautifully.

LOVE

At Christmas there is giving, and in the happiest instances, giving with joy is part of it. This act of love is not a natural instinct. The baby never gives up anything unless the frailty of his fingers forces his greedy grasp to surrender to the strength of someone stronger.

The wanting to give is only learned by learning to love. Though Christmas is the occasion when love makes a spectacular showing, there are other times, on some quiet calendar day, when a gift is given that no money can buy.

There was such a time, on a summer day, at the Flying Horses. My niece and nephew were six and seven, and here in Oak Bluffs for the long holiday. Their mother sent them a weekly allowance, which they changed into silver, and kept in glass jars on my kitchen shelf.

The boy's was gone by mid-week. I had to invent chores to help him exist until Saturday. His sister's jar was never empty, it was often half-full. I did not see how one child could be so wasteful with money while the other led as full a life on so much less.

Every day we walked to the Flying Horses. When we were ready the children opened their jars, and took out whatever money they planned to spend. Their planning always included two rides on the Flying Horses.

The little girl would cross the threshold as if she were entering a sacred place. There was no one in the world of children to whom the Flying Horses brought such ecstasy. When she sat astride her favorite horse, her imagination took the reins and transported her to enchanted places. Her face reflected the wonders she saw in flight.

The little boy had one practical purpose in mind. In his whole life, as he phrased it, he had never caught a gold ring. That was the goal he set for himself the summer that he was seven. As he rode his horse, his determined hand outstretched, he was reaching for the solid feel of a real prize.

The girl had a voice like little golden bells. It was irresistible. If her brother bought himself a second ice cream cone before she had bought herself her first one, I would say to her protectively, Don't you want one, too? The little golden bells would chime. I didn't bring enough money.

I would promptly open my purse. It seemed unfair to punish her for her prudence, while he was eating his second cone as if cones were two for a penny.

The boy was as open as the day. He was spending his money in a perfectly acceptable way. I was helping his sister hoard hers by encouraging her to spend mine. It was almost summer's end before I realized that I had let myself be beguiled.

I was firm thereafter, refusing to see my niece's hopeful eyes searching my face when her brother spent his money while hers was snug at home. I was trying to teach her a lesson, and it was her brother who taught her first, in a way far better.

That was the day he caught the gold ring on his second ride. He came running to me, his sister running behind him, both of them overwhelmed by his remarkable achievement. I praised him mightily. In his hand was his long-sought prize, a Flying Horse ticket for a free ride, the first time in his whole life that he would have three rides in one afternoon. I said, Run quick, before it starts.

He turned, then turned back and looked at his sister. He saw no envy, only awe. In her whole life she had never had three rides on the Flying Horses either.

He thrust the ticket into her hand. Here, Sisty, you can have it.

She stared at him unbelieving. She could never have given a Flying Horse ticket away. He was giving her one that he won with a gold ring. Her eyes filled with tears. My brother loves me, my brother loves me, she said. The golden bells had the sound of a heart running

That was the day she learned that all the money in her jar could not have bought that gift.

THE FLIGHT

One Monday in March I found myself at Logan Airport, sitting relaxed and even drowsy while waiting to board the plane that would return me to this blessed Island after a full and pleasant Sunday in Cambridge. All the unreasonable weather – snow, sleet, winds of high velocity, hazardous conditions – that had been projected for Sunday had never come to pass. The plane to Logan from the Martha's Vineyard Airport made perfect time, rode the air without a ripple, the view unmarred by the slightest film of fog, the blue sky and the cloud formations of extraordinary beauty.

Sunday having turned so fair, it would seem to follow that Monday, which had been projected at the time of Sunday's forecast as a morning of moderating winds and dissipating clouds with sun and rising temperatures by noon, would present no atmospheric problems. My plane should depart without delay and land at the Martha's Vineyard Airport at twelve-twenty, with Marlene's Taxi depositing me on my brick walk in less than twenty minutes, and my tea kettle on the boil shortly thereafter and then my familiar chair ready to soothe me into a catnap that would start the unwinding process and restore me to a peaceful pace again.

When I awoke Monday morning in the Sheraton Hotel and raised the shade to examine the day, I saw that a few snowflakes were falling halfheartedly, leaving very little trace of their failed life. I chose to believe that it had probably snowed lightly during the night to give some credibility to Sunday's forecast, and now, with Monday's promised rising temperatures, this was the dying end of it.

It was only the beginning. The snow began to fall a little faster and stick to the ground, which meant that the temperature had fallen on its face, too, and the earlier snow that had melted as it fell was now turning to ice.

At the hour arranged the taxi arrived, and when my bag and I were packed inside it, the cabman said, in reply to my nervous question, that the streets were getting very slippery, but he would take me on a route where the traffic was less intense than on the customary route. If it would cost a little more, though he said that it would not, these precious years still left to me were worth it.

We arrived at the airport in excellent time. I got my boarding pass and sat down for the short wait. But the waiting began to extend itself. The snow was now falling steadily, and the view outside the window was beginning to be eerie, as if seen through a descending fog.

Inside there was a lot of walking around by personnel, and talking back and forth, and talking over the telephone, and continuing shouts for a maintenance man, who was regularly appearing and disappearing through the exits and entrances. It was all a kind of bedlam, and since I had no idea what was happening, my advice to myself was to stay calm until, and if, there was reason for alarm.

There was finally an explanation from personnel. The runways were icy. The ice-cleaning machine had broken down. Maintenance had now fixed it. Very shortly the runway would be cleared. And those few of us scattered around the waiting room would be on our way to our separate destinations and, arguably, our destinies.

Through the window I could see the maintenance men behind the wheel, and thereby concluded that progress was now proceeding. In reasonable time I was told that my plane was ready for boarding. I was also told that I was the sole passenger.

I was struck by that. It seemed a sort of omen. Curiously I felt a great calm. I remember thinking, If something happens I'm glad I'm the only passenger. I'm glad there's no mother with children aboard, and no man aboard with wife and children at home, whose lives would change completely if something happened to him, and no young Vineyarder on a college break, whose grown-up life is just on the verge of beginning.

I had some feeling for the pilot. But he knew when he took the job that nothing in life is certain except death, and opted to take the risk. As for me, on Sunday in that Cambridge setting, I had seen some of the people I love best. My love had been a clear statement in my greeting, in my face. That thought was very satisfying. My life has been a long one. I've never had any expectations of being singled out to live forever. Though I've never had a compelling urge to see behind the heavenly curtain, the very thought of staying on earth for unnumbered years is numbing. Lingering is the thing I most fear. The quick, clean death is my idea – indeed my ideal – of leaving life with grace.

I got aboard and sat two seats behind the pilot instead of directly behind him, allowing him his space, allowing myself mine. He acknowledged my presence pleasantly, I, his. We made no other exchanges. If he wanted to be chatty, I knew he would be without my encouragement. As it was, I sensed that the plane and everything related to it was occupying his mind.

We were taxiing now, and he was busy with his instrument panel. Three times he opened his window, looked out and looked down, at what I could not determine. I did not ask the purpose of this procedure, my assumption being that he would have told me if the information would have been useful to me, and if my response would have been helpful to him.

It is a rule of mine never to ask unsolicited questions of people over twenty-one. I am only giving them the option of lying if they choose to. They would tell me the truth without my asking if they wanted me to know. To me that's fair enough.

I did say one thing to him when we began the take-off. I said, 'Are we flying by instrument?' I was trying to let him know I would be perfectly comfortable with his answer. His answer was 'Yes,' without elaboration.

From that moment on we were flying in total invisibility. And from that moment and for the next hour as we soared above land and sea, the pilot and the controller in the tower never stopped talking to each other. Two blinking red lights on the panel board never shut themselves off. The pilot never ceased to search for help from the various instruments on the panel.

I could not hear what the pilot was saying to the controller. But three times I heard the controller say over the loudspeaker, 'Use your own judgment.'

I had known from the beginning that we were due to find ourselves in trouble. Now I knew we were swirling in its center. I thought of the mother and her children, the man with a waiting family, the young college student with a still untested future. Just as before I had that feeling of calm and resignation that I had been chosen, not they.

The pilot and air controller kept up their nonstop exchange. The red lights relentlessly flashed their warning. The pilot's hands never ceased to search for solutions from the panel. Minutes passed, how many was hard to measure in a frame of such high intensity.

Then came the moment when the controller said – my ear retaining the pivotal phrases – two thousand feet . . . turn right.

Then a little while later the words were repeated. Then a third time that reinforced my sense of finally being on the right track. I now believed that we were holding course, a crashdown no longer an eventuality.

Above the noise of the plane, I spoke one more time to the pilot. I said in a clear and unexcited voice, 'We were in a bit of trouble, weren't we?' I think I was trying to tell him that I knew we were now out of it and were going to be all right, that I wasn't frozen in terror behind him. I wanted him to know that I had known all along that it was touch and go with us. I think I wanted a pat on the back for being brave and behaving so beautifully as my phantom passenger might not have.

We were descending now, out of the turbulence and the blind sky. We were on the ground, the ground fog had lifted. Everything was visible, yet everything looked crazy. Nothing looked familiar to the Island. We were being signaled to a stop, and having gotten my bearings, I said in astonishment to the pilot, not even trying to keep my voice from squeaking, 'We're back in Boston.'

He turned briefly, answered hurriedly, 'I'll tell you about it in a minute.'

When he brought his plane to a stop, his face relaxed, his tension easing, his mission accomplished. 'The front wheels had locked,' he said. I was glad that I didn't know that, having only a knowledge of cars that cannot navigate on two wheels. 'I had the option of taking a chance and going on to the Vineyard. I'd have done so in better weather,' he mildly boasted, 'but I thought in zero visibility it might be too chancy. So I used my best judgment and brought us back here. It shouldn't be long before we're on our way again. The mechanics are standing by.'

I remembered seeing a stark white emergency vehicle, maybe two, standing by when we put down, but because we were down, their reason for being there did not really register. I did not know that until the pilot could bring his plane to a stop without crashing it, we were still at risk.

I entered the waiting room, reluctant to believe I was back where I started almost four hours ago, four hours later than the time of arrival at the Vineyard imprinted on my ticket. I saw it as an undeserved punishment, a sort of slap in the face for all I had gone through to keep the mother and children, the family man, and the young college student intact in their lives.

I found my original resting place, made my nest in it, and tried to settle into a nap. I was through with feeling sorry for myself. I just wanted to sleep. After Sunday's long day, today's long ordeal, and with the total of my years, nothing was a better panacea.

An hour or so passed while I dozed in and out. After a while somebody behind the desk crossed the room to tell me, with apologies, that I was being transferred to another line to spare me further waiting. There was telephoning back and forth between the two lines with the human callers willing to shift me from one line to the other, but the computers having difficulty dealing with such deviant behavior. One computer had already swallowed up my fare. The other was being told to accept me on faith. Anyway, it was finally settled. I crossed to the other waiting room, and in a short time a plane was ready to take Vineyard and New Bedford passengers aboard.

The skies had cleared. It was a perfect flight. I touched Vineyard soil.

I have lived in various places, but the Island is my yearning place. All my life, wherever I have been, abroad, New York, Boston, anywhere, whenever I yearned for home, I yearned for the Island. Long before I lived here year-round, in my childhood, in the years of my exuberant youth, I knew the Island was the home of my heart.

'The Typewriter' was published in *Opportunity* (volume 4, July 1926).

'Jack in the Pot' was published in the *Daily News* (September 29, 1940).

'Mammy' was published in *Opportunity* (volume 18, October 1940).

'The Richer, the Poorer' was published in *The Best Short Stories by Negro Writers: An Anthology from 1899 to the Present*, edited by Langston Hughes (Boston: Little, Brown, 1967).

'Funeral' was published in the *Saturday Evening Quill* (volume 3, June 1930).

'The Penny' was published in the *Daily News* (June 25, 1941).

'Fluff and Mr. Ripley' was published in the *Daily News* (August 9, 1944)

'About a Woman Named Nancy' was published in the *Vineyard Gazette* (volume 141, no. 23, February 13, 1987).

'The Roomer' was published in the *Daily News* (March 31, 1941).

'The Maple Tree' was published in the *Daily News* (August 23, 1957).

'An Unimportant Man' was published in the *Saturday Evening Quill* (volume 1, June 1928).

'Rachel' was published as 'My Mother, Rachel West' in *Invented Lives: Narratives of Black Women 1860–1960* edited by Mary Helen Washington (Garden City, NY: Anchor Press, 1987).

'The Gift' was published in the *Vineyard Gazette* (volume 138, no. 36, January 20, 1984).

'The Sun Parlor' was published in the *Vineyard Gazette* (volume 138, no. 36, January 20, 1984).

'An Adventure in Moscow' was published in the *Vineyard Gazette* (volume 140, no. 1, May 10, 1985, page 3c).

'Elephant's Dance' was published in *Black World* (volume 20, November 1970).

'A Day Lost Is a Day Gone Forever' was published in the *Vineyard Gazette* (volume 141, no. 32, December 4, 1987).

'The Legend of Oak Bluffs' was published in *On the Vineyard* (Garden City, NY: Anchor Press, 1980).

'The Flight' was published in the *Vineyard Gazette* (volume 140, no. 1, May 10, 1985).